THE TRANSFORMATION OR RECONSTITUTION OF EUROPE

It is generally understood that EU law as interpreted by the ECJ has not merely reconstituted the national legal matrix at the supranational level, but has also transformed Europe and shaken the well-established, often formalist, ways of thinking about law in the Member States. This innovative new study seeks to examine such a narrative through the lens of the American critical legal studies (CLS) perspective.

The introduction explains how the editors understand CLS and why its methodology is relevant in the European context. Part II examines whether and how judges embed policy choices or even ideologies in their decisions, and how to detect them. Part III assesses how the ECJ acts to ensure the legitimacy of its decisions, whether it resists implementing political ideologies, what the ideology of European integration is, and how the selection of judges influences these issues. Part IV uses the critical perspective to examine some substantive parts of EU law, rules on internal and external movement, and the European arrest warrant. It seeks to determine whether the role of the ECJ has really been transformative and whether that transformation is reversible. Part V considers the role of academics in shaping the narratives of EU integration.

The Transformation or Reconstitution of Europe

The Critical Legal Studies Perspective on the Role of the Courts in the European Union

Edited by
Tamara Perišin and Siniša Rodin

·HART·

OXFORD · LONDON · NEW YORK · NEW DELHI · SYDNEY

HART PUBLISHING

Bloomsbury Publishing Plc

Kemp House, Chawley Park, Cumnor Hill, Oxford, OX2 9PH, UK

HART PUBLISHING, the Hart/Stag logo, BLOOMSBURY and the Diana logo are
trademarks of Bloomsbury Publishing Plc

First published in Great Britain 2018

First published in hardback, 2018
Paperback edition, 2020

A catalogue record for this book is available from the British Library.

Library of Congress Cataloging-in-Publication Data

Names: Perišin, Tamara, editor. | Rodin, Siniša, editor.

Title: The transformation or reconstitution of Europe : the critical legal studies perspective on the
role of the courts in the European Union / edited by Tamara Perišin and Siniša Rodin.

Description: Oxford [UK] ; Portland, Oregon : Hart Publishing, 2018. |
Includes bibliographical references and index.

Identifiers: LCCN 2017048790 (print) | LCCN 2017051412 (ebook) |
ISBN 9781509907274 (Epub) | ISBN 9781509907250 (hardcover)

Subjects: LCSH: Courts—European Union countries. | Law—European Union countries. |
Constitutional law—European Union countries. | Court of Justice (Court of Justice
of the European Union) | Justice, Administration of—European Union countries.

Classification: LCC KJE3666 (ebook) | LCC KJE3666 .T73 2018 (print) | DDC 347.24/012—dc23

LC record available at https://lccn.loc.gov/2017048790

ISBN: HB: 978-1-50990-725-0
PB: 978-1-50993-955-8
ePDF: 978-1-50990-726-7
ePub: 978-1-50990-727-4

Typeset by Compuscript Ltd, Shannon

To find out more about our authors and books visit www.hartpublishing.co.uk. Here you will find
extracts, author information, details of forthcoming events and the option to sign up for our newsletters.

CONTENTS

LIST OF CONTRIBUTORS

TAMARA ĆAPETA
Jean Monnet Professor at the University of Zagreb.

DANIELA CARUSO
Professor of Law and Jean Monnet Chair, Boston University School of Law.

DUNCAN KENNEDY
Carter Professor of General Jurisprudence Emeritus, Harvard Law School.

MITCHEL DE S-O-L'E LASSER
Jack G Clarke Professor of Law, Cornell Law School.

KOEN LENAERTS
President of the Court of Justice of the European Union, and Professor of European Union Law, University of Leuven.

FERNANDA NICOLA
Professor of Law, Washington College of Law, American University, Director of the Program on International Organizations, Law and Diplomacy.

TAMARA PERIŠIN
Professor of Law and Jean Monnet Chair, University of Zagreb.

SINIŠA RODIN
Judge, Court of Justice of the European Union, and Professor of European Union Law, University of Zagreb.

PIERRE SCHLAG
University Distinguished Professor and Byron R White Professor of Law, University of Colorado.

PIETER-AUGUSTIJN VAN MALLEGHEM
SJD candidate at Harvard Law School.

Part I

Introduction

1

Transformation or Reconstitution of Europe: The European Critical Legal Studies Perspective[*]

SINIŠA RODIN AND TAMARA PERIŠIN

I. Changing the Paradigm as a Response to Social Change

Introducing a new way of thinking to a well-established referential system is by no means an easy task. As Thomas S Kuhn suggested, '[n]ormal science does not aim at novelties of fact or theory and, when successful, finds none'.[1] In that sense, in the absence of a paradigm shift, innovation falls victim to the existing model's success. The same holds for law. The more successful a legal system is, the less likely it is to be open to change and innovation.

Change takes place in times of crisis and does not come about abruptly. It usually matures slowly within an existing way of reasoning. For example, before introducing the main tenets of his liberal theory, John Locke had to engage in religious debate with Sir Robert Filmer. Only after having refuted Filmer's assumptions within the referential framework of monarchist reasoning was Locke able to introduce his understanding of rights, separation of powers, and government limited by social contract.

This book looks into the legal dimension of the European integration process that has been recently characterised as 'undergoing its most acute multifaceted crisis'.[2] It has been suggested that a new element in the 'current crisis' is the

[*] We are grateful to Duncan Kennedy for lengthy conversations on this chapter and on discussions about CLS that have strongly influenced our text. We would also like to thank Daniela Caruso and Fernanda Nicola for their comments on earlier drafts. Thanks to Davor Petrić for his research assistance and to Mark Davies for his work in copy-editing this book.
[1] Thomas S Kuhn, *The Structure of Scientific Revolutions* 2nd edn (Chicago, University of Chicago Press, 1970) 52.
[2] 'Editorial Comments' (2015) 52 *CML Rev* 881.

'widespread mistrust of the positive force of law' and that '[t]he legal form—long associated with the success of European integration—is now perceived as an appendage to economic forces and governmental machines which undermine the social structures of the Member States, producing social commodification and cultural standardization'.[3] If this proposition is correct, it may indicate the success rather than the failure of European Union law. Distrust in positive law may mean that national entrenchments and patterns of legal reasoning have finally given way to a new methodological model, one that caters to the behemoth of functional spillover which is an essential element of the European Union's original design.[4] In that sense, the expansion of European Union law to areas, such as criminal justice, carries the same subversive seed that may develop in the direction of the Europeanisation of traditionally national domains. Or it may mean that European Union law is beating a dead horse: a once promising European economic and political construct which, in reality, due to rapid technological and social change, no longer exists.

How did these changes occur and why might law in general and European Union law in particular need to look for responses beyond the known? In recent decades, a number of authors, from economists to futurists, have written about how and why gaps in the world are growing. For example, the main thesis of Thomas Piketty's *Capital in the Twenty-First Century* is that the rate of return on capital is greater than the rate of economic growth.[5] Similarly, Ray Kurzweil argues in *The Singularity is Near* that the development of technology, specifically artificial intelligence, has reached the knee of the curve where returns yielded by technological progress grow exponentially at historically unprecedented speed leading to 'accelerating returns'.[6] This is in sharp contrast to the prevailing part of human history where growth was mainly linear. If all this is correct, then there are two important consequences.

First, affluent and technologically more advanced societies will crop exponential returns, while the returns of less developed societies will either remain linear or, in the better case, stay behind on the exponential curve. In either event, the gap between the returns of the two groups will widen. This holds equally between states and within a single state. In simple terms, technological development in Germany has a much higher growth rate than that in Portugal or Croatia or, indeed, in any other less technologically developed state. Moreover, this increasing gap cannot be easily compensated for, if at all.

Second, even within societies and states that have enjoyed accelerated returns, the participation rate of individuals benefiting from the returns of exponential

---

[3] ibid 882 and the references cited therein.

[4] For functional spillover, see Ernst B Haas, *The Uniting of Europe* (Stanford, Stanford University Press, 1958).

[5] Thomas Piketty, *Capital in the Twenty-First Century* (Cambridge, Harvard University Press, 2014).

[6] Ray Kurzweil, *The Singularity is Near* Kindle edn (London, Gerald Duckworth and Co, 2006) locations 1660 and 2718.

growth differs. Here again, the gap between those enjoying fast exponential growth and everyone else permanently increases. It should be noted that the nature of exponential growth is such that even the differences between the first and second most advanced are increasing and the gap between the two widens. More generally, while the difference between compared groups may still be small until the knee of the curve is reached, once that point is crossed, the gap will grow at an exponential rate. This does not mean that those on the linear curve will necessarily live worse off than usual, but it does mean that the future prospects of the members of that group will be substantially lower than the prospects of those who embarked on the path of accelerated returns. It is thus social exclusion from the stakes of the future and not necessarily economic distress that divide those who are on different growth curves.

When we spread social distribution along a graph where one axis describes population and the other social wealth extracted from accelerating returns, we obtain a bell curve. On the left of the curve we see socially deprived individuals (this also holds for regions or states), while the super-rich come at the far right. The vast majority of the population, however, is placed on the hill of the curve. The members of that vast majority can still live decent, even linearly improving, lives, but will, nevertheless, see themselves losing pace with the minority that is benefiting from the accelerated returns.

An extended period of accelerating returns that entails growing inequalities and deprivation from the stakes of the future opens a range of new questions, including, but not limited to, the question of how to pass on the returns to the majority of the population (for the European Union, this also concerns transfers to the Member States) that would suffice for a permissive consensus, on which future institutional, legal and social arrangements will be based. Insisting on arrangements that correspond to a dramatically different description of reality only aggravates distrust in law.

In addition, the quickening of technological development affects law as a regulatory mechanism of choice. Annelise Riles, writing in 2011, described the operation of securities markets as a routine consisting of 'a set of material practices of document production, filing and exchange—practices that in turn call for further routines and further documents'.[7] Gradually, routines, claims Riles, develop into an element of global private governance.[8] What is remarkable, due to the largely self-regulatory nature of financial markets, is that disputes arising from swap transactions, as described by Riles, escape judicial resolution.[9] Possible losses are

---

[7] Annelise Riles, *Collateral Knowledge, Legal Reasoning in the Global Financial Markets* Kindle edn (Chicago, University of Chicago Press, 2011).

[8] ibid 749.

[9] ibid 523: 'When disputes arise, therefore, often the parties' only formal recourse is to bring a lawsuit in a domestic court under ordinary common or civil law claims such as breach of contract or fraud. Since this is often impractical, the number of formal lawsuits arising out of swap transactions is remarkably low, given the notional amount of the transactions at issue'.

compensated on the market itself, due to the rapid speed of exchange, rather than in judicial proceedings. One can only ask in what other areas automation of work diverts dispute resolution from the legal to the factual. The courts must be aware of these societal changes.

II. Critical Legal Studies and European Legal Thought

The ambition of this book is not to revolutionise European legal thinking. It is rather to show that a different perspective is possible within the existing referential framework. In an attempt to bring this different perspective, contributors start their inquiry from fragments of what is generally known as critical legal studies (CLS), a fluid, allegedly leftist, stream of American legal thought that cannot be easily delimited.[10]

CLS emerged and developed in a specific social and legal environment. It sprouted from the soil of anti-formalism, particularly American legal realism often viewed as the dominant approach to law in the United States.[11] Already in the late nineteenth century, a German lawyer, Rudolph von Jhering, criticised formalist legal reasoning, and sought 'purposive' or 'teleological' or 'functionalist' jurisprudence.[12]

While the two world wars interrupted the reception of these ideas in Europe, they influenced legal realists on the other side of the Atlantic.[13] Realists considered that legal concepts themselves are indeterminate, so that the formalist approach to law led to 'the abuse of deduction, meaning that jurists habitually offered deductive justifications for interpretations that were in fact logically underdetermined'.[14] Instead of lawyers operating in a heaven of legal concepts where all legal questions are resolved by recourse to pure legal concepts, policy always pertains to law and decides legal questions. However, for each policy there is a counter-policy. What matters in law is not general propositions, but how judges decide cases.[15]

---

[10] Attempts to define CLS in this section are partly based on extensive in-person conversations with Duncan Kennedy, January 2016, and his subsequent comments.

[11] At the times when CLS was in full bloom, Rorty lamented how, '[e]veryone seems now to be a legal realist'. Richard Rorty, 'The Banality of Pragmatism and the Poetry of Justice' (1990) 63 *Southern California Law Review* 1811.

[12] Rudolf von Jhering, *Der Zweck im Recht* (Leipzig, Breitkopf & Härtel, 1877); Rudolf von Jhering, *Scherz und Ernst in der Jurisprudenz* (Leipzig, Breitkopf & Härtel, 1884).

[13] Felix Cohen, 'Transcendental Nonsense and the Functional Approach' (1935) 35 *Columbia Law Review* 809.

[14] D Kennedy, 'Legal Formalism' in *International Encyclopedia of the Social & Behavioral Sciences*, vol 13 (Amsterdam, Elsevier, 2001) 8634, 8635 http://duncankennedy.net/documents/Legal%20Formalism.pdf.

[15] Cohen (n 13) 809.

According to legal realists, when settling a case, a judge decides which interpretation is best 'here and now' and, in doing so, by necessity, sets a precedent that favours different interests (such as the majority versus the minority, capital versus labour, the lessor versus the lessee, freedom of choice versus the right to life, etc). According to Kennedy, judges began to develop the notion of balancing or proportionality as sometimes necessary to resolve conflicts.[16]

CLS takes this anti-formalist understanding of the law further, but also offers its critique, drawing on European critical social theory.[17]

CLS sees that there are not only two conflicting interests and interpretations in each case before a court, but, more broadly, that each legal norm is the product of a particular political conflict where one side won. Thus, legal norms are a snapshot of the distribution of power in political battles that created those norms. The set of legal norms can thus be characterised as more conservative, more liberal or more progressive depending on the political constellation. Typically, legal systems serve the interests of the dominant group, and their institutional structure works to the disadvantage of those on its margins.

The CLS critique of the anti-formalist approach to law that attempted to maintain the appearance of neutrality by balancing policies is based on the idea that policies (as well as law) are not neutral.[18] Policies also cause distributive effects, so deciding cases by balancing such policies cannot be neutral either. So nobody is neutral. While it is clear to most that the legislature and executive are not politically neutral, proponents of CLS highlighted how judges and doctrine cannot be neutral either.[19] They can be conscious, unconscious or partly conscious of their bias in reasoning, but being unconscious of their political bias does not make them neutral in deciding cases or in academic writing.[20]

What goes without saying is that both American legal realism and CLS developed within a liberal democratic environment and regulated a market economy with some elements of a welfare state. However, legal realism catered to emerging

---

[16] Duncan Kennedy, 'A Transnational Genealogy of Proportionality in Private Law' in R Brownsword, H-W Micklitz, L Niglia and S Weatherill (eds), *The Foundations of European Private Law* (Oxford, Hart Publishing, 2011).

[17] Duncan Kennedy sees CLS as influenced by Antonio Gramsci, Georges Gurvitch, Michel Foucault, Jacques Derrida, Jean-Paul Sartre, Franz Kafka and Wassily Kandinsky. See, eg, Duncan Kennedy, 'Antonio Gramsci and the Legal System' (1982) 6(1) *ALSA Forum* 32; Duncan Kennedy, 'Three Globalizations of Law and Legal Thought: 1850–2000' in David Trubek and Alvaro Santos (eds), *The New Law and Economic Development. A Critical Appraisal* (Cambridge, Cambridge University Press, 2006); Duncan Kennedy, 'The Stakes of Law, or Hale and Foucault!' (1991) 15 *Legal Studies Forum* 327; Duncan Kennedy, 'European Introduction: Four Objections' in Peter Goodrich, Florian Hoffman, Michel Rosenfeld and Cornelia Vismann (eds), *Derrida and Legal Philosophy* (Houndsmills, Basingstoke, Palgrave MacMillan, 2008); Duncan Kennedy, 'Freedom & Constraint in Adjudication: A Critical Phenomenology', reprinted in J Boyle (ed), *Critical Legal Studies* (New York, New York University Press, 1992); Duncan Kennedy, *A Critique of Adjudication [fin de siècle]* (Cambridge, Harvard University Press, 1997), most being available at http://duncankennedy.net/.

[18] Author's discussions with Duncan Kennedy, January 2016, Cambridge, MA.

[19] Kennedy, *Critique of Adjudication* (n 17).

[20] ibid.

social and economic needs by trying to design regulation and social laws reconciled with the changing social and regulatory environment of the New Deal.[21] In contrast, according to Duncan Kennedy, CLS was initially a critique of that same democratic social law that emerged from the New Deal. CLS rebellion against this system had two components.[22] The first was deconstructionist, a critique of the coherence or asserted legal logic of the private and public law rules of this status quo.[23] The second was a normative one, a critique of distributional inequity and gender and racial injustice of the outcome of the social democratic consensus.[24] The argument is that the status quo allows entrenched actors in the apparently neutral legal arena to have a 'foot on someone else's neck',[25] and law can be driven by greed and privilege.[26] CLS does not claim that this is a result of the continuous and deliberate bias of those who create or interpret the rules. However, it points out that not all groups are equal in the continuing political conflicts leading to the creation or interpretation of legal rules. CLS also does not claim that the legal order is entirely coherent so as to systematically represent the interest of a particular group. Rather, it claims that all regulation has distributive effects, and the status quo keeps the less privileged in such a position.

European legal history also shows that law can be proclaimed to be neutral or to serve one agenda, but in reality be serving another. In Central and Eastern Europe, the formal ideological narrative after World War II was that law serves the interests of the ruling class—the proletariat. The law was openly supposed to be biased not only in the courtroom where judges were expected to actively promote certain social and ideological ends,[27] but also institutionally and methodologically. However, in reality, the supreme authority for the interpretation of the will of the working class was located in the narrow and closed circles of the political elite and was transmitted to lower levels of law and policy-making.[28] Such a system was prone to creating distributive effects between other types of groups (eg on the basis of nationality, ethnicity, religion, gender, etc), and not just between workers and the rest. At some point the legal systems stopped being able to mitigate conflicts between various groups, leading to the breakup of the systems. The authoritarian nature of these regimes made the critique of law difficult. However,

---

[21] We are grateful to Duncan Kennedy for his comments that made us clarify this point.

[22] ibid.

[23] ibid.

[24] ibid.

[25] Duncan Kennedy, 'Liberal Values in Legal Education' (1986) 10 *Nova Law Journal* 603, 604.

[26] 'Greed and privilege play a major role in sustaining the rules in force. Other rules would often be ethically superior, but are not adopted because of greed and privilege'. Duncan Kennedy, 'Positive and Normative Elements in Legal Education: A Response' (1985) 8 *Harvard Journal of Law and Public Policy* 263, 266.

[27] Zdenek Kühn, 'Worlds Apart: Western and Central European Judicial Culture at the Onset of the European Enlargement' (2004) 52 *American Journal of Comparative Law* 531.

[28] Siniša Rodin, 'Croatian Parliament in Transition: From Authoritarian Past to European Future' in Ph Kiiver (ed), *National and Regional Parliaments in the European Constitutional Order* (Groningen, Europa Law Publishing, 2006) 97.

the absence of critique created another kind of reaction. The legal profession dug into an illusion of legal neutrality and abstraction. Legal rules were presented as objective and detached from social reality. They were safely locked in a heaven of juristic concepts[29] which contributed to a belated rebellion against formalism in Central and Eastern Europe.

At the same time, Western Europe was facing different problems. The starting point there was a different sort of legal formalism—a functional rather than conceptual one. While some might see this as anti-formalism, since legal and judicial reasoning is guided by some substantive aim (*telos*) which is beyond the form, for the purposes of this book we will call it functional formalism. This Western European functional formalism is not confined to the endless self-indulgent justification of abstract forms, but intentionally creates certain substantive outcomes.[30] Form is not typically an end in itself, but a means to reach an outcome. However, even the selection of aims can sometimes be formalised. For example, in EU law there are some obstacles to the movement of goods (distinctly applicable measures, ie, discrimination in the text) that can only be justified by reasons exhaustively listed in the Treaties. In contrast, other types of obstacles (indistinctly applicable measures, including discrimination in effect, but also non-discriminatory obstacles) can be justified not only on the basis of these Treaty grounds but by any other legitimate policy (mandatory requirements). The difference between these aims is not substantive, but formal. Furthermore, in the process of achieving the aim, the judge or another legal thinker is constrained by quite a formalised proportionality analysis. While the structure of legal analysis remains formal (legitimate aim, appropriateness, necessity and balancing *stricto sensu*), the result of the analysis is open ended and clearly policy driven. The result is not pre-determined by fidelity to a certain legal concept.

This Western European functional formalism, ie purposive interpretation with a proportionality test, has become part of the EU's own mainstream. It is also spreading to Central and Eastern Europe.

III. Critical Legal Studies in the European Union Context

The book title is inspired by Duncan Kennedy's monograph *A Critique of Adjudication [fin de siècle]* and poses the question whether the EU transforms the law or merely reconstitutes it within the existing conservative pattern.

---

[29] Rudolf von Jhering, 'Im juristischen Begriffshimmel' in von Jhering (n 12).
[30] We are not implying that conceptual formalism does not create substantive outcomes. However, such substantive outcomes are subordinated to legal concepts and often arise only incidentally, as a consequence of formalistic reasoning.

The impact of European Union law on the national legal orders of the Member States cannot be overstated. Propelled by the European Court of Justice, supremacy and the direct effect of EU law have empowered individuals and extended to them rights based on EU law that national courts must protect. The development of EU law, both substantive and procedural, has disturbed the well-established patterns of national law. The question, however, is whether EU law has genuinely transformed the way Europeans think about law or merely reconstituted national legal matrices at the supranational level. While the Court of Justice of the European Union (CJEU) is widely understood as an engine of European integration, its transformative potential in respect of traditional legal reasoning has not been fully explored.[31] Is the CJEU changing the way Europeans think about law or is traditional legal reasoning feeding into the European Court of Justice? Are national legal patterns now being reconstituted at the European level? Is European transformation reversible, is it still active, or has the transformative power of European law and of the European Court of Justice been exhausted?

What, then, makes CLS relevant for European Union law today? The answer is its method and its subversion.

The method itself is not unique or standard. One of the common methodological tools of the CLS is trashing. Mark G Kelman described it in the following words: 'Take specific arguments very seriously in their own terms; discover they are actually foolish ([tragi]-comic); and then look for some (external observer's) order (not the germ of truth) in the internally contradictory, incoherent chaos we've exposed'.[32] The target of trashing can be anything. Property, circular thinking, normativism, academic hierarchy, liberal thought, contract, just anything. The weapons are internal critique, ie critique of the object in its own terms and external critique which is usually based on a certain social agenda. The agenda itself is construed as against the prevailing and hitherto uncontested thought/concept/rule/principle. The more accepted and entrenched a principle is, the better. That said, CLS is inherently subversive in respect of the mainstream legal thought and prevailing institutional structure.

How does this relate to the European Union context? Apparently, just as the CLS is subversive in respect of mainstream legal reasoning and the structural distributive effects of the US legal and social order, the application of its methodology to an analysis of the law of the European Union has the potential to present an alternative, and ultimately to undermine some of the prevailing assumptions of national law of the Member States.

---

[31] Traditional understood as being constitutive of one's own identity, as being at the same time unique and differentiated from others. For an understanding of tradition, see Paul Feyerabend, *Science in a Free Society* (London, Verso, 1978). Feyerabend suggests that a tradition becomes susceptible to value judgements only when compared to some other tradition. Arguably, if there is such a thing as EU legal tradition, it is, at the minimum, a comparator against which national legal traditions can be evaluated.

[32] Mark G Kelman, 'Trashing' (1984) 36 *Stanford Law Review* 293.

It is well known that EU legislation and EU case law change the established distribution of power between various actors (domestic products and foreign ones;
labour and capital; private regulators and public ones; courts and political institutions, etc). The disruption of the status quo typically provides new opportunities
for those who have been less privileged. EU law has thus often helped the under-
privileged in Europe. It is equally true that EU law can have the opposite effect and
work to the advantage of those who are already better off. So, in terms of the CLS
social agenda, EU law can be both a desired outcome and the object of severe criticism. However, what is most relevant for this book is that both EU law and CLS
change the way one thinks about law. EU law requires one to step away from any
nationally accepted legal reasoning. So does CLS.

In fact, critical legal thought is vital for EU law if the latter is to establish and
maintain its autonomy from national legal orders on one hand and international
law on the other. European critical legal thinking establishes its agenda around the
process of Europeanisation, which, in turn, serves as a benchmark for an external
critique of national legal rules, principles and concepts. While the CLS agenda
is dominantly social, the EU critical agenda is primarily supranational. It is not
supranational in the sense that it would favour the complete harmonisation of
laws in Europe. On the contrary, the editors believe that in certain areas of law,
experimentation is necessary at national or local levels and that a uniform EU-
wide approach in certain fields could have adverse effects on some Member States
or certain groups.[33] However, the European critical legal studies agenda is supranational in the sense that one of its ideals is a better, larger life for all, and it under-
mines étatist protectionist policies.

In the current state of affairs in the EU, social rights have caused great tension between Member States and the people of Europe. Differences in social
rights, including healthcare,[34] education,[35] social benefits,[36] etc, have triggered
cases pushing the limits of the internal market and EU citizenship. This was often
frowned upon both by the wealthier states (eg when non-nationals received certain social rights) and by poorer states (eg when they had to pay for their citizens'

---

[33] For example, Roberto Unger claims that some of the internal market rules have adverse effects on
the less developed parts of the EU, and that more national experimentation with market rules would be
preferable. Roberto Mangabeira Unger, *Left Alternative* (London, Verso, 2005) 89–93. Similarly, Daniela
Caruso argues that the costs and benefits of EU-wide contract law harmonisation are not evenly distributed through the EU, and she calls for more tracking and measuring in this field. The false win-win
narrative must be abandoned, and losers must be identified and helped. Daniela Caruso, '(*Qu'ils man-
gent des contrats*) Rethinking Justice in EU Contract Law' in G de Burca, D Kochenov and A Williams
(eds), *Europe's Justice Deficit?* (Oxford, Hart Publishing, 2015).

[34] eg Case C-120/95 *Decker* [1998] ECR I-01831; Case C-158/96 *Kohll* [1998] I-01931; Case
C-372/04 *Watts* [2006] I-04325.

[35] Case 39/86 *Lair* [1988] ECR 3161; Case C-3/90 *Bernini* [1992] ECR I-1071; Case C-337/97
Meeusen [1999] ECR-3289; Case C-209/03 *Bidar* [2005] ECR I-2119; Case C-158/07 *Förster* [2008]
ECR I-08507; Case C-73/08 *Bressol* [2010] ECR I-02735; Case C-75/11 *C v Austria*, judgment of
4 October 2012; Joined Cases C-523/11 and C-585/11 *Prinz*, 18 July 2013; Case C-359/13 *Martens*,
26 February 2015.

[36] Case C-85/96 *Martínez Sala* EU:C:1998:217.

healthcare received in another state). The migration crisis has magnified this tension as refugees flee not only from war to safety, but also want to ensure better economic and other opportunities for themselves and family members. The migration route passes through the EU's 'periphery'[37] and goes to the wealthier centre. It seems that there are at least three possible ways of solving the tension arising from differences in social rights in the EU. The first is to lower the standards in all EU Member States to the lowest common denominator. The second is to maintain the differences, but to accept more limits on the internal market integration process. The third is to ensure the prerequisites for more integration and more movement within the internal market by setting up certain EU-wide social rights and EU-wide equality of opportunity, necessarily entailing more competences and funding for the EU.

European critical legal thought (or is it ECLT? Ho, ho, ho, a pattern seems to be emerging here) is not limited to the critique of national law or legal reasoning. This book examines to what extent ECLT is possible, ie whether CLS methodology can be applied to thinking about EU law, and in particular about the case law of the European Court of Justice. At the EU level, there is a double problem. First, against which target, within the EU legal tradition, should a critical legal thinker be pointing her blade once the tradition has emancipated itself from national legal traditions. Is there an ideology hidden behind EU law worth debunking, and can this ideology be subsumed under the terms 'left' versus 'right' or any other typology? Second, how may the arguably independent EU legal tradition assert its claims concerning the objectivity (or is it the universal validity) of EU law and claim to impose itself[38] on national legal systems, having in mind Feyerabend's warning that apparently objective statements make sense only within a tradition.[39]

Ultimately, how then does CLS/ECLT help a legal thinker, if at all? Ironically, CLS/ECLT is largely descriptive and often does not offer normative proposals. It merely tells a legal thinker something like: 'if you want to think about law, you had better take these things into account. But, be prepared to discover how deep the rabbit hole is and be aware that answers to legal questions often lie beyond law'. In other words, CLS/ECLT offers the legal thinker a methodological toolbox for dealing with legal problems. How the tools are to be used is for the legal thinker to decide, and in the vast majority of cases there is no textbook solution.

Following this introductory chapter, the book develops through a further four parts. The second part, 'Adjudication and the Transformation of Law and Society' (Schlag, Kennedy), examines whether and how judges embed policy choices in their decisions, and how to detect hidden policies and even ideologies in judicial

---

[37] Damjan Kukovec, 'Economic Law, Inequality and Hidden Hierarchies on the EU Internal Market' (2016) 38(1) *Michigan Journal of International Law*.

[38] Suffice it to mention concepts of supremacy and direct effect of EU law.

[39] Feyerabend (n 31).

decisions. The third part on 'The Role of the ECJ in the Transformation or Reconstitution of Europe' (Lenaerts, Ćapeta, Lasser) assesses how the European Court of Justice acts so as to ensure the legitimacy of its decisions, whether and how it resists implementing political ideologies through its decisions, and what the ideology of European integration is. It also examines how the selection of judges influences these issues. The fourth part, 'Substantive EU Law and the Transformation of Europe' (Perišin, Rodin), uses the critical legal studies perspective to examine some substantive parts of EU law, the internal market, external trade, and the European arrest warrant. It shows how the CJEU manages policy choices to achieve certain objectives. The final part, 'Academic Discourse and the Transformation of Europe' (Van Malleghem, Caruso, Nicola), examines the role of academics in influencing the way practising lawyers think about law, adjudication and their respective roles. It considers to what extent scholars or other commentators can politicise EU law or manipulate the narratives of EU integration, and whether this in turn affects judicial interpretation.

Part II

Adjudication and the Transformation
of Law and Society

2

On Textualist and Purposivist Interpretation (Challenges and Problems)

PIERRE SCHLAG[*]

In law, interpretation seems to be everywhere. And everywhere it seems to be, it turns out to be very much a localised, context-sensitive, text-specific affair. Does this mean then that nothing of theoretical value can be said about legal interpretation? No. Not at all. What it does mean is that we need to develop a theoretical approach to legal interpretation that respects its local, contextual, text-specific character. We need to recognise that legal interpretation will not necessarily conform to high-order theoretical directives or prescriptions.

Taking this caution to heart, I try to sketch here an approach to legal interpretation that respects its local, contextual and text-specific character. Hence, rather than trying to organise an understanding of legal interpretation in terms of systematic solutions or over-arching prescriptions, I try to organise an understanding of legal interpretation in terms of stereotyped interpretive challenges and problems as these might be encountered or raised by a judge or lawyer.

Here in this chapter, I will deal with two predominant modes of legal interpretation—namely, textualism and purposivism. These two modes seem to recur frequently across many different national and international legal regimes. The inquiry here will focus on the stylised challenges and problems that arise *within* each mode of interpretation. Such an 'intra-modal' focus presumes the interpreter is already committed to a particular mode of interpretation rather than having to decide between different modes of interpretation (the 'inter-modal'). The focus on the intra-modal allows the identification of the stereotyped decision-points that a judge or lawyer confronts when practising a particular mode of interpretation.[1] Before turning specifically to the two modes of interpretation,

[*] University Distinguished Professor and Byron R White Professor of Law, University of Colorado.
[1] Much of my other work on legal interpretation has focused on the 'inter-modal'. See, eg, Pierre Schlag, 'Hiding the Ball' (1996) 71 *New York University Law Review* 1681.

however, a few general observations are warranted on what might be called 'the interpretive situation'—namely, the contexts, conflicts and tensions within which legal interpretation happens.

I. The Interpretive Situation—Recurrent Tensions and Conflicts

The various modes of interpretation—textualism and purposivism—share some common challenges. These challenges stem from recurrent tensions and conflicts that pervade the attempt to discern legal meaning. A thorough appreciation of these tensions and conflicts allows recognition of the many possibilities that are generally available in the interpretation of legal texts.

A. The 'Legal' in the Legal Text

Many jurists and legal theorists have infused their understandings of interpretation by borrowing from literary critics, linguists and philosophers. Much of this has been helpful. Some of it has not. Be that as it may, there are certain aspects of legal interpretation that distinguish the endeavour relative to, for instance, literary or philosophical interpretation. One of them is that the interpretation of legal texts is and must be shaped, guided and directed by law itself. Jurisprudence, in this sense, impinges upon interpretation—in theory as well as in practice.[2]

Because law and laws provide prescriptive directives for the interpretation of legal texts, legal interpretation is *never just* a question of getting the semantic meaning of a legal text right. It is also a question of following jurisprudential and legal directives for how legal interpretation is to proceed.[3] And this remains the case *even if*—(and now comes the vexing part)—those jurisprudential and legal directives miscast or misunderstand the nature of texts or interpretation.[4]

The practical issue thus arises: what is to be done when the texts at issue and the relevant interpretive directives seem to be at odds? Does one follow the interpretive directives or does one instead try to conform to the text being interpreted? This practical question arises because law ('*le droit*') is fundamentally unclear or

---

[2] For two opposed accounts of legal interpretation demonstrating this general point, see William Baude and Stephen E Sachs, 'The Law of Interpretation' (2017) 130 *Harvard Law Review* 1079; and Mark Greenberg, 'What Makes a Method of Legal Interpretation Correct? Legal Standards vs Fundamental Determinants' (2017) 130 *Harvard Law Review Forum* 105. The disagreement turns upon a jurisprudential dispute over the scope and content of the 'law' that governs interpretation.

[3] ibid.

[4] This is why the work of Stanley Fish, Steven Knapp and Walter Benn Michaels is instructive, but nonetheless somewhat askew where '*legal* interpretation' is concerned.

perhaps more accurately ambivalent about the degree to which legal interpretation is a matter of *producing* legal meanings in accordance with interpretive directives as opposed to a matter of *finding* the meaning of the legal text at issue. Clearly, we have some of both going on. This is a very complicated problem. There is a great deal to be said about it—indeed far too much to pursue the question here.

Moving on, then.

B. The Interpretive Contexts

Among legal academics, the topic of legal interpretation is often approached in very abstract ways. Indeed, 'legal interpretation' is its own abstract stand-alone topic—frequently addressed outside any substantive issue or procedural context. This abstract perspective is very different from that of the judge or the lawyer who encounters an interpretive problem typically in a fact-rich and institutionally localised context where interpretive conclusions have discernible concrete consequences. In what follows, I elaborate on these various aspects of the judge's and the lawyer's situation.

i. Fact-rich

Judges are not, as academics sometimes intimate, called upon to interpret legal texts in general—but rather to interpret a legal text (or usually a small part thereof) as it might bear on a particular case, a particular factual scenario. It may be that some degree of generality is required to resolve the particular interpretive question posed. This generality may be required by a judge's commitment to a certain kind of 'principled' decision-making.[5] Or it may be required by a certain degree of pragmatism (eg, the 'where do you draw the line?' kind of pragmatism). But either way, the *degree* and *direction* of this generality will be shaped by the factual scenario at hand.

ii. Institutionally Localised

The judge is constrained by a series of professional imperatives and restraints, such as heed the law, resolve disputes, preserve order, do justice, clear dockets, establish sensible regimes, respect litigants, and explain and justify decisions. These are fairly role-specific tasks, not common to academics or other mortals. The judge resolves an interpretive issue by working it through these institutional imperatives and restraints, as well as by working the institutional imperatives and restraints through his or her interpretations. It is important to note that

---

[5] Some jurisprudential approaches, of course, explicitly demand a high degree of generality. See, eg, Herbert Wechsler, 'Toward Neutral Principles of Constitutional Law' (1959) 73 *Harvard Law Review* 1.

the judge's professional role (how he or she views the mission at hand) is itself susceptible to (and perhaps demands) interpretation. Indeed, the insightful judge will learn to read legal texts not simply for the doctrines, policies and principles they announce, but for what the legal texts reveal about his or her own roles, tasks, responsibilities and limitations.

iii. Procedural Posture

Judges and lawyers are called upon to interpret legal texts at certain stages in the proceedings. The legal texts they must or are permitted to examine may well depend upon the specific identity of the court, its jurisdiction, and other institutional and procedural matters. While these are themselves subject to interpretation, it is nonetheless the case that judges will often have a much more localised focus than other kinds of interpreters such as academics, journalists and the like.

iv. Discernible Specific Consequences

When a judge rules on a question of legal interpretation (unlike, say, a journalist or an academic offering his or her views), discrete specific consequences ensue. Someone pays (or does not), goes to jail (or does not), ceases and desists (or does not), and so on. Judicial interpretation has consequences—some of them rather determinately laid out by the law itself. When the judge writes, he or she does so in the medium of law. His or her opinion registers automatically in the networks of law and has certain discrete automatic juridical effects.[6] It can be argued, of course, that such discrete specific effects ought not to be considered by the judge. But it can also be argued back that if the judge does not consider such effects, then he or she has a blinkered understanding of the identity and character of law and judgment. Again, one can find in the law a certain ambivalence about what must, can and cannot be taken into consideration. Insofar as the polar extremes (one can *never take any* consequences into account/one *must take all* consequences into account) seem generally unacceptable, judges are left with what will sometimes be a difficult jurisprudential choice about just which consequences must, can and cannot be taken into account. This, of course, will present not merely a conceptual challenge (specifying concepts), but a cognitive one as well (bending one's mind to conceptual demands).

C. The Textual Feedback Loop

Every relatively complex text provides clues and even imperatives as to how it should be read. This is certainly true of legal texts. As we strive to interpret

---

[6] Robert Cover, 'Violence and the Word' (1986) 95 *Yale Law Journal* 1601.

a text (however we may do it) the text acquires meaning for us. That meaning which we ascribe or derive in turn informs us as to how we are to read the text itself.[7] Interpretation begets meaning, and, in turn, meaning begets further interpretation.

While an integrated meaning is often what the judge or other legal officials seek, legal interpretation, if taken seriously, often leads in other directions. Some believe that this interpretive feedback loop can, in the image of an inward running spiral, lead to a stable unitary, integrated meaning.[8] But there is no reason to suppose that this is invariably true.[9]

The important thing for the interpreter is to take notice of how her interpretation affects and sometimes changes the character of the text she is reading, thus requiring further efforts at interpretation. After a while, a legal text can begin to look less like a sharply delineated stable identity and more like an interactive constellation of meanings. The task and challenge of the judge and the lawyer will often be to morph the constellation into a manageable directive.

D. The Plurality of Contexts

It is commonplace that the meaning of a text is a function of context. This commonplace bears some elaboration, however, because the contexts that can potentially affect the meaning of the text are numerous and varied.

i. The Context of Application

The idea here is that the meaning of a law must be understood in light of the context of application—that is to say, the particular social or economic or historical context to which the law is to be applied. This might be conceptualised as a problem of interpretation as translation. That is to say, how does one translate a legal text that means X in context A to context B (where context B turns out to be significantly different)? Does X still mean X (ie, literal transposition) or does X now need to be translated into Y because X in A means Y in B (analogical extrapolation)?[10]

ii. The Authorial Context

Even when we put intentionalism aside, as we have here, the determination of authorship remains important. There are legal issues of competence, or scope

---

[7] Hans Georg Gadamer, *Truth and Method* (New York, Continuum, 2004) 366–67.
[8] Ronald Dworkin, *Law's Empire* (Cambridge, Harvard University Press, 1986).
[9] Schlag (n 1) 1688–714.
[10] Lawrence Lessig, 'Fidelity in Translation' (1993) 71 *Texas Law Review* 1165, 1189–92.

of authority, that can arise. The purview of legitimate concerns, goals or values served by a legal text can be ascertained in part by an examination of what agent or agency created a legal text.

iii. The Addressee Context

A legal text is potentially addressed to many different kinds of addressees: states, parties, lawyers, courts, other governmental bodies and more. The meaning of the text may well vary depending upon which parties are taken to be the (primary) addressees of the legal text.[11] Additionally, different addressees may be authorised or compelled to read the text differently or in some cases (ie non-justiciability) not to 'read' parts of it at all.

iv. The Functional Legal Context

The immediate legal entourage of a text may affect its meaning. Thus, it matters whether the object of interpretation is found in a legal text that has a prohibitory, delegative, permissive, distributive, etc, effect. It also matters whether the text to be interpreted is understood to be embedded in a legal field rich with principles, policies, procedures, discretion (or not). In other words, even if one focuses on the interpretation of a singular identified legal text, the interpretation cannot help but take into account the surrounding functional entourage.

v. Contexts Generally

By exploring the multiple contexts in which a legal text is embedded, it is possible to enrich the interpretive possibilities. Such an exploration serves to multiply the perspectives that can be taken in trying to figure out the meaning of a legal text.

One last point to be noted: the text/context distinction is neither necessarily fixed nor necessarily perspicuous. That is to say that the activity of interpretation itself, precisely because it yields meaning as it happens, can produce a change in what is considered text and context. The point is difficult to appreciate until one recognises that not only is the text a function of context, but context is a function of text (ie, the text points to its relevant contexts) and both (as well as the distinction between the two) are a function of interpretive activity.

E. Fidelity to the Original Meaning

This familiar difficulty arises in a variety of settings. It is particularly salient in those circumstances where the legal text was drafted in a historical, social, linguistic

---

[11] Meir Dan Cohen, 'Decision Rules and Conduct Rules—Acoustic Separation in Criminal Law' (1984) 97 *Harvard Law Review* 625 (exploring the idea that criminal law rules communicate simultaneously different meanings to the public and to the courts).

and economic context different from our own. As technology leads to ever more accelerating developments in social, economic and cultural life, this difficulty will intensify. Indeed, the experience or sense of historical lag in law will occur across smaller time segments.[12]

What then is one to do in transposing the meanings of a text crafted in a particular time and place (that of enactment or ratification) to another very different time and place (the facts of the case in issue)?

The classic response is that the interpreter must show fidelity to the authoritative law. But what does that mean? Is meaning best preserved and honoured by a *literal transposition* that disregards changes in context or is it best preserved and honoured by *analogical extrapolation* in response to changes in context?[13] Notice that this crucial question cannot be answered by saying that the interpreter is obliged to show fidelity to the original meaning. On the contrary, both approaches—literal transposition as well as analogical extrapolation—claim to be (and, *in their own way*, are) honouring the original meaning.

A more radical problem for fidelity to the original meaning is that there may not be an 'original meaning' for the simple reason that a *legal* text, even as it might claim to be 'original' or 'constitutive', cannot possibly mean that in any strong sense of the term. No legal text is ever a complete *rupture* with its antecedents. On the contrary, any *legal* text variously incorporates, depends upon, borrows, modifies and disavows antecedent legal meanings and traditions in order to give effect to its own. This, of course, places on the interpreter the challenge of trying to discern what has been carried over from what has not.

F. Summary

These then are but a few of the stereotyped tensions and conflicts within which legal interpretation happens. Understanding and appreciating these tensions and conflicts allows the potential opening of a whole set of interpretive possibilities and attendant arguments. We turn now to textualism and purposivism to discuss their specific conflicts and tensions.

II. Textualism

In addition to the general conflicts and tensions articulated above, textualism presents certain stereotyped interpretive challenges that give rise to interpretive

---

[12] cf Ray Kurzweil, *The Singularity is Near* (New York, Viking Press, 2006).
[13] See Lessig (n 10).

disputes. Here I describe some that are sufficiently stereotyped and recursive to warrant discussion.

One challenge lies in identifying the object of interpretation—is it a word, a phrase, a sentence, or just what precisely? (*The Individuation Problem*). A second challenge lies in respecting the meaning of the entire text (*Intratextual Integrity*). And a third challenge lies in respecting the meaning of texts related to the one interpreted (*Intertextual integrity*).

A. Individuation: What is the Unit of Interpretation?

Treaties, Constitutions, statutes and regulations typically contain titles, which in turn contain sections, which contain subsections, which contain sentences, which contain phrases, which contain words. One might ask, in a given case, which unit is to serve as the unit of interpretation—the section, the subsection, the sentence, the phrase, or the word? This is a particular instance of what is sometimes called 'the individuation problem'.

In Anglo-American jurisprudence, the most famous example that is used to illustrate this problem is HLA Hart's famous hypothetical about an ordinance that 'prohibits vehicles in the park'.[14] The question is whether the ordinance covers tricycles, bicycles, the statue of a World War II tank (and so on). Hart believed that the key inquiry would have to turn on the semantic meaning of the term 'vehicle'. Fuller, his antagonist in the dispute, thought that one had to interpret the ordinance as a whole in terms of its ostensible purpose.

Among the several interpretive challenges raised by this hypothetical, one of the more interesting ones is the individuation problem: just what is the unit (in this case, a single word, the entire ordinance or something even broader) that is to be the object of interpretation? On this question, the law and the learning are rather unhelpful. (The individuation problem has an interesting similarity to the generally intractable 'level of abstraction' or 'level of generality' problem—which also tends to defy meaningful resolution.) What is clear, however, and this matters very much to the interpreter, is that a focus or emphasis on different units of interpretation may very well affect the outcome—or at least make one interpretation more plausible than another.

---

[14] See HLA Hart, 'Positivism and the Separation of Law and Morals' (1958) 71 *Harvard Law Review* 593, 606–15. For an explanation of the jurisprudential context giving rise to the dispute between Hart and Fuller, see Frederick Schauer, 'A Critical Guide to Vehicles in the Park' (2008) 83 *New York University Law Review* 1109. For Lon Fuller's response, see Lon L Fuller, 'Positivism and Fidelity to Law—A Reply to Professor Hart' (1958) 71 *Harvard Law Review* 630, 661–69. Since the original Hart-Fuller dispute, the hypothetical has taken on a life (several, actually) of its own. For my take, see Pierre Schlag, 'No Vehicles in the Park' (1999) 23 *Seattle University Law Review* 381.

B. Intratextual Integrity

Sophisticated textualists understand that the meaning of a text is not exhausted simply by summing up the meanings of individual words. They understand that texts are structured in all sorts of internal relations (hierarchies, cross-references, dependencies, encroachments, and so on and so forth). Similarly, they understand that the meaning of a term might well turn on its immediate syntactical entourage (eg, the clause of which it is a part) or instead on a technical use that remains constant throughout the text.[15] On the whole, sophisticated textualists understand that terms mean in an interactive way. In this interaction, the terms 'do' things to each other (modify, qualify, enhance, confirm, extend, and so on and so forth). Deciding what 'impact' words, clauses, sentences, paragraphs, and so on have on each other creates many pathways for interpretive argument.

C. Intertextual Integrity

Law, as already suggested, is 'layered' in multiple ways. The interpretation of a given law has implications not just for that law, but also for other laws to which it may be related. With just about any interpretation of a law, the question arises: must the interpretation offered conform to or accommodate other associated laws (and, if so, how)? This is the paradigmatic question of intertextual integrity. It is a question with both interpretive as well as jurisprudential aspects.[16]

III. Purposivism

Purposivism, as the term is used here, includes both principled interpretation and policy analysis when they are turned to the enterprise of interpretation. This is arguably an unusually encompassing use of the term. Indeed, some legal thinkers would greatly object (and for non-trivial reasons) to the conflation of principle and policy. Nonetheless, given a certain degree of abstraction, there are sufficient similarities in principle and policy interpretation that, for the limited purposes here, we can treat them together.

Purposivism, as its name indicates, calls for an examination of the purpose or purposes of a particular law. In the 'no vehicles in the park' hypothetical, a purposivist would try to figure out what sensible purpose might be served by prohibiting vehicles from the park.

---

[15] For one exploration, see Akhil Amar, 'Intratextualism' (1999) 112 *Harvard Law Review* 747.
[16] See, eg, Koen Leanerts, 'Discovering the Law of the EU: The European Court of Justice and the Comparative Law Method' in this volume.

Right away, the prohibition of vehicles from the park could be seen as serving a number of different purposes—among them: safety, noise abatement, aesthetic enjoyment, environmental concerns, wildlife preservation, landscape preservation or indeed some combination of the foregoing. The wording of the ordinance itself provides few contextual cues. One significant cue is often the least noticed—the notion of park.[17] An inquiry into the kind of park we are talking about—a city park, a national preserve, a skateboarding arena, a botanical garden—might give an indication of the function of the park at stake and thus what kind of purpose is to be served.[18]

But, as the hypothetical illustrates, the big challenge for purposivism lies in identifying and articulating the purposes ostensibly served by a law. Unfortunately, legal professionals tend to underestimate the difficulties in selecting purpose. As but one example, Henry Hart and Albert Sacks, the great US mid-century legal process thinkers, advanced the notion that statutory meaning is to be derived by assuming that legislators are 'reasonable men pursuing reasonable purposes reasonably, unless the contrary is made unmistakably to appear'.[19] Whether or not making this assumption is itself reasonable (an interesting question) it seems clear that it is not altogether all that helpful.

A. Multiple Purposes

Any mildly complex decision generally involves multiple purposes. Imagine you are going on a vacation to the Alps. Whatever purposes might be served by such an action, it is unlikely to be singular. The purposes for taking a vacation are multiple: exercise, change of scenery, revitalisation, challenge, time to think and more. As a general matter, human beings and groups (eg, institutions) do not generally act for singular or unitary purposes. The same is true of law. When one thinks about what the purpose for a particular provision might be, numerous possibilities come to mind. We have already seen this with regard to the 'no vehicles in the park' hypothetical above.

How is one to select, then, among several different purposes? Should a judge interpreting a legal text simply assume that all 'reasonable' purposes should be included in the interpretation of the ordinance? That is a possible strategy, but what happens when the purposes seem to indicate different conclusions? Moreover, consider that no one is ever willing to pursue any single legal objective endlessly. There is always a point at which one decides that pursuing a single objective (eg, accident deterrence) has become too costly, unreasonable, or something

---

[17] Steven Winter, 'An Upside/Down View of the Countermajoritarian Difficulty' (1991) 69 *Texas Law Review* 1881, 1886–88.

[18] ibid.

[19] Henry Hart and Albert Sacks, *The Legal Process: Basic Problems in the Making and Application of Law*, University Casebook Series 10th edn (Minnesota, Foundation Press, 1958) 1415.

of the sort. At some point, one encounters other objectives or values thought to be more compelling. Almost regardless of how we define the functions of a law (or the legal system generally) we will run up against a certain limit set forth in another law, or in the general policies, principles, values or other considerations of the legal system. We should recognise that to do legal analysis or legal interpretation by deriving our conclusions from a single legal imperative is never the right way to proceed: all legal imperatives are always embedded in and circumscribed by other legal imperatives that pull or push in other directions.

Moreover, all reasonably complex laws, despite what may seem to be their singular form (eg a prohibition), will nonetheless effectuate multiple ends. Take a simple traffic code law that prohibits driving without proof of liability insurance. At first one thinks about what it is in form: a prohibition. But, de facto, it is not just a prohibition. For one thing, it is a subsidy to insurance companies. It is a delegation of authority to police officers to check for liability insurance. It is a tax or revenue-raising mechanism for the state. It is a measure to assure social confidence—namely, the possibility of corrective intervention by way of damages, risk spreading and the like. Already then we see that the plausible purposes of a law are multiple—even if the form seems to be singular (eg a prohibition). Most laws will serve multiple purposes in exactly this way.

The difficulty from an interpretive standpoint lies in selecting which purposes are to be honoured and which not and how they are to be arranged in terms of their relative priority.

B. Selection

Confronted with many different purposes—as in the examples above—the immediate question becomes which of the several possible purposes are to be honoured and which are to be discounted? How much so? And on the basis of what criteria? These selection questions must be answered when indeed the purposes are in tension and point to different conclusions.

These are very tough questions. At one extreme one might say, as some legal thinkers have, that some coherent principles or criteria must be used to select which purposes are to be honoured.[20] But formulating such principles or criteria is surely no easy task. On the one hand, one wants to avoid particularist situationism (along this line lies the descent of law into managerialism). On the other hand, one wants to avoid rigid monism (along this line lies mechanistic formalism). But if we reject these two polar extremes and opt for some 'middle ground', just how much context-sensitivity should we demand of our coherence?

Applicable legal authorities tend to be ambivalent and vague on these problems. And understandably so: in law, we are interested in the kind of coherence that

---

[20] Wechsler (n 5); Dworkin (n 8).

takes due account of differences and dissimilarities ... which is to underscore the somewhat nebulous and elusive character of that which we seek.

C. The Structure of Purpose

Purpose is structured and organised in multiple ways—it can be seen as layered, conflicted, provisional, mutable, conditional and so on. That is, once one turns to the interpretation of a particular law or provision, it becomes apparent that it has many conceivable purposes, some of which will be disjunctive or conflicting. This realisation presents not just a selection question as described above, but an organisational one: how does one organise the various purposes identified? How do they relate to each other? Which, if any, are to be accorded primacy? What kind of structure can we give to the array of purposes?[21] And from where are we to derive this structure?[22]

IV. Conclusion

Just about any non-trivial legal issue can be presented as one involving interpretation. Once that framing of the issue is in place—that is, once the judge or other legal official recognises that there is an interpretive dimension to the legal issue— all kinds of questions (namely those described in this chapter) can be posed and a wide array of arguments can be advanced to address the legal issues at stake. Whether any of the questions turn out to be salient and whether the attendant arguments are deemed persuasive or not—these are altogether different matters. But at least it may help to have an index of possibilities to consider.

---

[21] See generally Robert S Summers, *Instrumentalism and American Legal Theory* (Ithaca, Cornell University Press, 1982); Robert S Summers, 'Pragmatic Instrumentalism in Twentieth Century American Legal Thought—A Synthesis and Critique of Our Dominant General Theory About Law and Its Use' (1981) 66 *Cornell Law Review* 861.

[22] This is where legal ontology kicks in—implicitly or explicitly. See Sinisa Rodin, 'Useful Effect of the Framework Decision on the European Arrest Warrant' in this volume.

3

Proportionality and 'Deference' in Contemporary Constitutional Thought

DUNCAN KENNEDY[*]

In a recent piece called 'Critical Perspectives on Social and Economic Rights, Democracy and Separation of Powers',[1] Karl Klare developed a novel and important argument in favour of judicial activism on behalf of constitutionally entrenched social and economic rights. His argument aims at both the legislature and the executive, and includes both invalidating and requiring particular actions. The innovation is that he treats the norm of judicial deference to the elected legislature and executive as a 'consideration' among others, one that might or might not lead the judge to uphold a statute in spite of his personal view that it is unconstitutional. It is of variable weight, according to him, depending on the particular context, rather than a categorical command.[2]

In an article called 'Freedom and Constraint in Adjudication',[3] I tried some years ago to imagine what it would be like to be a left liberal activist judge faced with a labour law dispute in which the law seemed to favour what he saw as an unjust result. The case was between private parties, with constitutional overtones, but not involving judicial review of legislation.

In this chapter I deploy the phenomenological method of 'Freedom and Constraint' to interpret and extend Klare's analysis, not necessarily in the direction he would have chosen. A phenomenological account of the judge thinking about deference has to start with a 'situation'. I will try to reconstruct the experience of a

[*] Carter Professor of General Jurisprudence Emeritus, Harvard Law School. Thanks to Karl Klare and Pascal McDougal, and to Jirhan Zang for research assistance. Errors are mine alone.
[1] K Klare, 'Critical Perspectives on Social and Economic Rights, Democracy and Separation of Powers' in HA García, K Klare and LA Williams (eds), *Social and Economic Rights in Theory and Practice: Critical Inquiries* (New York, Routledge, 2014).
[2] ibid.
[3] D Kennedy, 'Freedom and Constraint in Adjudication: A Critical Phenomenology' (1986) 4 *Journal of Legal Education* 518.

judge who has a specific place in a typology of judges and is operating in a specific political and legal cultural context. Of course, there are many other dimensions of the situation that might be relevant.

I. Contemporary Legal Thought

My judge is firmly situated in 'contemporary legal thought'.[4] By this I mean the set of typically contradictory jurists' ideas and attitudes that have come to dominate, transnationally, following the weakening of faith in socially oriented legal thought[5] and the partial revival of elements of classical legal thought.[6] There are three aspects of contemporary legal thought that are directly relevant to the topic addressed here.

A. Proportionality

The first of these is the slow transformation of the teleological jurisprudence developed by the social jurists between the 1890s and the 1940s into a jurisprudence of 'balancing' or 'proportionality'. Constitutional courts around the world sometimes deploy formal proportionality analysis as the reasoning technique for resolving conflicts between constitutionally protected rights and government powers, between protected private rights, between central and federated powers (the US, the EU), and between international courts and treaty signatories. In all its variants, the method is a complex amalgam of elements from social and classical legal thought.[7]

Jurists typically present the procedure as having three steps, only the third of which will concern us in this chapter. The first step is to decide whether the challenged action falls within the power of the defendant, whether a state or private actor, and at the same time whether the plaintiff has suffered an injury to the right (or subordinate power) alleged. This step seems typically to be performed in a conceptual or inductive/deductive manner, reminiscent of classical legal thought, by 'defining the scope' of power and right. The second step is to determine whether there was a 'less intrusive means' by which the actor could have accomplished

---

[4] See D Kennedy, 'Three Globalizations of Law and Legal Thought: 1850–2000' in DM Trubek and A Santos (eds), *The New Law and Economic Development: A Critical Appraisal* (Cambridge, Cambridge University Press, 2006).

[5] ibid 25.

[6] ibid 37.

[7] ibid; D Kennedy, *A Critique of Adjudication [fin de siècle]* (Cambridge, Harvard University Press, 1997); J Bomhoff, *Balancing Constitutional Rights: The Origins and Meanings of Postwar Legal Discourse* (Cambridge, Cambridge University Press, 2013); A Marzal Yetano, *La dynamique du principe de proportionnalité: Essai dans le contexte des libertés de circulation du droit de l'Union européenne* (LGDJ/ Institut Universitaire Varenne, 2014).

the legitimate objective established in the first part. The notion is that if the goal could have been accomplished by another means that would have a smaller (or negligible) impact on the plaintiff's entitlement, the means is illegitimate. This step is derived from the teleological jurisprudence characteristic of social legal thought.[8]

The third step, or 'true' or 'per se' balancing or proportionality, is the only one that will concern us here. The jurist performs it only if the first two steps yield neither a conceptual nor a teleologically convincing resolution of the case. In this sense, (true) balancing is the legal reasoning method of last resort.

The conflicting considerations to be balanced include the legal desiderata identified by the social jurists as 'interests' to be taken into account when interpreting 'law as a means to an end' (certainty, flexibility, security, innovation, social cohesion, social welfare, individual autonomy, and so forth).[9] But they also include the canonical classical categories of rights, powers, duties, privileges and so forth.

A typical jurisprudential reflection of this development was Ronald Dworkin's argument for including 'principles' with 'weight' (eg *pacta sunt servanda*, no one should profit by their own wrong, but also rights 'as trumps') into the formal definition of law, thereby overthrowing the mode of positivism according to which law was rules.[10] Dworkin to the contrary notwithstanding,[11] proportionality in contemporary practice has always included policies as well as principles, rights and powers.[12]

In both classical and social legal thought, and in both common law and civil law jurisdictions, the technique of proportionality was only marginally acknowledged, perhaps more in the US than elsewhere. In the US, it was present before World War II in nuisance, negligence and antitrust, and in the law of the federal 'commerce clause'. In the civil law, it found a prominent place in administrative law and in variants of abuse of right doctrine.[13]

---

[8] Thus legal ontogeny recapitulates legal phylogeny. In these first two steps the jurist may very well be covertly balancing in deciding the scope of rights and powers and the intrusiveness of means. cf R Alexy, *A Theory of Constitutional Rights* (New York, Oxford University Press, 2010) 399. Indeed, one way to understand the formal structure is that it permits courts to decide the vast majority of cases by manipulating these first conceptual or teleological steps, to make the outcome seem less discretionary and so less controversial than it would be if reached through the third 'true balancing' step. Critics of the outcome then bring to bear the 'hermeneutic of suspicion' described in s I.C below, to show legal error in the service of ideology. See D Kennedy, 'The Hermeneutic of Suspicion in Contemporary American Legal Thought' (2014) 2 *Law and Critique* 91.

[9] RV Jhering, *Law as a Means to an End*, trans I Husik (Boston, Boston Book, 1913).

[10] RM Dworkin, 'The Model of Rules' (1967) 1 *The University of Chicago Law Review* 14.

[11] RM Dworkin, 'Hard Cases' (1975) 6 *Harvard Law Review* 1057.

[12] Kennedy (n 7) 119.

[13] Kennedy (n 7); See D Kennedy, 'From the Will Theory to the Principle of Private Autonomy: Lon Fuller's "Consideration and Form"' (2000) 1 *Columbia Law Review* 94; D Kennedy and MC Belleau, 'La place de René Demogue dans la généalogie de la pensée juridique contemporaine' (2006) 56 *Revue interdisciplinaire d'études juridiques* 163; D Kennedy, 'A Transnational Genealogy of Proportionality in Private Law' in R Brownsword et al (eds), *The Foundations of European Private Law* (Oxford, Hart Publishing, 2011); A di Robilant, 'Abuse of Rights: The Continental Drug and the Common Law' (2010) 3 *Hastings Law Journal* 687.

It seems obvious, but only in retrospect, that it was covertly pervasive in both systems, but regarded as inconsistent with the basic idea that legal interpretation is a rational practice. Today overt recognition that 'the law', as narrowly defined by, say, Hartian positivism, sometimes 'runs out', and that the proper *and fully 'legal'* last resort response is balancing, is common but controversial.[14] This has meant that many but by no means all contemporary practitioners of legal reasoning in 'hard cases' live with a measure of self-doubt.[15]

B. Institutional Competence Arguments

The second relevant aspect of contemporary legal thought is the gradual emergence within the discourses of legal justification (whether lawyers' briefs, judgments, legal academic literature or legal philosophy) of what are commonly called 'institutional competence' arguments, a phrase popularised by Hart and Sacks in their famous *Legal Process Materials*.[16] These are typically based on the idea that founding documents (Constitutions, charters, treatise, see Teubner)[17] define distinct roles for different institutions in a system, and that these role constraints are in some sense binding or valid.

i. Institutional Competence in General

In the conventional understanding of these systems of separated powers, the role of the judge is to 'interpret and apply' the law that defines the competences of the institutions, to ensure that each operates only within its allocated 'sphere' or 'zone'. The conventional understanding sharply contrasts 'interpreting' with 'making' law, understood to be a legislative function, not authorised for judges. Thus the 'sphere' of the judge is defined *both* by the role of policing everyone else's sphere ('competence competence') *and* by the methodological imperative that he do this through legal interpretation alone.

This means that there are two different kinds of critique of a judicial decision. It might be wrong substantively: the wrong party won, the rule enunciated was the

---

[14] See generally Alexy (n 8); D Kennedy, 'A Left Phenomenological Alternative to the Hart/Kelsen Theory of Legal Interpretation' in D Kennedy, *Legal Reasoning: Collected Essays* (Aurora CO, The Davies Book Publishers, 2008).

[15] See Kennedy, 'From the Will Theory' (n 13); Kennedy (n 8); D Kennedy, 'A Social Psychological Interpretation of the Hermeneutic of Suspicion in Contemporary Constitutional Thoughts' in J DeSautels-Stein and C Tomlins (eds), *Contemporary Legal Thought* (Cambridge, Cambridge University Press, forthcoming).

[16] HM Hart and AM Sacks, *The Legal Process: Basic Problems in the Making and Application of Law*, tentative edition in 1957, published version edited by WN Eskridge Jr and PP Frickey (Westbury, New York, Foundation Press INC, 1994).

[17] G Teubner, 'Societal Constitutionalism: Alternatives to State-Centred Constitutional Theory?' in C Joerges, I-J Sand and G Teubner (eds), *Constitutionalism and Transnational Governance* (London, Hart Publishing, 2004).

result of a mistake in legal reasoning. The observer attacks the court's decision as legally unjustifiable, because, for example, it incorrectly constrains or fails to constrain the legislature when it passes a law that impinges civil liberties.

The second kind of critique adds to the substantive objection that the court reached its wrong result by overtly or covertly abandoning correct interpretive method, which would have precluded that outcome. The judgment consciously or unconsciously reasons on bases that are appropriate only to a co-equal legislative or executive power.[18] The defender of the judgment will respond with an institutional argument in the opposite direction, to the effect that the court's methodology was fully 'legal', as well as substantively correct. These arguments are loosely associated with the notions of judicial 'passivism' and 'activism', referring to greater or lesser willingness of the court to challenge the other powers in the system.

ii. Institutional Competence and the 'Counter-majoritarian Difficulty'

Institutional competence arguments emerged and were gradually abstracted and systematised in the United States during two periods, 1895–1937, and 1954–80, of intense controversy over decisions of the US Supreme Court striking down first progressive and then conservative legislation that had strong political and legislative support. The paradigmatic cases were *Lochner v New York*[19] and *Brown v Board of Education*.[20] The arguments developed in those contexts have been globalising since the Second World War, as Constitution-making bodies in many countries have established constitutional courts with the power of final judicial review of legislation.[21] In the US and in other national contexts of review of legislation under a bill of rights, the focus of the institutional competence argument is the 'counter-majoritarian difficulty'.[22]

In the American balancing debate of the 1950s, the blurring of the line separating judicial from legislative power was sometimes condemned because it forfeited the social benefits of role specialisation, with 'competence' meaning something like effectiveness and skill in judicial, legislative and administrative practice. In contemporary constitutional discourse, the issue is typically that of 'usurpation' by judges of legislative power. The accusation is that a particular instance of judicial activism violates the rules of constitutional law and the principle of democracy. 'In a democracy', the argument goes, law-making power belongs to 'the people', and they are represented in the separation of powers by the elected legislative

---

[18] Kennedy (n 7) 23–38.

[19] *Lochner v New York* 198 US 45, 25 S Ct 539 (1905).

[20] *Brown v Bd of Educ*, 347 US 483, 74 S Ct 686 (1954).

[21] See eg, CN Tate and T Vallinder (eds), *The Global Expansion of Judicial Power* (New York, New York University Press, 1995) 5.

[22] I believe that this phrase was coined by Alexander M Bickel in AM Bickel, *The Least Dangerous Branch: The Supreme Court at the Bar of Politics* (New Haven, Yale University Press, 1962) 19; and elaborated by John H Ely in JH Ely, *Democracy and Distrust: A Theory of Judicial Review* (Cambridge, Harvard University Press, 1980).

branch. The judges, because they are not elected, do not represent the democratic or majority will. Therefore if they 'make law', they usurp the legitimate powers of the other branches.

Sophisticated jurists have affirmed for more than a hundred years that what judges do and indeed have to do in important constitutional cases is more than 'just' interpretation in the classical mode of induction/deduction and conceptualism. They have recognised a consequent problem for the conventional view of the separation of powers. In exceptionally difficult questions of constitutional law, the court doing judicial review would have to go beyond straightforward conceptual reasoning (the law runs out) and open itself to the charge that it was usurping legislative power.

They have responded over time with perhaps a dozen sophisticated and often interesting explanations of how judges make law, but in a way that constrains them so as to make them very different from legislators. Then they have argued that judicial review can 'make law', in the restricted sense that is appropriate to the judicial role, and avoid the counter-majoritarian difficulty, by adopting their proposed method. An early example was Roscoe Pound's argument for teleological against formalist constitutional interpretation.[23]

Hart and Sacks, for another example, argued that if a decision invalidating a statute as unconstitutional could not be justified by 'reasoned elaboration' of the legal materials, it usurped legislative power both by inappropriate reasoning and by displacing the legitimate law maker.[24] Herbert Wechsler, a famous American jurist of the 1950s and 1960s, argued that the limit of judicial power was defined by the requirement of justification by 'neutral principles'.[25] As we will see in the next section, surprisingly and controversially, in the current 'age of proportionality' numerous contemporary jurists think that proportionality as a method is up to the justificatory task.

Competence arguments are of course not limited to the national individual rights situation. They have abstracted and generalised across the same wide range of institutional situations in which proportionality has become an important method, including, for example, judicial review of administrative action, judicial review by courts at the various levels of a federal system, and judicial review by national and international courts under human rights treaties. In Gunther Teubner's 'pluralist' transnational legal order, institutional competence issues, or something like them, arise when 'court-like' organs in non-governmental organisations interpret their founding documents.[26] Resistance to judicial power will be more complex when the opposition is no longer simply 'elected representatives of the people versus unelected judiciary'. For example, in the federal and transna-

---

[23] R Pound, 'Mechanical Jurisprudence' (1908) 8 *Columbia Law Review* 605.
[24] Hart and Sacks (n 16) 362–545.
[25] H Wechsler, 'Toward Neutral Principles of Constitutional Law' (1959) 1 *Harvard Law Review* 1.
[26] Teubner (n 17).

tional contexts, the argument for democracy mixes in an often puzzling way with the argument that the court applying constitutional or treaty norms should defer in some cases out of respect for the 'sovereignty' of the entity being judged. The discussion here is limited to the variant of institutional competence argument that is directed against or in support of a national court that is reviewing national legislation challenged as an interference with constitutionally protected fundamental rights.

iii. Deference and Proportionality

In a controversy about whether the court decided correctly when striking down a statute, the losers will argue that the judgment was incorrect as constitutional interpretation. Because it was incorrect, a valid legislative choice has been displaced by a wrong judicial one, and that is a misfortune for the losing litigants and for the separation of powers. But a 'deference' argument goes a step further.

It is to the effect that, in a particular case, the court should defer to the legislature by upholding a statute against constitutional challenge (or by refusing to impose an affirmative law making obligation). Deference occurs when the justices in the majority vote to uphold the law in spite of their own best legal judgment that it is unconstitutional. A closely allied variant of this argument in European constitutional discourse is that in cases of judicial review there exist 'margins of appreciation', meaning bounded areas or 'zones' of discretion, within which courts should defer to co-equal powers.[27]

The oldest version of the institutional competence argument for deference in the constitutional context is that a judge should vote to defer unless the case for unconstitutionality is 'clear'.[28] If there is doubt, he should vote to uphold the legislation. Suppose that, *as a legislator*, he would have regarded the case as close and difficult, but would ultimately have decided that the statute was unconstitutional and voted against it for that reason. *As a judge*, the argument goes, he should defer because of the particular kind of counter-majoritarian difficulty,[29] or democratic deficit,[30] implied in displacing the elected legislator in questions for which there is no clear legal answer.

Against this background, the rise of proportionality poses serious difficulties for the traditional doctrine of deference. On the one hand, it threatens to vastly expand the number of plausible challenges to the validity of statutes. On the other,

---

[27] See Alexy (n 8); and V Jackson, 'Constitutional Law in an Age of Proportionality' (2015) 8 *Yale Law Journal* 3094, 3144–47.

[28] Famously put forward in 1893 by JB Thayer, 'The Origin and Scope of the American Doctrine of Constitutional Law' (1893) 3 *Harvard Law Review* 129.

[29] See s I.B.i and I.B.ii above.

[30] cf JHH Weiler, 'Eurocracy and Distrust: Some Questions Concerning the Role of the European Court of Justice in the Protection of Fundamental Human Rights within the Legal Order of the European Communities' (1986) 3 *Washington Law Review* 1103.

its widespread use leads to fear that important questions of constitutional validity can never have clear answers in the sense required by the traditional doctrine. Something close to every single rule of public and private law can today be conceptualised as striking a balance between abstract rights, powers, values, interests and goals enshrined in the national constitution. For this reason, at the interpretive moment, every single rule is a candidate for proportionality analysis. This is Matthias Kumm's 'total constitution'.[31]

Sometimes the enemy of the judgment argues something more than that because the case was not clear there should have been deference. Suppose that the judgment invalidates the statute, using proportionality on the ground that the conceptual and teleological methods have 'run out' (the first two steps of the formal analysis are inconclusive) and there is no alternative to 'true balancing' other than 'denial of justice'.

The critic or dissenting judge answers that the method itself is not sufficiently distinct from the avowedly political method of the legislature to justify using it as a supposedly 'legal' constraint on legislative power. If unconstitutionality can be established only by balancing, the answer cannot be 'clear' in the requisite sense. The separation of powers requires that when the only possible basis for judgment is proportional, the court should defer unless there is 'no reasonable basis' for the statute.[32]

At this point, the parties will find themselves embroiled in a third aspect of contemporary legal thought, namely 'the hermeneutic of suspicion'.

C. The Hermeneutic of Suspicion[33]

The 'hermeneutic of suspicion' animates contemporary constitutional discourse when the legal question under discussion involves large political or social or economic stakes. The judge knows that there is a high consciousness among jurists of the indeterminacy of legal argument, associated with critiques revealing the prevalence of gaps, conflicts and ambiguities in standard legal materials. This goes along with a sense that both conceptual and teleological methods turn out to be frequently manipulable, with indeterminacy masked by the 'abuse of deduction'[34] (or of teleology).[35] Proportional argument is if anything more vulnerable than the

---

[31] M Kumm, 'Who's Afraid of the Total Constitution?' in AJ Menéndez and EO Eriksen (eds), *Arguing Fundamental Rights* (Netherlands, Springer Science & Business Media, 2006).

[32] TA Aleinikoff, 'Constitutional Law in the Age of Balancing' (1987) 5 *Yale Law Journal* 943.

[33] Kennedy (n 8); Kennedy (n 15).

[34] The phrase was coined by Francois Geny in F Geny, *Méthode d'interprétation et sources en droit privé positif: essai critique* (Paris, F Pichon Et Durand-Auzias, 1919); but the earliest example of this kind of critique seems to be Jhering (n 9) Ch VIII, p 381 et seq. See generally Kennedy, 'From the Will Theory' (n 13).

[35] For a classic example of the critique of the abuse of teleology by the social jurists, see K Klare, 'Judicial Deradicalization of the Wagner Act and the Origins of Modern Legal Consciousness, 1937–1941' (1978) 3 *Minnesota Law Review* 265.

other methods, and serves as no more than a weakly rational last resort when the other methods do not produce convincing answers (the 'law runs out').

Jurists habitually suspect that jurists other than themselves have instrumental-ised these indeterminacies to justify interpretations that are based on their politi-cal ideology rather than on the law.[36] They accuse their opponents of dressing up ideological judgments as legal judgments for the purpose of usurping legislative power. While the hermeneutic of suspicion has been a feature of constitutional law debates in the US from the end of the nineteenth century, it has generalised across all politically salient domains of law (with the 'juridification of social fields') and globalised (along with judicial review of legislation) in the contemporary period.

When the hermeneutic is directed at conceptual and teleological reasoning, the accusation is of 'motivated error' in interpretation by abuse of deduction or one-sided teleology. When directed at proportional reasoning, it is likely to have an added complexity. The accuser is likely to point out that the proportional method is in itself an invitation to usurpation of the legislative role because it requires the judge to assess the weights of conflicting considerations without any plausibly 'objective' measuring tool. The rise of proportionality has in this way multiplied occasions for suspicion of ideological corruption of adjudicative processes.

II. A Hypothetical Judge in a Hypothetical Situation

A. The Institutional Setting and the Legislation

My judge is sitting in the fifth year of a 10-year term on the nation's constitutional court, which has final authority to decide on the constitutionality of legislation. Like the other eight justices, he was nominated by the president and confirmed by the national legislature. The legislature is unicameral and elected from single member districts with a run-off system. He was elevated to the High Court from a lower court in a period of social democratic control of both the presidency and parliament. Centre right and far right parties now control both the executive and the legislature.

New legislation now challenged before the Court as unconstitutional denies non-citizens, whether legally or illegally present in the country, both various criminal due process rights granted to citizens and access to various social and economic benefits. The legislation is justified in its preamble through highly controversial factual claims about immigration, national security, personal secu-rity against crime, and equity given the alleged unequal fiscal contributions of the two groups to social provision.

---

[36] Kennedy (n 7) 209–12; Kennedy (n 8).

It is the common view of the legal community that the clauses of the Constitution referring to discrimination, to equality, to due process and social and economic rights, as well as to the powers of the legislature to protect national security, personal security and social welfare, are general and vague and sometimes at least apparently contradictory, and that their meanings are contested.

B. What Kind of Judge?

Now we need to specify just what kind of judge we are dealing with. There are a number of finely graded spectra along which we assess judicial attitudes. A given judge may have attitudes that it is hard or even impossible to locate along the relevant spectrum, but in our case the categories allow us to describe him accurately. The spectra:

— Formalist ('positivist', conceptualist, inductive/deductive, 'traditional') versus teleological vs proportional (balancing) versus eclectic;
— Centre left versus neoliberal versus nationalist/authoritarian/populist (NAP) versus eclectic;
— Activist versus passivist versus eclectic in relation to legislative power.

These dimensions are independent. A centre-left formalist passivist attitude toward legislation is perfectly possible and happens all the time, and moreover is not inconsistent with an opposite attitude toward executive or private power.

i. His Positions on the Spectra of Judicial Attitudes

— He believes the proportional method is in many important cases the only rational one, but is adept at conceptualist and teleological argument, and often finds one or the other convincing (easy cases).
— My judge understands that viewed from outside, his positions very roughly correspond to those of the social democratic party whose president nominated him and whose legislative members confirmed him five years ago. But he was never a member of a political party and regards himself as completely independent of party or factional discipline of any kind. He is opposed both to the NAP positions of the main right-wing party and to the neoliberal views of the conservative wing of the social democratic party.
— My judge is a judicial activist. This requires some specification.
   a. Looked at from the external perspective of a political scientist or a journalist, he has been relatively willing to make legal decisions that are understood to go counter to the interests and desires of power holders in the legislative, executive or civil society spheres.
   b. Looked at from the internal legal point of view, these decisions have been controversial because they depart from what the typical jurist's first impression is as to the likely outcome of conceptual/doctrinal reasoning.

His alternative argumentative strategy may be nonetheless conceptualist, albeit surprising, or may involve teleological or proportional argument.

c. The pattern of his activist decisions corresponds in a very general way to the agenda of the social democratic party, although he was never a member, and has often reached results inconsistent with its programme.

ii. His Judicial 'Philosophy' is Dworkinian

In his own mind, my judge understands his commitment to the rule of law in the following way: if the result of conceptual reasoning that seems plausible on first impression strikes him as unjust, he has a duty to try to find an alternative legal argument (which might be conceptual, teleological or proportional) that will lead to a just outcome. If he fails to find such an argument, he is bound to and will in fact reach the unjust result (except where he feels obliged to openly defy the law).[37]

In cases that involve the constitutionality of legislation, it is part of his conception of his oath to judge according to the law that he cannot strike a law unless he believes that the best interpretation of the Constitution is that it is invalid. In other words he fully accepts that he has a 'duty of interpretive fidelity'.[38]

Where conceptual and teleological reasoning 'run out' he has to resort to proportionality. In that case, he sees himself as bound to decide according to the balance in the particular factual context of the abstract ideals, rights, powers, principles, policies and values that are evoked in the general and particular clauses of the Constitution. These include civil, political and social rights, equality, national security, personal security, social welfare and so on.[39] Unlike Dworkin, he fully embraces 'policies' as elements in the analysis.[40]

C. His View of this Case

Although he thinks that cases sometimes have right answers when decided according to the deductive/inductive or teleological methods, it is clear to him that this case is not one of them. The law conceived that way 'runs out' so that there is no alternative to employing the method of proportionality. Entering into that procedure, he has concluded that (a) the measures enacted are within the powers of the government, and (b) that there are not available equally efficacious means that would be less detrimental to the rights of legal and illegal aliens.

However ... (c) the benefits to national security, personal security and tax equity are not proportional to the harm to the rights to equality, due process, and

---

[37] Kennedy (n 7) 161–64.
[38] R Dworkin, 'Law as Interpretation' (1982) 1 *Critical Inquiry* 179.
[39] Dworkin (n 11).
[40] See Kennedy (n 7) 124–30.

social protection guaranteed by the Constitution. He has therefore determined in his own mind that the statute is unconstitutional *unless* the doctrine of separation of powers requires him to defer to the decision of the legislature.

This means that he has in his own mind a clear answer to the typical lay argument that because his activist decisions seem consistently to be on the side of his social democratic party colleagues, he is deciding to strike the statute on political grounds and therefore usurping the power the people have conferred on the NAP adversary. His answer is that it is the Constitution itself that, faithfully interpreted, supports the social democratic position. He has subjected himself to the discipline of producing his own legal 'right answer' (Dworkin again), namely the result and the reasoning that he considers correctly proportional given constitutional values.

It follows that he does not see himself as having usurped legislative power, in the simple sense of making a 'wrong' legal judgment for political ends. Of course, pursuant to the hermeneutic of suspicion his political adversaries will condemn a decision against the statute as a politically motivated legal error. But this kind of exchange is just part of the territory of contemporary legal debate. If he chooses to defer, his erstwhile social democratic colleagues in the legislature will accuse him of betraying the activist legal truth through cowardice or opportunism.

III. Deference

The much more difficult question is whether the doctrine of separation of powers requires him to defer to the legislative judgment and uphold the statute in spite of his conviction that the best interpretation of the Constitution condemns it.

A. The Origins: Deference Linked to Proportionality

As far as I know, the first clear articulation of the argument that he should indeed do so is in Felix Frankfurter's famous concurrence in the 1951 case of *Dennis v United States*,[41] in which the US Supreme Court upheld the constitutionality of a statute criminalising speech advocating 'violent overthrow' of the government, aimed at the US Communist Party.

> The demands of free speech in a democratic society, as well as the interest in national security are better served by candid and informed weighing of the competing interests, within the confines of the judicial process, than by announcing dogmas too inflexible for the non-Euclidian problems to be solved.

---

[41] *Dennis v United States* 341 US 494, 71 S Ct 857 (1951) 525.

But how are competing interests to be assessed? Since they are not subject to quantitative ascertainment, the issue necessarily resolves itself into asking, who is to make the adjustment?—who is to balance the relevant factors and ascertain which interest is in the circumstances to prevail? Full responsibility for the choice cannot be given to the courts. Courts are not representative bodies. They are not designed to be a good reflex of a democratic society. Their judgment is best informed, and therefore most dependable, within narrow limits. Their essential quality is detachment, founded on independence. History teaches that the independence of the judiciary is jeopardized when courts become embroiled in the passions of the day and assume primary responsibility in choosing between competing political, economic and social pressures.

Primary responsibility for adjusting the interests which compete in the situation before us of necessity belongs to the Congress. The nature of the power to be exercised by this Court has been delineated in decisions not charged with the emotional appeal of situations such as that now before us. *We are to set aside the judgment of those whose duty it is to legislate only if there is no reasonable basis for it.*[42]

Dennis is one of the earliest, if not the earliest, discussions[43] of proportionality as a legitimately legal although last-resort form of legal reasoning in the exercise of judicial review of legislation (as opposed to private and administrative law).[44] It is striking that right from this beginning it was linked to the idea of deference.

Since the end of the nineteenth century, American judges when striking statutes routinely stated that they acted only in clear cases, and dissents routinely argued that the case was not clear (See eg, *Lochner v New York*[45] and the famous article by Thayer on 'The American Doctrine of Judicial Review').[46] But in this case, Frankfurter seems to be saying something much more specific. It is because the case can only be decided by balancing that the court must defer, and the standard of 'no reasonable basis' goes far beyond the ritual requirement that the case against the statute be clear.

When *Dennis* was decided, at the dawn of the third globalisation (contemporary legal thought), there were very few acknowledged balancing cases in American constitutional law (it was several years before the German constitutional court would decide the *Luth* case).[47] It was, I imagine, plausible that balancing would be an unusual procedure, so that a requirement of extreme deference in a few cases would have little impact on the law. As it happened, balancing cases proliferated and the US court soon developed an elaborate structure of 'degrees of scrutiny' corresponding to different levels of deference. Meanwhile proportionality became the basic doctrine first of the German Constitutional Court and then of

---

[42] ibid, emphasis added.
[43] Aleinikoff has nothing earlier in his history. See Aleinikoff (n 32).
[44] Kennedy, 'Transnational Genealogy of Proportionality' (n 13).
[45] *Lochner v New York* (n 19).
[46] Thayer (n 28).
[47] 7 BVerfGE 198 (1958).

the European Court of Justice and the European Court of Human Rights.[48] After the 'transition' around 1989 from left and right dictatorships to at least nominal constitutional democracy, it globalised along with judicial review.[49] In the US, paradoxically, at the moment of the global triumph of an American innovation the practice went underground.[50]

Writing about the 1950s, Martin Shapiro, to my mind the period's most astute analyst of constitutional law as political discourse, predicted that balancing would be an excuse for judicial surrender to the legislature.[51] Because it lacks compelling rational structure, it would be hard to defend a balancing ruling against the charge of usurpation of the legislative prerogative of deciding political questions. To the contrary, it has long since been obvious that proportionality has been the vehicle of a radical expansion of judicial vis-à-vis legislative power. Balancing turned out to be the activists' language of choice for constructing an alternative after destabilising a targeted rule's conceptual or teleological rationale as formalist.

Judicial review as an aspect of the globalisation of contemporary legal thought means that my imaginary judge has to deal, if he wants to decide in good faith according to fidelity to law, with the separation of powers argument. According to that argument, he should uphold the statute, even though he believes that it is unconstitutional, on the ground that the legislature is the proper body to decide contestable questions of constitutional proportionality.

B. The Conceptual Arguments for and against Deference

i. The 'Legalist' or No-deference-at-all Argument

My judge could but will not respond by rejecting the whole notion of deference. He could but will not appeal to the version of the separation of powers that requires the judge to perform judicial review according to strictly legal criteria. In this view, to refuse to apply the law as he believes it to be, on the ground that 'courts are not

---

[48] Bomhoff (n 7) chs 1 and 3; AS Sweet and J Mathews, 'Proportionality, Balancing and Global Constitutionalism' (2008) 47 *Columbia Journal of Transnational Law* 72.

[49] D Beatty, *The Ultimate Rule of Law* (Oxford, Oxford University Press, 2004) 162–63; Sweet and Mathews, ibid.

[50] Thus Aleinikoff writing in 1987 described balancing in US con law as 'widespread, if not dominant'. See Aleinikoff (n 32) 943–44. In 2015, Jackson sees 'the relative dearth of proportionality analysis in US jurisprudence' as an interesting phenomenon worthy of explanation, and develops an elaborate account. It includes a role for 'distinctively American fears about judging and the role of judges, in part an inheritance of Legal realism and critical legal studies', that are absent in Europe. See Jackson (n 27) 3125. She ignores the (Republican) elephant in the room, which is the political right-wing campaign against left judicial activism under the slogans of strict construction and original intent and the liberal regression under pressure, surrendering their own advanced thought from sociological jurisprudence to Legal Process. Jackson, ibid 3125. See also Bomhoff (n 7) 156–89.

[51] MM Shapiro, *Freedom of Speech: the Supreme Court and Judicial Review* (Englewood Cliffs NJ, Prentice-Hall, 1966) 103.

representative bodies', is to betray his role, rather than perform it. It is a 'refusal of justice'. This argument was skilfully made by Gerald Gunther, 'The Subtle Vices of the Passive Virtues',[52] against Alexander Bickel's *The Least Dangerous Branch*.[53]

My judge's reason for rejecting the categorical argument is that it is based on a simplistic distinction between legal interpretation and law making. As a contemporary, he cannot escape the usurpation charge simply by ignoring the role of politics in law.

In this case, according to him, conceptual and teleological reasoning run out. His solution, though held in good faith as his Dworkinian 'right answer', is based on last-resort proportional analysis of the general desiderata of national security, due process, and so forth. His understanding of these concepts as well of the Constitution as a whole corresponds roughly to that of the social democratic party that chose him, but lost the last election to the nationalist/authoritarians/populists.

NAP jurists have a very different construction of the very same constitutional text, one that supports a different assessment of the weights of the contending considerations, and a judgment that the statute is a valid exercise of legislative power. My judge believes that this reading is 'wrong', and like the other participants in contemporary legal consciousness, he is quick to apply the hermeneutic of suspicion to their argument. He thinks that they are committing an ideologically motivated legal error and are in denial about the flaws in their reasoning.

But ... he does not believe that the statute has 'no reasonable basis' or that its unconstitutionality is 'clear' according to widely accepted non-partisan canons of legal reasoning. He is perfectly capable of placing himself in a 'third' position vis-à-vis himself and his opponent and applying the hermeneutic of suspicion to his own good faith conviction about the right answer. He recognises that his view is in all probability influenced, first, by his own ideological priors, which guide his work of legal interpretation,[54] and second by the history of interpretive work by others of his ideological persuasion.

At this point, he has to ask himself whether there is a meaningful difference between his debate with his conservative colleagues on the bench and the debate in the legislature. Judicial review in this case may be distinctively 'legal',[55] and may sometimes dictate or exclude particular outcomes, but not in this case: it is not plausible here that professional judgment under a duty of fidelity to the materials is a 'check' on the political passions of the moment. It appears merely to substitute highly technical but eminently manipulable legal language of judges for the more open politics of the legislators. Since judicial review is final (absent constitutional amendment), the political judgment of the elected legislature has been overruled by the political judgment of the judges.

---

[52] G Gunther, 'The Subtle Vices of the "Passive Virtues"—A Comment on Principle and Expediency in Judicial Review' (1964) 1 *Columbia Law Review* 1.

[53] Bickel (n 22).

[54] Dworkin (n 11).

[55] Klare (n 1) 6.

True they were selected by the president with the consent of the parliament, but they are not now subject to any electoral check. The judge concedes that in cases such as this, their power to decide against the will of the legislative majority faces a 'democratic deficit' or 'counter-majoritarian difficulty'. Under the right circumstances (to be considered below), our judge believes he will be obliged to defer.

ii. The Conceptual Argument for Deference in Proportionality Cases

Having rejected the conceptual argument against deference, the judge will consider the conceptual argument in its favour. The reader will already have guessed that if this argument fails, as the 'legalist' or 'no-deference-at-all' argument did, the judge will have to choose a 'last resort'.

Here again is Frankfurter's argument for the position that deference is always required when the judgment must be based on proportionality:

> Courts are not representative bodies. They are not designed to be a good reflex of a democratic society. Their judgment is best informed, and therefore most dependable, within narrow limits. Their essential quality is detachment, founded on independence. History teaches that the independence of the judiciary is jeopardized when courts become embroiled in the passions of the day and assume primary responsibility in choosing between competing political, economic and social pressures.[56]

Given (1) the reconcepualisation of the rules of public and private law as compromises of constitutionally protected rights, powers, principles, values and interests (Kumm, 'total constitution');[57] (2) the pervasive sense of the indeterminacy of the constitutional law rules supposedly regulating these conflicts; and (3) the concomitant rise of proportionality as an accepted, fully 'legal' methodology, the Frankfurter proposal to defer unless the legislation has 'no rational basis' would seem to reduce the scope of judicial review so radically as to be inconsistent with the 'normal' understanding of the separation of powers.

If we view the doctrine of separation of powers as a 'valid norm' of the constitutional order, it appears to have two components. The first is that the court is to interpret and apply the Constitution as law to strike down legislation that violates it. The second is that the court is to restrict itself to interpreting and applying, and never to exercise the law-making power conferred on the legislature. As Martin Shapiro argued in 1966, in the contemporary situation, the Frankfurter 'no reasonable basis' test amounts to allowing the second command to abolish the first.[58] In other words, the situation appears to be one in which the conceptual method for applying the separation of powers as a legal norm 'runs out'.

---

[56] *Dennis* (n 41) 525.
[57] Kumm (n 31).
[58] Shapiro (n 51).

iii. Splitting the Difference: Alexy's Solution

In the 2010 Postscript to his *A Theory of Constitutional Rights* (1986),[59] Robert Alexy developed a complex theory of deference in the specific context of his theory of proportionality as the master method of legal reasoning. It is striking that it was written specifically for the English translation of the work. It signals something like the merger of the American and German debates on the issue.

Alexy starts from the premise that democracy and constitutional rights are contradictory ideas, each claiming supremacy over the other. Moreover, 'the problem of epistemic or knowledge-related discretion can be resolved by balancing formal and substantive principles'.[60] My best effort at a translation would be: 'the problem of the discretion of the legislature in situations of uncertainty about the right answer can be resolved by balancing the principle of the separation of powers against the principle of respect for constitutional rights'.

Alexy might have developed his prescriptions for deference from this starting point in a direction like the one suggested by Klare. Instead he produced a set of conceptual distinctions that define spheres or zones without the need for case-by-case assessment of pros and cons. The distinctions are:

— First distinction: Between questions of constitutional validity that have certain versus uncertain answers under the test of proportionality. Where the answer 'is' certain, there is no room for deference. The judge must apply the law, as in the 'legalist' position above, *unless* the proportional method produces 'stalemate'. In that case, the legislature can choose between equally valid alternatives.

— Second distinction: Between questions of constitutional validity that 'are' uncertain because relevant facts are uncertain, and questions that 'are' uncertain because the correct balance of legal reasons is uncertain. The determination of uncertain facts is a part of law-making (not interpretation) and therefore belongs to the democratically legitimated legislature.

— Third distinction: Among situations where the legal answer is uncertain, between those where two solutions are equally likely legally correct, and situations in which one is more likely correct than the other ('there are constitutional rights on both sides [so] there is an epistemic stalemate between them'). In the stalemate, there is no 'definitive Ought'. 'The principle of the decision-taking competence of the democratically legitimated legislature' means that the legislature can decide the constitutional question.[61]

My judge, much more American than German, will experience each of Alexy's distinctions as unable in practice to answer the question of deference. The distinctions—between certainty and uncertainty, between factual and normative

---

[59] Alexy (n 8).
[60] ibid 414.
[61] ibid 421–22.

uncertainty, and between legal uncertainty with or without stalemate—are themselves obviously uncertain, subject to inflection by the very passions they are supposed to tame. In the case before my judge, each of them could go either way, to indicate or forbid deference.

Alexy's approach is at the extreme opposite pole from the phenomenological, because it posits the truth of law as external to the practitioner, denying the practitioner's experience of its relativity to his work on the materials. The hermeneutic of suspicion makes short work of justifying upholding a statute because the correct balance 'is' uncertain. It will seem obviously preferable to confront directly the pro and con arguments about deference that will be masked by a certainty test.

C. The Proportional Approach to Deference: The Separation of Powers as a 'Consideration'

Confronted with what looks like a choice between two evils, my judge will explore the argument that he should regard the separation of powers as one of the 'conflicting considerations' that the judge should consider when trying to decide whether to uphold a statute he would reject as unconstitutional if he were a legislator rather than a judge. It is worth quoting at length Karl Klare's argument that it is a wrong interpretation of the rule of law to say that, *no matter what the context*, a judge conscious of the at least partially political character of his choice of interpretation should defer to the legislature.

> For time-honored theoretical and historical reasons, the countermajoritarian concern is always a respect-worthy consideration. Limitations of institutional competence should always be considered. But that is precisely what the countermajoritarian and institutional competence concerns are—*considerations* in a complex balancing of multiple sometimes conflicting factors. How powerful the countermajoritarian and institutional competence factor is in any given case depends on the circumstances. Within an overall proportionality template, it may sometimes be appropriate to subordinate those concerns to other considerations. Surely we cannot rule out this possibility a priori.[62]

In his canonical argument for deference to the legislature, Frankfurter offers no considerations on the other side. He proposes nothing that would push a judge who believes that the statute 'is' unconstitutional to refuse deference and strike it down, other than the judge's own hypothetical preference for free speech over national security in the case at hand.

This is not surprising given that Frankfurter was methodologically strongly committed to the teleological, rather than proportional method, and the latter was barely beginning to seem an inevitable last resort in important cases. In the

---

[62] Klare (n 1) 19 (footnotes omitted).

teleological method, the purposes or interests on the winning side are listed as conclusive and there is no overt balancing.[63]

i. Considerations against Deference

In the judge's proportional judgment, the gains to national security, personal security and tax equity were not worth the loss to equality, due process and social and economic rights. The first argument against deferring is that he believes that the statute entails a serious departure from the true meaning of the Constitution: it impairs the value of the rule of law which binds the legislature no less than the judiciary. Second, the constitutional distortion moves the Constitution away from what the judge understands to be true (social democratic) values.

These are considerations against deference to be weighed against the argument that the representative legislature is a better reflection of democratic will, and more competent to deal with broad issues of policy (courts perform well only 'within narrow limits').

ii. Dimensions of Strength of the Deference Argument (cf Alexy)[64]

In making his proportional argument against deference in the South African Supreme Court's interpretation of the constitutional clauses about social and economic rights, Klare points out[65] that there is a wide variety of more or less activist approaches the judge can take if he decides to challenge the legislature with regard to this statute. He could demand a 'second look', give a chance to amend within a given time or risk invalidation, choose to invalidate some or many parts with variable effect on the viability of the legislation, invalidate but suggest means by which the aims could be constitutionally accomplished, and many more. It will be a consideration against deference that the statute's bad effects can be prevented or mitigated in a way that only minimally, though effectively, challenges legislative power.

The proportional argument will incorporate the notion of a gradient of more or less intrusive action in review, along with the variability of the gains and losses to the competing considerations that favour and oppose deference. Imagine the degree of deference on the Y axis and the degree of impairment of civil, political and economic rights on the X axis. More impairment means less deference, and vice versa.

a.   The more serious the consequences for the values that lost out in the legislative determination, the weaker the argument for deference.

---

[63] See Kennedy, 'From the Will Theory' (n 13) 116–21.

[64] These considerations are analogous to Alexy's 'laws of balancing' but applied to deference rather than to the substantive balance. See Alexy (n 8) 102.

[65] Klare (n 1) 19–20.

b.   The more gentle and nuanced the proposed challenge to the legislative judgment, the weaker the deference argument.

There are doubtless a number of similar gradients in play, for example:

c.   The stronger the legal case against the law, according to conventionally accepted standards, and the greater the judge's subjective certainty that his 'right answer' is indeed right, the weaker the case for deference.
d.   The greater the judge's certainty as to the factual consequences of upholding versus striking the statute, the weaker the case for deference.
e.   As Klare argues,[66] the weaker the democratic pedigree of the statute, the weaker the case for deference. An apartheid or communist era statute whose continued enforcement allows strong parties to exploit others with no relation to the goals and values of the democratic regime should be struck down, in a way that invites the legislature to find its own new solution to the question posed.

iii. Should the Democratic Defects of the Legislature be a Consideration Affecting the Strength of the Argument for Deference in Judicial Review?

Suppose that the judge considers that in the present political situation a NAP elected president and a NAP elected legislature are frequently violating constitutional guarantees of civil, social and economic rights. The discriminatory legislation against non-citizens is part of a general right-wing political programme.

Suppose that electoral procedures, including the drawing of electoral boundaries, vote-counting procedures, the financing of campaigns and control of the media, have been continuously revised so as to keep the NAP regime in power. The revisions make the rules of electoral competition more favourable to incumbents than those of any other European democracy. Voter participation in parliamentary elections, partly because of the new rules, hovers around 50 per cent.

The judge is committed to a proportional approach to answering the legal question. Is it forbidden, permissible or required, in assessing the argument for deference, to take into account the actual quality of the democratic process? The argument that 'Courts are not representative bodies. They are not designed to be a good reflex of a democratic society', has force. But what if the legislature is not even arguably a good reflex, and the consequences of deference for democratic values appear likely to be severe? To exclude consideration of the democratic quality of the legislature seems irrational. When the stakes are high for democratic

---

[66] Klare (n 1) 20.

values, the judge should be less deferential in reviewing statutes produced by only nominally democratic institutions that threaten those values than in reviewing statutes produced in better conditions, subject of course to the multiple grids already mentioned. As Klare puts it:

> Traditional SOP discourse under-weighs or entirely ignores the democratic shortcomings of shabby, dysfunctional, or corrupt legislative processes. Complacency about democratic deficits in modern parliamentary politics may blind constitutional theory to 'routine political ineffectiveness and quiescence—rooted in social and economic inequality—of masses of ordinary citizens'.[67]

iv. Should there be Less Deference where Judges are More Democratically Accountable?

The argument for deference depends on the idea that the judiciary is a 'counter-majoritarian' institution. Suppose the constitutional judges are selected for life terms by the president, without legislative advice and consent, from the ranks of senior sitting judges who are themselves co-opted from the corps of lower court judges.

The argument that this court suffers from a 'democratic deficit' will be strong. But what if the legislature elects the court from its own members, under a requirement of approval by three quarters of legislators in office, to staggered renewable 10-year terms (so that no legislative session will elect a majority, barring deaths in office), and judges have the possibility of re-election by their legislative peers (so they have something to lose by flouting them).

Now imagine that our judge was elected through a complex compromise between social democratic and NAP forces in the legislature, made necessary by the complex selection procedure I just described. At the same time, imagine that a new NAP majority has gerrymandered the electoral map so effectively that future social democratic electoral victories will be impossible even if the party secures a substantial majority of the votes overall. In this hypothetical, the legislature is more 'democratically defective' than the judiciary and the counter-majoritarian difficulty close to non-existent. In such a case, our judge would regard the argument for deference as weak.

Of course, these are counterfactual examples the judge uses to decide whether in his much more nuanced case he can even consider the actual democratic quality of legislature and judiciary. He will conclude from the hypothetical that he is not just permitted but obliged to at least consider the possibility that there is no judicial deficit.

---

[67] Klare (n 1) 21, citing RD Parker, 'The Past of Constitutional Theory—and Its Future' (1981) 42 *Ohio State Law Journal* 223.

D. The Problem of 'Universalisation'

The alternatives to the 'proportional deference' (PD) test that our judge has adopted seem to be the 'no reasonable basis' test on one side, and the 'legalist' or no-deference-at-all approach on the other. In the view of our judge, neither is conceptually required by the Constitution regarded as basic law. The basic objection to each alternative is that it purchases a measure of clarity (at least clarity in theory) at the expense of potentially disastrous arbitrariness from the point of view of constitutional values. In short, too much deference or too little. But of course PD as an answer is open to many and serious objections as well, several of which come under the rubric of universalisation. In this part, assume that our judge is going to base his judgment on PD, and explain it in his opinion, giving the arguments outlined above.

i. *Goose and Gander Universalisation: Will You Accept it when they do the Same Thing to You?*

There is what one might call a Kantian universalisation question here: if the 'maxim' of his judgment is PD, can our judge 'will it to be law universal?' That would mean judging it equally right for a NAP judge facing a symmetrically reversed legal/political issue to apply PD to justify nullifying progressive legislation.

I think our judge will fully accept that his NAP adversary is 'entitled' to do PD. Sauce for the gander. Of course, our judge is likely to disagree very strongly, indeed to regard as contrary to law and legality, the results that the NAP judge arrives at. But these will be objections to the legal reasoning by which the NAP judge concluded that the statute was unconstitutional, and to the NAP judge's application of the standard of proportional deference. They will not be objections to the norm of PD through which the NAP judge approaches the problem.

This is not quite the end of the story, for two reasons. First, the judge may be of the view that if he adopts PD as his maxim, it will indeed be used by NAP judges, with disastrous legal results. These might far outweigh, he fears, the beneficial legal results that flow from his and like-minded colleagues adopting and then using the standard in this and future cases when they are in the majority.

If this is the situation, the argument against announcing PD as a norm is obviously strong. If we assume (for the moment) the judge's duty to declare his true reasons for his judgment, this is also a strong motive to adopt one of the alternatives (defer unless 'no reasonable basis' or 'one right answer'). Of course, it might also be the case that our judge believes that what he or his majority say about PD will have little or no effect on NAP judges in future cases.

In the US context, in the 1950s, several very prestigious conservative federal judges practised (or said they practised) strong deference toward liberal legislation. They might have been less deferential if their liberal adversaries had put forward PD to justify activist review. But it is not clear that there are any deferential conservatives remaining in the US context. If they have instead adopted some covert version of PD, our judge might well think it is he who is evening things up by doing it openly.

All this assumes that the national political system is operating 'normally' so that it at least plausible for our judge to see it as like a long running game with rules that are pretty much accepted by everyone. This is in part because everyone assumes that over the long run the 'sides' can expect gains and losses to be relatively stable and at least minimally acceptable to all players.

It is worth noting that in the post-'transition' period of globalising judicial review, no small number of national systems around the world have descended into a Schmittian 'crisis of parliamentary democracy'.[68] In such a crisis, political actors come to believe that they cannot treat politics as like a game in which the point is to win or lose 'by the rules'. In a crisis, particular decisions that are legitimate under the present rules appear likely to the actors to have irreversible rule-transforming and system-transforming future effects. In the US context, this is a plausible interpretation of the *Citizens United* decision.[69] At that point, it may appear that resolving the crisis in the 'right' way is much more important than any consequences that might follow after the fact from the framing of a norm of PD.

ii. Administrable Universalisation: Will Any Imaginable Standard of Proportional Deference Violate Minimum Rule of Law Norms of Legal Certainty and Restraint of Judicial Arbitrariness?

A second kind of universalisation objection is distinct from the goose/gander question. Again, we imagine a debate about whether judges should declare PD as the governing interpretation of what separation of powers requires in judicial review of legislation.

It is the traditional objection to proportionality tests in private, public and international law that they are uncertain on multiple dimensions. 'Proportion' or 'balance' is a metaphor not an intelligible prescription. According to the critique, the relevant considerations are not specified by positive law and the choice of 'weights', once considerations are specified, seems blatantly subjective, as compared to conceptual or teleological reasoning.

The resulting uncertainty is arguably a violation of the rule of law because it deprives the citizenry of assurance that they can avoid sanction by obedience. More important, the use of a proportionality test in the context of deference is in itself arguably a violation of separation of powers doctrine, because it poses no

---

[68] C Schmitt, *The Crisis of Parliamentary Democracy* (Cambridge MA, MIT Press, 1985).
[69] *Citizens United v FEC*, 558 US 310, 130 S Ct 876 (2010).

meaningful restraint on the usurpation of legislative power by the constitutional court. The considerations our judge proposes for PD seem either hopelessly indefinite (harm to constitutional values) or blatantly ideological or political (democratic deficits).

The first response to this argument, almost always ignored by it proponents, is that proportionality in the PD argument is a last resort. To attack it without defending either no-deference-at-all or 'no reasonable basis' is just wasting our time.

Proportionality is the dominant mode of reasoning in difficult constitutional law cases throughout Europe. Since the end of the nineteenth century, proportionality has been the basic technique of European administrative law in cases where the conflict is between the 'legitimate interests' of the citizen and the public interest. It is far too late to claim that it is fundamentally illegitimate, inconsistent with the rule of law or separation of powers in the abstract.

In the US, it corresponds to some overt practice, eg in the Fourth Amendment, but corresponds to sub rosa actual practice across the whole domain of the law of individual rights against the state, because judges are unwilling to accept either alternative in practice. This is most obvious in 'degrees of scrutiny' of legislation depending on the imputed importance of the infringed right and the imputed 'compellingness' of the state interest. The avoidance of the word 'proportionality' has to do with the odd rhetorical battles between liberal and conservative constitutional jurists in the US (eg strict constructionism versus living constitutionism).

The permissible considerations in proportionality are restricted by the requirements that they be themselves universalisable (ie, not explicitly partisan, ideological, religious, etc) and that they be derivable from the legal materials that are sources of positive law.

Proportional deference if adopted as a norm would evolve through application, like other norms of the same type. While not likely to become a highly administrable standard, it would develop, for example, by working out lists of permissible and impermissible factors and through the force of precedent. The common objection that proportional judgments cannot have precedential force is obviously incorrect, for two reasons.

First, the proportionality test produces a new norm, which in many cases will be highly 'material' and therefore administrable, in spite of its origin in the only weakly rational balancing calculus. For example a rule of restricted deference to a statute enacted under dictatorship and never reconsidered after the transition to democracy would be easy to apply. Even when the court chooses not a bright line rule, but an ad hoc 'standard', requiring balancing in each case, the balance in a particular case will determine a future case by a fortiori reasoning if there is no plausible argument that at least one losing argument from that case is stronger in this one.

In short, the arguments against PD based on the general critique of proportionality are subject to responses developed by its partisans over the last decades.

They may be stronger or weaker in this case, but they do not seem to be different in kind. And for our judge, the first is still the most important: there is no viable alternative to PD, given the arbitrariness of either the 'reasonable basis' test or the no deference position.

IV. Deciding on the Basis of Proportionality to Cast Proportionality as Deduction or Teleology to Avoid Bad Consequences of Candour

We know already that jurists are divided in terms of their explicit positions between the formalist/positivists, teleologists, proportionalists and eclectics. We also know that they practice a hermeneutic of suspicion amongst themselves, accusing one another of letting political ideology bias their judgment causing them to adopt incorrect legal positions. Now suppose that the informed politically active public (or at least the relevant lay elites) have a somewhat different view. They tend to be uninformed formalists, believing that there are always correct answers, but also confirmed cynics, convinced that judges like all other officials are very often corrupt, personally or politically.

In spite of his proportional beliefs, the judge may anticipate quite reasonably that if he is going to vote to invalidate the statute, he should cast his activist attack in formalist conceptual or teleological terms, even though he does not think those methods can answer the legal question ('the law runs out'). A fortiori, he should treat the separation of powers issue in conceptual (no deference) rather than proportional language. The reason being that if the public were to realise the extent to which his centre left solution rests on a partially political method, they would react in one of two ways, each undesirable.

Some might lose their naive belief in the objectivity of judicial review and conclude that the power is such a serious danger to democracy that it should be eliminated. By eroding faith in the distinction between courts and the other branches, left judicial activism might kill the formalist goose that lays the golden eggs of left judicial power. But of course the consequences are incalculable. Other parts of the public might conclude that liberal judges are usurpers, using their political method in violation of the rule of law, which could be restored by the selection of true jurists, namely right-wing formalist/positivists.

My view is that it is permissible for the judge to write and speak in bad faith, making himself plausible as a formalist/positivist, so long as *but only so long as* he honestly believes it is (a) necessary to prevent serious bad consequences for the body politic (b) taking into account the negative consequences. In other words, there is always the possibility that there will be a third moment of proportional judgment. This time it will be neither about the substance of the legal case for or against the statute nor about the weight of the democratic deficit in the decision whether or not to defer. The judge will take into account all the same kinds of concerns about universalisation, administrability and unintended consequences that he brought to bear in deciding on PD, but this time he will decide case by case whether to try to mislead at least part of the public.

This view has been, I think, very generally rejected among the scholars associated with critical legal studies, including Karl Klare, whose analysis I have followed closely up to this point.

A. Always Already in Bad Faith

Rather than defend this 'outrageous' position at length, I will argue for it by analogy. There are three analogous institutional 'situations' that, I have argued elsewhere, put the judge as a matter of course in a similar kind of dilemma. They derive from one of the role conflicts that in my view define his existential situation. The conflict in question is between, on one side, his duty to state his reasons in good faith, and on the other his obligation to see that justice is done in fact, in the world.[70]

In the situations I have in mind, the judge's duty to think about the real life consequences for constitutional values, as he understands them, may legitimately lead him to give reasons in bad faith if doing otherwise has bad enough consequences. In this case, we are supposing that terrible consequences may follow if our judge openly casts the underlying legal question in terms of proportionality (deductive/teleological reasoning having 'run out'), and then in terms of PD, and then turns the democratic deficit into a factual question.

It seems plain to 'sophisticated observers' that many a judge responds to this dilemma by 'abusing deduction'. He persuades himself that (what seems to the observer) a patently false deductive or teleological argument settles the case. He does this not as a conscious strategy, as proposed above, but 'in denial' of what he is 'really' doing to escape the psychic pain of role conflict. This is bad faith in the particular Sartrean sense of self-deception that avoids taking responsibility for one's actions.[71] According to my argument here, the judge will not be departing, conceptually or ethically, from his everyday rhetorical practice if he abandons denial and consciously and deliberately casts his argument in this case in the seriously misleading rhetoric of legal necessity.

It will seem to him that the direness of the decision to mislead is further palliated by the inevitability that the wielders of the hermeneutic of suspicion on the other side will attack his bad faith argument as just that. In other words,

---

[70] Kennedy, *Critique of Adjudication* (n 7) 192–212; Kennedy (n 8); Kennedy (n 15).
[71] See Kennedy, *Critique of Adjudication* (n 7).

his dishonesty is not as bad as it at first appears because it is in the context of a struggle to persuade, rather than in the context of authoritative pronouncement that his first guilty intuition might have suggested it might be.

B. The Duty to Persuade in the Collective Judicial Decision Process[72]

Because he is part of a collective rather than individual decision process, the judge has regularly to deal with questions of good faith in argument that are analogous, at least loosely, to his problem vis-à-vis the public. In this context of struggle, the judge has already to deal with the question of bad faith argument vis-à-vis his colleagues. Within that process, he will as a matter of course argue to his colleagues about how the court should decide, that is, he will argue to them that they should vote in one way rather than another. The dilemma of good faith arises when he is convinced that to state his true, proportionality-based reasons for an outcome will be unconvincing or even counterproductive in mustering a majority for that outcome. When good faith argument threatens to bring about a result that is seriously disastrous from the point of view of legal truth as he sees it, he has to make a difficult choice. He will not think it obvious that he should choose frankness '*et ruat Justitia*' ('though justice perish').

Now suppose that his position wins out in the sense that he is part of a majority coalition that will vote for some part of, but not all of, what he thinks is the correct legal outcome. The good faith problem will present itself once again if he is charged with drafting a majority opinion. All insiders understand that the 'author' of the majority opinion justifying the compromise outcome as legally correct will present the compromise as legally compelled from top to bottom, rather than as an incoherent assemblage. The justices on both sides who participated in the negotiation understand that this is a misrepresentation of the reasoning behind the outcome, but it is hardly bad faith as to them. (The dissenting opinions will take issue in equally legalist terms.) The general public, as we are imagining, has no access to what happened in the negotiation. In this hypothetical, the judge first offers what he regards as a bad but convincing argument for his preferred outcome and then justifies what he regards as an only partly just result through the abuse of induction/deduction or proportionality.

This example is supposed to make the proposal, that the judge should misrepresent his proportional argument for striking down the statute as formalism, seem close to the normal or routine of judicial practice.

---

[72] Kennedy (n 15).

C. Should the Liberal Activist Judge Back off if Backlash Threatens?

Suppose that an activist attack on the discriminatory statute will produce first a legislative and then a popular backlash, orchestrated by the regime and its captive media. Suppose that there is a real possibility that the executive and legislature will collaborate to restrict judicial power, for example by constitutional amendment, or adding judges to the court, or by impeachment, or restricting financing or changing selection procedures. Is it permissible to take these into account?

I would say yes, citing the hoary precedent of Chief Justice Marshall's famous tactics of delay and equivocation on the path to successfully imposing judicial review. Here the judge upholds the statute although he thinks it is unconstitutional and that there is no proportional case for deference. His opinion explaining the outcome, in whatever legalist terms, will be a good deal more misleading than the recasting of proportionality as deduction or teleology.

Felix Frankfurter[73] and his disciple Alexander Bickel thought it a sometimes-plausible alternative to this mode of bad faith for the court to deploy American constitutional procedural devices that allow deference without discussing the merits. By denying standing, denying a justiciable case or controversy, and refusing to judge 'political questions', a court defers without affirming. In Bickel's version, the Court manipulates the doctrines on the basis of an unacknowledged political calculus in which deference stores legitimacy for Schmittian cases in which the judiciary is the last bastion against disaster.[74]

D. Bad Faith Deference in Hopes of Reversal

It may be helpful in addressing this question to add a third typical situation which is one in which the national constitutional court is in some complex way subject to review by a transnational court. This might be the European Court of Human Rights, or the European Court of Justice, or the Inter-American Court of Human Rights. In the American federal context, state supreme courts are subject to US Supreme Court review when, for example, they impose or prevent the legalisation of gay marriage (if they do so on federal constitutional grounds).

The analogy to the situation of an intermediate appellate court subject to review by a supreme court is real but imperfect. It is well known, indeed obvious, that lower courts strategise to avoid reversal. In our hypothetical situation, if the transnational instance has meaningful power to reverse the national court, our judge

---

[73] Felix Frankfurter, 'The Supreme Court of the United States' in A Macleish and EF Pritchard Jr (eds), *Law and Politics: Occasional Papers of Felix Frankfurter* (New York, Harcourt, Brace, 1939).
[74] Bickel (n 22) 169–99.

will surely adjust his argument with that in mind. But it is by no means obvious that the sole strategic goal is to avoid reversal.

Suppose that our judge is reasonably certain that if his court upholds the statute it will be taken to the transnational instance, which will strike it down. If this is the case, there might be a strong argument that a majority that regards the statute as unconstitutional should uphold it, arguing deference, hoping to divert the backlash to the international level. Is it possible to argue that doing so would violate the ethical duty of the judge, no matter how serious the consequences for the court if it challenged the executive and legislative power of the NAP forces at this particular juncture? If the court's jurisdiction might not survive the backlash, 'deference in bad faith' is arguably the ethically obligatory posture.

The point of the argument by analogy is that for the judge to deliberately reformulate his proportional argument in conceptual or teleological language in order to avoid seriously evil consequences is consistent with, indeed milder than, a number of other practices that constitutional judges legitimately engage. In contrast with 'backing off' or 'deferring in hope of reversal from above', the judge is acting to achieve what he himself believes to be the legal 'right answer'.

Moreover, as I pointed out at the beginning of this section, he writes within contemporary legal consciousness imbued with the hermeneutic of suspicion, and therefore knows that his formulation will be subject to critique as exactly what it is: a motivated error in legal reasoning in pursuit of an ideological project. He can pride himself that at least he knows what he is doing, unlike many of his colleagues who manage to maintain themselves in denial while producing identical words.

To spare you, dear reader, the ennui of infinite regress, I will not ask: if the judge believes he must sometimes lie, should he announce this position at some point in advance of any particular case arising?

V. Conclusion: Judging and Politics as a Vocation

Finally, the judge will appeal directly to Max Weber's famous essay, *Politics as a Vocation*.[75] According to Weber:

> [A]ll ethically oriented action can be guided by either of two fundamentally different, irredeemably incompatible maxims: it can be guided by an 'ethics of conviction' or an 'ethics of responsibility.' … In the former case this means, to put it in religious terms: 'A Christian does what is right and leaves the outcome to God,' while in the latter you must answer for the (foreseeable) *consequences* of your actions.[76]

---

[75] M Weber, 'Politics as a Vocation' in D Owen, TB Strong (eds) and R Livingstone (trans), *The Vocation Lectures*, (Indianapolis, Hackett, 2004).
[76] ibid 83.

The ethic of conviction is Kantian, prohibiting doing things that are wrong 'in themselves', such as, in our case, lying. The ethic of responsibility holds that it may be necessary to violate that ethic without a universalisable counter-ethic that will tell you when the violation is justified:

> [N]o ethic in the world can say when, and to what extent the ethically good end can 'justify' the ethically dangerous means and its side effects.[77]

> ...

> In truth, politics is an activity of the head but by no means *only* of the head. In this respect the adherents of an ethics of conviction are in the right. But whether we *should* act in accordance with ethics of conviction or an ethics of responsibility, and when we should choose one rather than the other, is not a matter on which we can lay down the law to anyone else.[78]

With Dostoyevsky, Kierkegaard and Nietzsche in the background, the Weberian judge in the post-formalist, post-absolutist age has to decide 'without a warrant' and suffer the moral consequences if after the fact he turns out to have done wrong.

---

[77] ibid 84.
[78] ibid 91–92.

Part III

The Role of the ECJ in the Transformation or Reconstitution of Europe

4

Discovering the Law of the EU: The European Court of Justice and the Comparative Law Method

KOEN LENAERTS[*]

The central topic of this book, edited by Judge Siniša Rodin and Professor Tamara Perišin, appears to be quite challenging and innovative. Applying the American Critical Legal Studies (CLS) Perspective on the Role of Courts in the European Union is indeed a complex endeavour. The reason for this can actually be found in Professor Duncan Kennedy's *A Critique of Adjudication: Fin de Siècle*,[1] where he argues that European judicial discourse has, unlike its American counterpart, *not* been affected by a 'native movement of viral internal critique', according to which there are no correct legal answers to resolve particular gaps, conflicts and ambiguities in any legal order without resorting to policy.[2] European judges, Kennedy posits, have not crossed the Rubicon of using 'deductive argument supplemented or "guided" by policy argument'.[3] Even when 'the law runs out', he writes, European scholars maintain a naïve belief in abstraction, deduction and coherence.[4] Whereas the 'hybrid' model of judicial discourse is 'universally recognized and accepted' in the US,[5] it is said to be foreign to European judges.

In Professor Kennedy's *Critique*, the term 'policy' is to be understood broadly so that it encompasses any non-deductive argument.[6] However, given that the term 'policy' is politically charged and could be misleading to a European audience, this chapter uses the term 'non-deductive argument' instead.

In the context of a symposium organised by the *Cardozo Law Review* to celebrate Professor Kennedy's book, Professor Mitchel Lasser respectfully challenged

---

[*] President of the Court of Justice of the European Union, and Professor of European Union Law, University of Leuven. All opinions expressed herein are strictly personal to the author. I would like to congratulate my friend and colleague, Judge Siniša Rodin, and Professor Tamara Perišin for this initiative.

[1] D Kennedy, *A Critique of Adjudication (fin de siècle)* (Cambridge, Harvard University Press, 1997).
[2] ibid 81.
[3] ibid 104.
[4] ibid 94–95.
[5] ibid 109.
[6] ibid 109.

Kennedy's argument on the distinctiveness of American judicial discourse,[7] pointing out that European judges have also had recourse to non-deductive arguments. For example, whilst at first sight the rulings of the French Cour de cassation appear to be composed of 'single-sentence syllogisms', one may, upon closer examination, find that French *magistrats* measure 'the advantages and disadvantages of adopting one interpretive decision over another'.[8] In the same way, Opinions of Advocates General, whose role it is to assist the European Court of Justice (the ECJ), are imbued with large-scale substantive policy issues. As the main thrust of their reasoning, Advocates General often engage in a reconstruction of existing case law guided by a method of interpretation that is purpose-driven.[9] The idea, then, is that, where the ECJ decides to follow the Opinion of the Advocate General, it is endorsing the non-deductive arguments contained in the Opinion.

In my view, in order for the ECJ to carry out its constitutional task properly, its role cannot be confined to that of judges acting as a mouthpiece for the law, as Montesquieu describes it.[10] Ever since the landmark decision in *van Gend en Loos*,[11] the ECJ has consistently held that the EU is a distinct and autonomous legal order. Yet autonomy could hardly be attained in a legal system that is not self-sufficient and complete. For the EU legal order to find its own space between Member State law[12] and international law, the fragmentation resulting from constitutional and legislative gaps could not be allowed to persist. Although inspired by the constitutional traditions of the Member States or by international treaties, solutions intended to fill gaps must come from within the EU legal order itself.[13] The very raison d'être of EU law thus pushes the ECJ to take its responsibility for 'finding' the law (*'Rechtsfindung'*), notably by fashioning general principles of EU law.[14]

However, it goes without saying that neither American nor European courts should embark on what Professor Kennedy calls 'judicial legislation'. I concur with him in that 'to make [non-deductive] arguments is not to ask the judge to violate his role constraint by usurping the legislative function'.[15] When called upon to resolve particular gaps, conflicts and ambiguities in the existing regime, judges

---

[7] M Lasser, 'Do Judges Deploy Policy?' (2001) 22 *Cardozo Law Review* 863, 864.

[8] ibid 872.

[9] ibid 873–77.

[10] K Lenaerts and JA Gutiérrez-Fons, 'To Say What the Law of the EU Is: Methods of Interpretation and the European Court of Justice' (2013–14) 20 *Columbia Journal of European Law* 3, 35.

[11] Case 26/62 *van Gend en Loos* EU:C:1963:1.

[12] For the sake of clarity, I shall, where possible, avoid the use of the adjective 'national' when referring to the Member States, given that this could be misleading for an American audience for whom that adjective refers not to the component states, but to the federal government.

[13] P Pescatore, 'La carence du législateur communautaire et le devoir du juge' in *Rechtsvergleichung, Europarecht und Staatenintegration: Gedächtnisschrift für Léontin-Jean Contantinesco* (Köln, Heymanns Verlag, 1983).

[14] K Lenaerts and JA Gutiérrez-Fons, 'The Constitutional Allocation of Powers and General Principles of EU Law' (2010) 47 *Common Market Law Review* 1629.

[15] Kennedy (n 1) 109–10.

should have a sincere feeling of constraint that inhibits them from engaging in strategic behaviour to dispose ideological stakes.

Logically, for the ECJ the question is whether there is a method of interpretation that prevents the Court from crossing the dividing line between law and politics, whilst allowing it to 'discover the law of the EU' by means of non-deductive arguments. As you know, some members of the CLS movement are rather pessimistic in that respect because, as Professor Kennedy points out, a non-deductive argument may operate as 'a Trojan horse for the introduction of ideology into law'.[16] However, my 28 years on the bench—first, at the European General Court (the EGC) and, currently, at the ECJ—tell me to remain optimistic. It is indeed my experience that the comparative law method serves as a crucial interpretative tool that enables the ECJ to resolve particular gaps, conflicts and ambiguities without embarking on judicial legislation.

To argue this, this chapter is divided into two parts. Part I relates to the comparative law method as such. Part II focuses on the precise use made by the ECJ of that method. In doing so, I shall add a twist to this topic by drawing some comparisons with the US Supreme Court's reliance on State law as a canon of federal constitutional interpretation. Even the ECJ's comparative law method will thus be examined from a comparative law perspective.

I. The Comparative Law Method

The following sections seek to address three different, albeit interconnected, questions. First, what are the constitutional bases for the comparative law method? Second, is that method limited to constitutional adjudication or may it also serve as a tool for statutory interpretation? Third, and last, does the comparative law method fit well with what Pierre Schlag defines as 'key ontological identities'?[17]

A. The Constitutional Bases for the Comparative Law Method

By virtue of Article 19 of the Treaty on European Union (TEU), the ECJ is required to solve the cases over which it enjoys jurisdiction. Accordingly, where a case is brought before the ECJ and the Treaties do not contain any rules for its solution, 'unless the [Court] is to deny justice it is therefore obliged to solve the problem by reference to the rules acknowledged by the legislation, the learned writing and the case-law of the [Member States]'.[18] It follows that Article 19 TEU provides the

---

[16] ibid 111.
[17] P Schlag, 'Empty Circles of Liberal Justifications' (1997) 96 *Michigan Law Review* 1.
[18] Joined Cases 7/56 and 3/57 to 7/57 *Algera and Others v Assemblée commune* EU:C:1957:7, 55.

general constitutional authority for the ECJ to engage in a comparative study of the laws of the Member States.[19]

Apart from Article 19 TEU, two additional Treaty provisions explicitly refer to the laws of the Member States, namely Article 6(3) TEU and Article 340(2) of the Treaty on the Functioning of the European Union (TFEU). Those two provisions relate respectively to the protection of fundamental rights and to the EU's non-contractual liability.

Article 6(3) TEU mandates the EU to respect '[f]undamental rights, as guaranteed by the [ECHR] and as they result from the constitutional traditions common to the Member States, [which] shall constitute general principles of the Union's law'. That Treaty provision is no less than an explicit endorsement by the authors of the Maastricht Treaty of the case law of the ECJ in the field of fundamental rights protection. Likewise, Article 52(4) of the Charter of Fundamental Rights of the European Union (the 'Charter') imposes the same obligation on the ECJ as it states that '[in] so far as [the] Charter recognises fundamental rights as they result from the constitutional traditions common to the Member States, those rights shall be interpreted in harmony with those traditions'.

Furthermore, by stating that the principle of non-contractual liability of the EU is to be developed 'in accordance with *the general principles common to the laws of the Member States*',[20] Article 340 TFEU clearly indicates that the authors of the Treaties envisaged recourse to the comparative law method as a means of filling lacunae in the legal order of the EU.

This point is illustrated by *FIAMM*,[21] in which the ECJ held that the EU could not be held liable in the absence of an unlawful act or omission on its part. The ECJ reached that determination by engaging in a comparative examination of the Member States' legal systems from which it deduced that there was no convergence of those legal systems 'as regards the possible existence of a principle of liability in the case of a lawful act or omission of the public authorities, in particular where it is of a legislative nature'.[22]

---

[19] Joined Cases C-46/93 and C-48/93 *Brasserie du pêcheur and Factortame* EU:C:1996:79, para 27 (holding that '[s]ince the Treaty contains no provision expressly and specifically governing the consequences of breaches of [EU] law by Member States, it is for the [ECJ], in pursuance of the task conferred on it by Article [19 TEU] of ensuring that in the interpretation and application of the Treaty the law is observed, to rule on such a question in accordance with generally accepted methods of interpretation, in particular by reference to the fundamental principles of the [EU] legal system and, where necessary, general principles common to the legal systems of the Member States'). See, in this regard, Lenaerts and Gutiérrez-Fons (n 10) 44 and 45.

[20] See Art 340(2) TFEU (emphasis added).

[21] Joined Cases C-120/06 P and C-121/06 P *FIAMM and Others v Council and Commission* EU:C:2008:476.

[22] ibid para 175. The EGC had, however, taken a different view, by recognising the existence of such a principle. See Case T-69/00 *FIAMM and FIAMM Technologies v Council and Commission* EU:T:2005:449, paras 157–60. See also Joined Cases C-120/06 P and C-121/06 P *FIAMM and FIAMM Technologies v Council and Commission* EU:C:2008:98, Opinion of AG Poiares Maduro, paras 54ff.

More recently, in *Gascogne*,[23] the ECJ was asked to find the right remedy for the EGC's failure to adjudicate within a reasonable time in competition cases. Existing case law offered two different approaches, ie either a reduction, by the ECJ, of the penalty imposed on the infringing undertaking (the *Baustahlgewebe* approach)[24] or a separate action for damages brought against the EU under Article 340 TFEU before the EGC (the *Der Grüne Punkt* approach).[25] At the outset, AG Sharpston noted that there was no common remedy across the EU for failure to adjudicate within a reasonable time in competition cases.[26] In addition, any approach was likely to be imperfect, in the sense that it would have both advantages and dis-advantages. Accordingly, in the absence of a common approach, she posited that the right remedy had to be compatible with Article 47 of the Charter.[27] Whilst it was tempting to opt for the 'procedural economy' of reducing the fine, she urged the ECJ to discard the *Baustahlgewebe* approach. The reason was threefold. First, the 'delay in the [EGC] is conceptually quite distinct from the anti-competitive conduct that led the Commission to impose the fine in the first place'.[28] Second,

> [w]ithin the EU legal order, it is the [EGC], rather than [the ECJ], that is the jurisdiction that is concerned with detailed fact-finding and the weighing of evidence. That would seem ... to be a further element in favour of concluding that a free-standing action for damages before the [EGC] is preferable to trying to grant an effective remedy by reduc-ing fines on appeal.[29]

Third and last, no provision could be found in the Treaties allowing the EU judi-ciary to reduce a fine when 'there are no substantive grounds for modifying the Commission's assessment of *the fine that was appropriate to the infringement*'.[30]

The ECJ followed, in essence, the Opinion of the Advocate General. It held that

> having regard to the need to ensure that the competition rules of [EU] law are com-plied with, the [ECJ] cannot allow an appellant to reopen the question of the validity or amount of a fine, on the sole ground that there was a failure to adjudicate within a

---

[23] Case C-58/12 P *Groupe Gascogne v Commission* EU:C:2013:770.

[24] Case C-185/95 P *Baustahlgewebe v Commission* EU:C:1998:608.

[25] Case C-385/07 P *Der Grüne Punkt—Duales System Deutschland v Commission* EU:C:2009:456.

[26] Case C-58/12 P *Groupe Gascogne v Commission* EU:C:2013:360, Opinion of Advocate General Sharpston, para 118 (holding that '[c]ertain Member States order a reduction in the penalty imposed or mitigate its execution where there has been excessive delay [Austria, Belgium, Germany, Finland, the Netherlands, Spain and the United Kingdom]. Other Member States only provide financial com-pensation rather than a reduction in the fine [France, Italy, Poland and Romania]. Some have adopted specific provisions concerning compensation for an infringement of the right to a fair hearing within a reasonable time [Germany, Finland, Italy and Poland]. Others consider that a judgment finding that there has indeed been a failure to adjudicate within a reasonable time suffices as just satisfaction [Germany and Greece]. In at least one Member State [the Netherlands], there are specific rules govern-ing the percentage reduction in penalty that is to be applied for a failure to adjudicate within a reason-able time in competition matters').

[27] ibid para 121.

[28] ibid para 125.

[29] ibid para 127.

[30] ibid para 131.

reasonable time, where all of its pleas directed against the findings made by the [EGC] concerning the amount of that fine and the conduct that it penalises have been rejected.[31]

Accordingly, it ruled that

a claim for damages brought against the European Union pursuant to Article 268 TFEU and the second paragraph of Article 340 TFEU constitutes an effective remedy of general application for asserting and penalising such a breach, since such a claim can cover all the situations where a reasonable period of time has been exceeded in proceedings.[32]

B. The EU's 'Federal Common Law'

Apart from the fact that the comparative law method provides analytical support for the discovery and development of general principles of EU law, it may also be relied upon with a view to clarifying specific provisions of secondary EU law.

In other words, it provides a good framework for the ECJ to undertake 'federal common law-making'.[33] For instance, in *Reed*,[34] the ECJ was called upon to interpret the term 'spouse' for the purposes of Article 10 of Regulation No 1612/68.[35] In particular, the referring court asked whether Article 10 of Regulation No 1612/68 could be interpreted as meaning that a person who is in a stable relationship with a worker who is a national of another Member State but is employed and resides in the host Member State could be treated as a 'spouse' for the purpose of that provision. The ECJ replied in the negative. As the starting point of its reasoning, the ECJ followed the comparative law method: it observed that, since Regulation No 1612/68 applied 'in all of the Member States, ... any interpretation of a legal term on the basis of social developments must take into account the situation in the whole Community, not merely in one Member State'.[36] It found that, at the material time, there was no consensus among the Member States on whether unmarried companions should be treated as spouses. Accordingly,

[i]n the absence of any indication of a general social development which would justify a broad construction, and in the absence of any indication to the contrary in the

---

[31] *Groupe Gascogne v Commission* (n 23) para 78.

[32] ibid para 82. In that regard, the ECJ pointed out that '[i]t is ... for the [EGC], which has jurisdiction under Article 256(1) TFEU, to determine such claims for damages, sitting in a different composition from that which heard the dispute giving rise to the procedure whose duration is criticised'. ibid para 90. See also Case C-50/12 P *Kendrion v Commission* EU:C:2013:771 and Case C-40/12 P *Gascogne Sack Deutschland v Commission* EU:C:2013:768.

[33] K Lenaerts and K Gutman, '"Federal Common Law" in the European Union: A Comparative Perspective from the United States' (2006) 54 *American Journal of Comparative Law* 55.

[34] Case 59/85 *Reed*, EU:C:1986:157.

[35] Reg (EEC) No 1612/68 of the Council of 15 October 1968 on freedom of movement for workers within the Community [1968] OJ L 257/2, which was repealed by Reg (EU) No 492/2011 of the European Parliament and of the Council of 5 April 2011 on freedom of movement for workers within the Union Text with EEA relevance [2011] OJ L 141/1.

[36] *Reed* (n 34) para 13.

regulation, it must be held that the term 'spouse' in Article 10 of the Regulation refers to a marital relationship only.[37]

Fifteen years later, in *D and Sweden v Council*,[38] the ECJ refused to interpret the expression 'married official' set out in the Staff Regulations as meaning that same-sex partnerships recognised by some Member States were comparable to the situation of a married official. To that effect, it held that '[i]t is not in question that, according to the definition generally accepted by the Member States, the term "marriage" means a union between two persons of the opposite sex'.[39]

However, since those two judgments were delivered, the legal and social context has evolved at both Member State and EU level. For example, according to the most recent Staff Regulations, EU officials in a non-marital relationship recognised by a Member State as a stable partnership who do not have legal access to marriage should be granted the same range of benefits as married couples. At Member State level, the ECJ has held that, in so far as Member State law treats marriage and same-sex partnerships alike, any discriminatory treatment regarding benefits deriving from an employment relationship would be contrary to the principle of non-discrimination on grounds of sexual orientation as given expression in Directive 2000/78.[40] For example, if under Member State law marriage and same-sex partnerships stand on an equal footing in the relevant respect, a Member State measure limiting survivors' benefits under a compulsory occupational pensions scheme to surviving spouses would run counter to the principle of equal treatment.[41]

Furthermore, it will be interesting to see how the ECJ will interpret the term 'spouse' for the purposes of secondary EU law, notably Directive 2004/38.[42] This is because the interpretation of that term raises a difficult constitutional question that requires the ECJ to strike the right balance between competing interests.

On the one hand, no one would question the proposition that legalising same-sex marriage is a political decision to be taken at Member State level. In the absence of consensus among the Member States, that question gives rise to value diversity within the EU.[43] At the time of writing, whilst 12 Member States allow

---

[37] ibid para 15.

[38] Joined Cases 122/99 P and C-125/99 P *D and Sweden v Council* EU:C:2001:304.

[39] ibid para 34.

[40] Council Dir 2000/78/EC of 27 November 2000 establishing a general framework for equal treatment in employment and occupation [2000] OJ L 303/16. See also Art 4 of Council Dir 2003/86/EC of 22 September 2003 on the right to family reunification [20013] OJ L 251/12.

[41] See, in this regard, Case C-267/06 *Maruko* EU:C:2008:179; Case C-147/08 *Römer* EU:C:2011:286; Joined Cases C-124/11, C-125/11 and C-143/11 *Dittrich and Others* EU:C:2012:771; and Case C-267/12 *Hay* EU:C:2013:823.

[42] See Art 2(2)(a) of Dir 2004/38 which does not provide a definition of the term 'spouse'. See, in this regard, K Lenaerts, 'Federalism and the Rule of Law: Perspectives from the European Court of Justice' (2009–10) 39 *Fordham International Law Journal* 1338, 1355ff. See also C-673/16 *Coman and Others* (pending).

[43] Fundamental Rights Agency, 'Protection against Discrimination on Grounds of Sexual Orientation, Gender Identity and Sex Characteristics in the EU—Comparative Legal Analysis—Update 2015', 85ff, available at http://fra.europa.eu/en/publication/2015/lgbti-comparative-legal-update-2015.

for same-sex marriage,[44] the Constitutions of seven Member States define specifi-cally marriage as a union between a man and a woman.[45] That said, a significant majority of Member States provide for some sort of legal recognition for same-sex couples, often equivalent to marriage,[46] and applicable to marriages legally entered into in another Member State.[47]

On the other hand, the term 'spouse' defines the scope *ratione personae* of free movement law: it is only where same-sex married couples move to a Member State where their civil status is recognised that they can fully benefit from the pro-tection of EU law. That is even more so where one of the same-sex spouses is a third-country national, since he or she may only enjoy a derived right to free movement.[48]

It is worth recalling that Directive 2004/38 adopted a broad definition of the expression 'family member', so as to include registered partnerships.[49] However, the European Parliament was unable to persuade the Council to stipulate expressly that the term 'spouse' laid down in Article 2(2)(a) of that Directive also applies to spouses of the same sex. The Council opted for a hands-off approach, leav-ing this sensitive decision to judicial interpretation.[50] Indeed, if a Member State court were to ask for guidance in the interpretation of this term, the ECJ would have no choice but to provide a definition through the medium of common-law-making.[51] As I have argued elsewhere, when confronted with the need to interpret the term 'spouse', the ECJ has three alternatives.[52]

First, the ECJ could adopt its own independent definition of 'spouse' without referring to either the laws of the home or the host State (the 'autonomous concept' approach). The ECJ could choose, for example, to exclude or to include same-sex marriages when defining the scope of Article 2(2)(a) of Directive 2004/38. Such a solution would foster uniformity and legal certainty, but

[44] Belgium, Netherlands, Spain, Sweden, Portugal, Denmark, France, the United Kingdom, Luxembourg, Finland, Ireland and Germany.

[45] See, eg, Bulgaria, Croatia, Hungary, Latvia, Lithuania, Poland and Slovakia.

[46] See *Oliari and others v Italy* CE:ECHR:2015:0721JUD001876611, App nos 18766/11 and 36030/11 (ECtHR 21 July 2015), paras 53 to 55 and 178.

[47] For free movement purposes, same-sex couples who get married in another Member State keep their civil status in Croatia. See Art 74 of the Same Sex Life Partnership Act, 15 July 2014, available in English at www.zivotnopartnerstvo.com/wp-content/uploads/2015/06/same-sex-life-partnership-act-croatia.pdf.

[48] See, eg, Case C-456/12 *O and B* EU:C:2014:135, para 36.

[49] The non-registered partner of an EU citizen is not considered as a family member under Dir 2004/38/EC. However, Art 3 provides that the host Member State must facilitate the entry and resi-dence of persons with whom an EU citizen has a durable relationship, provided that it can be duly attested.

[50] See H Toner, *Partnership Rights, Free Movement, and EU Law* (Oxford, Hart Publishing, 2004) 60–68 (who notes that the regime laid down in Dir 2004/38 was the result of a political compromise among conservative and liberal Member States). In the same way, see E Guild, S Peers and J Tomkin, *The EU Citizenship Directive: A Commentary* (Oxford, OUP, 2014) 33ff.

[51] See K Lenaerts and K Gutman, 'The Comparative Law Method and the European Court of Justice: Echoes Across the Atlantic' (2016) 64 *American Journal of Comparative Law* 841.

[52] Lenaerts (n 42) 1355.

it would disregard the sensitivities of some Member States in favour of those of others. It would also encroach upon the prerogatives of the Member States in the field of family law.

For present purposes, two recent rulings of the US Supreme Court, namely *United States v Windsor* and *Obergefell v Hodges*,[53] are of great comparative law value. In the first case, the US Supreme Court was called upon to rule on the constitutionality of the Defence of Marriage Act (DOMA),[54] a federal statute that defined 'marriage' as 'a legal union between one man and one woman as husband and wife', and the term 'spouse' as 'a person of the opposite sex who is a husband or a wife'. In so doing, not only did Congress rule out federal common law in interpreting marriage, but Section 2 of DOMA also exempted states from giving effect to marriages (or equivalent relationships) contracted under the laws of a sister state.[55]

In *United States v Windsor*, the US Supreme Court noted that DOMA provided for 'unusual deviation from the usual tradition of recognizing and accepting state definitions of marriage'. Congress had done so in order 'to deprive same-sex couples of the benefits and responsibilities that come with federal recognition of their marriages'.[56] Writing for the majority, Justice Kennedy found that DOMA created in-state inequality based on moral considerations where a state recognises same-sex marriage. 'DOMA', he wrote, 'forces same-sex couples to live as married for the purpose of state law but unmarried for the purpose of federal law, thus diminishing the stability and predictability of basic personal relations the State has found it proper to acknowledge and protect',[57] creating two contradictory marriage regimes within the same state.[58] Accordingly, the US Supreme Court held that, since 'the principal purpose and the necessary effect of [DOMA was] to demean those persons who [were] in a lawful same-sex marriage, [that statute was] unconstitutional as a deprivation of the liberty of the person protected by the Fifth Amendment of the Constitution'. In addition, DOMA also violated the Equal Protection Clause given that it 'singl[ed] out a class of persons deemed by a State entitled to recognition and protection to enhance their own liberty'.[59]

---

[53] *United States v Windsor*, 133 S Ct, 2675 (2013), and *Obergefell v Hodges* 135 S Ct, 2584 (2015).

[54] See the Defence of Marriage Act (DOMA)—1 USC §7, 28 USC 1738C (2000) (originally 110 Sta, 2149 [1996]).

[55] s 2 of DOMA also states that '[n]o State, territory, or possession of the United States, or Indian tribe, shall be required to give effect to any public act, record, or judicial proceeding of any other State, territory, possession, or tribe respecting a relationship between persons of the same sex that is treated as a marriage under the laws of such other State, territory, possession, or tribe, or a right or claim arising from such relationship'.

[56] *United States v Windsor* (n 53) 2693.

[57] ibid 2694.

[58] For the case at hand, this meant that a same-sex surviving spouse whose marriage had been recognised by the state of New York could not claim a federal estate tax exemption, whilst surviving spouses of opposite sex living in that same state could do so.

[59] ibid 2695.

After *United States v Windsor* was delivered, some US scholars noted that several passages of that judgment suggested that the scope of the personal liberty protected under the US Constitution could include a federal constitutional right to same-sex marriage.[60] To that end, they quoted a passage of that judgment in which the US Supreme Court stressed the fact that DOMA 'demean[ed] the couple, whose moral and sexual choices the Constitution protects'.[61] The argument then ran that state laws whose purpose and effect were similar to those of DOMA would also demean those choices and thus constitute a violation of the Fourteenth Amendment. That aspect of the judgment was in fact criticised by Chief Justice Roberts in his dissenting opinion, who accused the majority of prejudging 'challenges to state marriage definitions affecting same-sex couples'.[62] Two years later, this was precisely the question with which the US Supreme Court was confronted in *Obergefell v Hodges*.

In that case, the US Supreme Court began by endorsing an evolving understanding of marriage, in keeping with 'new dimensions of freedom [that] become apparent to new generations', such as the progressive recognition of rights for homosexuals. Again writing for the majority, Justice Kennedy pointed out that when a person decides to get married, he or she exercises a personal choice that is central to his or her dignity and autonomy because such a choice defines that person's identity and beliefs. The right to marry is thus a fundamental right inherent in the liberty of the person protected under the Due Process Clause of the Fourteenth Amendment.[63] Furthermore, the US Supreme Court relied on four principles and traditions that define the central meaning of that right and that demonstrate that 'the reasons marriage is fundamental under the [US] Constitution apply with equal force to same-sex couples'.[64] It also found that state laws that deny same-sex couples the benefits afforded to married couples of opposite sex created inequality.[65] Those considerations led the US Supreme Court to rule that state laws depriving same-sex couples of the right to marry run counter to both the Due Process and Equal Protection Clauses of the Fourteenth Amendment.

---

[60] See, for example, MJ Klarman, '*Windsor* and *Brown*: Marriage Equality and Racial Equality' (2013–14) 127 *Harvard Law Review* 127; and W Baude, 'Interstate Recognition of Same-Sex Marriage After *Windsor*' (2013–14) 8 *New York University Journal of Law & Liberty* 150.

[61] *United States v Windsor* (n 53) 2675, 2694 (2013) (referring to *Lawrence v Texas*, 539 US 558 (2003)).

[62] ibid 2697 (CJ Roberts, dissenting). In the same way, Justice Scalia wrote that 'the view that this Court will take of state prohibition of same-sex marriage is indicated beyond mistaking by today's opinion'. See *United States v Windsor* (n 53) 2675, 2709 (2013) (J Scalia, dissenting).

[63] *Obergefell v Hodges* 135 S Ct 2584, 2597 (2015).

[64] Those principles and traditions are: (1) 'the right to personal choice regarding marriage is inherent in the concept of individual autonomy', ibid 2599; (2) 'the right to marry is fundamental because it supports a two-person union unlike any other in its importance to the committed individuals', ibid 2599; (3) '[that right] safeguards children and families and thus draws meaning from related rights of childrearing, procreation, and education', ibid 2600; (4) '[the US Supreme] Court's cases and the Nation's traditions make clear that marriage is a keystone of our social order', ibid 2601.

[65] ibid 2604.

The same applied to state laws refusing to recognise the civil status of same-sex marriages registered out-of-state, as the US Constitution guaranteed that right in all states.[66]

If the ECJ were to follow in the footsteps of the US Supreme Court, this would mean that, when Member States implement EU law, the Charter provides a right to marry to same-sex couples. The term 'spouse' laid down in Directive 2004/38 would have to be interpreted in the light of that right. However, it is worth noting that the explanations relating to the right to marry enshrined in Article 9 of the Charter state that '[t]his Article neither prohibits nor imposes the granting of the status of marriage to unions between people of the same sex'.[67] Thus, unlike the Due Process and Equal Protection Clauses of the Fourteenth Amendment, the Charter appears to be 'gender-neutral' regarding the right to marry of same-sex couples,[68] thus leaving that question to the laws of the Member States.[69]

As a second option, the ECJ could defer to the laws of the host Member State (the 'host State principle') when interpreting the term 'spouse'. This option has been followed by the EU legislator when defining the legal effects of registered partnerships. Article 2 of Directive 2004/38 states that registered partners are considered family members only 'if the legislation of the host Member State treats registered partnerships as equivalent to marriage and in accordance with the conditions laid down in the relevant legislation of the host Member State'.[70] However, as noted by some scholars, this option might give rise to obstacles to the right of free movement, since the exercise of that right might entail a change in the civil status of incoming same-sex couples.[71]

As a third option, the term 'spouse' might be interpreted in accordance with the civil law under which the marriage is entered into (the State of origin principle). This option would be the most favourable to same-sex couples, since the exercise

---

[66] ibid 2607 (holding that 'if States are required by the Constitution to issue marriage licenses to same-sex couples, the justifications for refusing to recognize those marriages performed elsewhere are undermined').

[67] It is worth noting that, unlike the wording of Art 12 ECHR which states that '[m]en and women … have the right to marry', Art 9 of the Charter is silent in that regard.

[68] See, in that regard, S Choudhry, 'Art 9—Right to Marry and Right to Found a Family' in S Peers, T Hervey, J Kenner and A Ward (eds), *The EU Charter of Fundamental Rights: A Commentary* (Oxford, Hart Publishing, 2014) 283.

[69] In order to comply with the ECHR, Member State laws do not need to provide for such a right. See, in that regard, *Schalk and Kopf v Austria* CE:ECHR:2010:0624JUD003014104, ECHR 2010-IV 409. However, where those laws do not provide for same-sex marriage, Art 8 ECHR imposes on Contracting States a 'positive obligation to ensure respect for [same-sex couples'] private and family life, in particular through the provision of a legal framework allowing them to have their relationship recognised and protected under domestic law'. See, in this regard, *Oliari and others v Italy* (n 46) para 164.

[70] See Art 2 of Dir 2004/38.

[71] See S Titshaw, 'Same-Sex Spouses Lost in Translation? How to Interpret "Spouse" in the EU Family Migration Directives' (2016) 34 *Boston University International Law Journal* 45, 109; A Tryfonidou, 'EU Free Movement Law and the Legal Recognition of Same-Sex Relationships: The Case for Mutual Recognition' (2014–15) 21 *Columbia Journal of European Law* 195, 222ff (suggesting that application by analogy of the judgment in Case C-148/02 *Garcia Avello* EU:C:2003:539).

of free movement rights would have no adverse repercussions on their civil status. However, the host Member State could object that this interpretation would be too intrusive, amounting to excessive interference in its jurisdiction both over family law and with regard to the exercise of police powers on its territory.

A more nuanced approach would be for the ECJ to apply the principle of mutual recognition when interpreting the term 'spouse':[72] a marriage entered into under the laws of the home Member State is to be recognised in the host Member State unless the latter puts forward overriding reasons of general interest in order to deny its legal recognition. This approach would facilitate free movement, whilst having regard to legitimate justifications that might be put forward by the host Member State in the field of family law. Since the EU legislator deferred to the judiciary the definition of the term 'spouse', this approach also has the advantage of allowing the ECJ to proceed on a case-by-case basis,[73] engaging in a balancing exercise that scrutinises whether the reasons put forward by the host Member State pass muster under free movement law and the Charter.

C. The Comparative Law Method and the Autonomy of the EU Legal Order

Writing extra-judicially, Judge Rodin supported the contention that the 'key ontological identities' of the European Union may explain why its constitutional setting offers an ideal ground for the interpretation of EU law in the light of public international law and the constitutional traditions common to the Member States.[74]

Those identities suggest that the EU is, as the ECJ held in its Opinion 2/13, not a state;[75] that EU constitutionalism cannot be apprehended from a foundational but from a functional perspective,[76] and that the democratic legitimacy of the EU is shared between the Member States and European citizens.[77] It follows from

---

[72] Lenaerts (n 42) 1338. See also Titshaw, ibid 112–13; and J Rijpma and N Koffeman, 'Free Movement Rights for Same-Sex Couples Under EU Law: What Role to Play for the CJEU?' in D Gallo, L Paladini and P Pustorino (eds), *Same-Sex Couples before National, Supranational and International Jurisdictions* (Berlin Heidelberg, Springer, 2014) 445. See Tryfonidou (n 71) 240 (opining that the best solution would be for the EU legislator to take action in applying the principle of mutual recognition to the word 'spouse'. To that end, she suggests redrafting Art 2(2)(a) of Dir 2004/38 as follows 'the spouse, irrespective of sex, according to the relevant legislation of the home State').

[73] Lenaerts (n 42) 1338.

[74] S Rodin, 'Constitutional Relevance of Foreign Court Decisions' (2016) 64 *American Journal of Comparative Law* 815.

[75] Opinion 2/13 EU:C:2014:2454, para 193.

[76] K Lenaerts and JA Gutiérrez-Fons, 'The European Union: A Constitutional Perspective' in R Schütze and T Tridimas (eds), *Oxford Principles of European Union Law, Volume I: The European Union Legal Order* (Oxford, Oxford University Press) (forthcoming).

[77] See generally K Lenaerts, 'The Principle of Democracy in the Case Law of the European Court of Justice' (2013) 62 *International and Comparative Law Quarterly* 271.

those identities that the EU is an autonomous legal order that seeks to find its own constitutional space between the laws of the Member States and international law. Thus, as Judge Rodin concludes, those identities find concrete expression in the EU notion of autonomy. This means, in essence, that the comparative law method may not be relied upon where its application would call into question the constitutional tenets on which the EU is founded.[78]

Yet, the autonomy of the EU legal order should not be confused with complete detachment.[79] It follows from settled case law that the ECJ seeks to define the EU constitutional space without denying that EU law influences and is influenced by the legal orders that surround it.

From a substantive perspective, the comparative law method promotes value diversity, provided that the Member States do not adversely affect the essential interests of the EU.[80] For example, in *Omega* and *Sayn-Wittgenstein*,[81] the ECJ held that

> it is not indispensable for the restrictive measure issued by the authorities of a Member State to correspond to a conception shared by all Member States as regards the precise way in which the fundamental right or legitimate interest in question is to be protected and that, on the contrary, the need for, and proportionality of, the provisions adopted are not excluded merely because one Member State has chosen a system of protection different from that adopted by another State.[82]

In accordance with Article 4(2) TEU, the EU is to respect the national identities of its Member States.[83] The comparative law method takes due account of that

---

[78] Lenaerts and Gutiérrez-Fons (n 10) 7–8.

[79] K Lenaerts, 'The Court of Justice as the Guarantor of the Rule of Law Within the European Union' in G De Baere and J Wouters (eds), *The Contribution of International and Supranational Courts to the Rule of Law* (Cheltenham, Edward Elgar Publishing, 2015) 242.

[80] Lenaerts and Gutiérrez-Fons (n 10) 47–48.

[81] Case C-36/02 *Omega* EU:C:2004:614; and Case C-208/09 *Sayn-Wittgenstein* EU:C:2010:806.

[82] *Omega*, ibid paras 37 and 38; and *Sayn-Wittgenstein*, ibid para 91.

[83] In this regard, the ECJ has held that, for the purposes of Art 4(2) TEU, the expression 'national identity' includes, for example, 'the status of the State as a Republic' (see *Sayn-Wittgenstein* (n 81) para 92) and 'the protection of a State's official national language' (see Case C-391/09 *Runevič-Vardyn and Wardyn* EU:C:2011:291, para 86; Case C-51/08 *Commission v Luxembourg* EU:C:2011:336, para 124; and Case C-202/11 *Las* EU:C:2013:239, para 86). cf Case C-393/10 *O'Brien* EU:C:2012:110, para 49, where the ECJ held that the fact of extending to part-time judges remunerated on a daily fee-paid basis the scope of the principle of equal treatment, as given expression in secondary EU legislation, and the fact of protecting them against discrimination as compared with full-time workers could not have any adverse effect on the national identity of the Member State concerned. Moreover, Member State measures which, whilst aiming to protect a Member State's identity, derogate from EU law must be proportionate to that objective. This means that the national identity of the Member States is not absolute but must be weighed against the requirements laid down by EU law. See, in this regard, Case C-202/11 *Las* EU:C:2013:239, paras 29ff. See generally E Cloots, *National Identity in EU law* (Oxford, OUP, 2015). See also S Rodin, 'National Identity and Market Freedoms after the Treaty of Lisbon' (2011) 7 *Croatian Yearbook of European Law and Policy* 11, 41 (who argues that '[t]he role of Article 4(2) TEU is twofold. As a competence rule, it imposes limits on EU regulation, even in cases where such regulation would otherwise be permissible. As an interpretative rule, it provides guidance for the [Court of Justice] and [Member State] courts on how to interpret the relationship between EU and [Member State] law').

constitutional mandate as it promotes 'value diversity'. However, that diversity is not absolute. As the ECJ ruled in *Melloni*, 'Member States are free to apply [their own] standards of protection of fundamental rights, provided that the level of protection provided for by the Charter, as interpreted by the [ECJ], and the primacy, unity and effectiveness of EU law are not thereby compromised'.[84]

From a structural perspective, it is safe to say that the comparative law method fits well with the preliminary reference procedure which 'by setting up a dialogue between one court and another, specifically between the [ECJ] and the courts and tribunals of the Member States, has the object of securing uniform interpretation of EU law', is the keystone of the [EU] judicial system.[85]

First, by embarking on a comparative analysis of the laws of the Member States, the ECJ favours a judicial dialogue with Member State courts. If the ECJ decides to depart from the solution used by a particular Member State legal system, it must explain why that solution does not fit well with the needs of the EU or, as the case may be, why the solution favoured by the legal systems of other Member States is better suited to the problem with which EU law is confronted. Second, where the solution adopted by the ECJ mirrors that set out in the laws of the Member States, the effectiveness of EU law is better achieved.[86] Third, the use of the comparative law method gives rise to a constructive interaction between the legal order of the EU and those of its Member States. Initially, the dialogue between the ECJ and Member State courts may serve to highlight the advantages and disadvantages of the different solutions adopted at Member State level, thus enabling the ECJ to choose the approach that seems most appropriate. Subsequently, by highlighting, in some cases, the fact that the approach adopted by the ECJ does not achieve the outcome expected, Member State courts may invite the ECJ to reconsider its approach. This illustrates how the comparative law method and the judicial dialogue go hand-in-hand.

II. The ECJ's Evaluative Approach

As understood by the ECJ, the comparative law method may be defined as an interpretative tool that serves the ECJ to resolve particular gaps, conflicts and ambiguities, be they at constitutional or legislative level. Whilst the comparative law method focuses on the laws of the Member States, it does not rule out

---

[84] Case C-399/11 *Melloni* EU:C:2013:107, paras 60 and 61. See K Lenaerts and JA Gutierrez-Fons, 'The Place of the Charter in the EU Constitutional Edifice' in Peers, Hervey, Kenner and Ward (eds) (n 68) 1586ff.

[85] Opinion 2/13 (n 75) para 176.

[86] K Lenaerts, 'Interlocking Legal Orders in the European Union and Comparative Law' (2003) 52 *International and Comparative Law Quarterly* 873, 880.

international law, or even the law of third countries such as the US.[87] This stands in sharp contrast to the intense controversy generated in the US by the use of foreign law in constitutional adjudication.

The reason why the comparative law method focuses on the laws of the Member States is due to the fact that those laws are not seen as 'external' to the EU legal order, but as norms that inform and nourish the interpretation and formulation of EU law.[88] To some extent, the comparative law method is similar to the way in which the US Supreme Court 'bases federal constitutional doctrine on state law'.[89] That method of interpretation is known as the 'national consensus doctrine'. Notably, that doctrine has been applied in the context of the Eighth Amendment of the US Constitution where the US Supreme Court has relied on a collective evaluation of state laws in order to interpret the notion of 'cruel and unusual punishment' set out therein.[90] As Chief Justice Warren wrote in the seminal *Trop v Dulles* case, '[t]he [Eighth] Amendment must draw its meaning from the evolving standards of decency that mark the progress of a maturing society'.[91] The national consensus doctrine has also been applied in the context of the Fourth, Sixth and Fourteenth Amendments.[92] Indeed, unlike the use of foreign law in constitutional adjudication,[93] the use of state law as a canon of constitutional interpretation has not led to the same level of controversy.[94]

Arguably, the use of the national consensus doctrine as such is not being criticised by Supreme Court Justices and scholars, but rather the way in which the US Supreme Court deploys it in order to find national consensus. Criticisms have thus focused on the methodology of the US Supreme Court, leaving the foundations of that doctrine untouched.[95] For example, whilst state legislation is deemed to constitute objective evidence of contemporary values,[96] other indicators, such as

---

[87] K Lenaerts and K Gutman, 'The Comparative Law Method and the Court of Justice of the European Union: Interlocking Legal Orders Revisited' in M Andenas and D Fairgrieve (eds), *Courts and Comparative Law* (Oxford, OUP, 2015).

[88] ibid.

[89] RM Hills, 'Counting States' (2009) 32 *Harvard Journal of Law & Public Policy* 17.

[90] The Eighth Amendment of the US Constitution states that '[e]xcessive bail shall not be required, nor excessive fines imposed, nor cruel and unusual punishments inflicted'.

[91] *Trop v Dulles* 356 US 86, 101 (1958).

[92] As to the Fourth Amendment, see, eg, *Mapp v Ohio* 367 US 643 (1961). As to the Sixth Amendment, see, eg, *Burch v Louisiana* 441 US 130 (1979). As to the Fourteenth Amendment (right to privacy), see *Lawrence v Texas* 539 US 558 (2003).

[93] *Atkins v Virginia* 536 US 304, 325 (2002) (J Rehnquist, dissenting) (holding that '[f]or if it is evidence of a national consensus for which we are looking, then the viewpoints of other countries simply are not relevant').

[94] See, eg, Note, 'State Law as "Other Law": Our Fifty Sovereigns in the Federal Constitutional Canon' (2006–07) 120 *Harvard Law Review* 1670.

[95] RJ Smith, BJ Sarma and S Cuilt, 'The Way the Court Gauges Consensus (and How to Do it Better)' (2013–14) 35 *Cardozo Law Review* 2397, 2405.

[96] *Penry v Lynaugh* 492 US 302, 331 (1989) (holding that '[t]he clearest and most reliable objective evidence of contemporary values is the legislation enacted by the country's legislatures').

opinion polls, statistical data and experts' reports appear to be more questionable.[97] In any event, it is not clear what the relative importance of these indicators is.[98]

It follows that, on both sides of the Atlantic, the existence or absence of consensus is important in order for the ECJ or the US Supreme Court to refer respectively to the laws of the European and American States. For example, cases such as *FIAMM*, *Gascogne*, *Reed* and *D and Sweden v Council* demonstrate that there is a strong correlation between the degree of convergence existing among the different Member State legal systems and the deference shown to Member State law by the ECJ.[99] The same applies in the US where the US Supreme Court examines state laws in order to determine whether there is a national consensus regarding contemporary societal norms that should be taken into account for the purposes of interpreting the US Constitution.

A. The Existence of Consensus

The more convergence there is among the legal orders of the Member States, the more the ECJ will tend to follow in their footsteps.[100] Where convergence is not total but a particular approach is common to a large majority of Member State legal systems, then the ECJ will normally follow that approach, adapting and developing it to fit within the EU context.[101] A good example is provided by the *Berlusconi* case, where the ECJ held that '[t]he principle of the retroactive application of the more lenient penalty forms part of the constitutional traditions common to the Member States'.[102] In so doing, the ECJ implicitly relied on the comparative study undertaken by AG Kokott who stressed the fact that '[that principle is] established in the ... legal systems of almost all 25 Member States'.[103]

The same applies in the US. For example, in *Coker v Georgia*, a case concerning the imposition of the death penalty for rape of an adult woman, the US Supreme Court observed that Georgia was the only state that imposed capital punishment for such a crime. Accordingly, it ruled that such an objective indicator 'weigh[ed] very heavily on the side of rejecting capital punishment as a suitable penalty for raping an adult woman'.[104]

---

[97] *Atkins v Virginia* 536 US 304, 326 (2002) (J Rehnquist, dissenting).

[98] Smith, Sarma and Cuilt (n 95) 2415–18. Compare *Atkins v Virginia* 536 US 304 (2002) and *Roper v Simmons* 543 US 551 (2005) (legislative enactments) with *Graham v Florida* 560 US ___ (2010) (actual sentences practices).

[99] Lenaerts and Gutiérrez-Fons (n 10) 49.

[100] Lenaerts (n 86) 886.

[101] See, regarding the recognition of the right of property as a general principle of EU law, Case 44/79 *Hauer* EU:C:1979:290. Regarding the right of access to documents, Case C-353/99 P *Council v Hautala* EU:C:2001:661; and Case C-58/94 *Netherlands v Council* EU:C:1996:171.

[102] Joined Cases C-387/02, C-391/02 and C-403/02 *Berlusconi and Others* EU:C:2005:270, para 68.

[103] Joined Cases C-387/02, C-391/02 and C-403/02 *Berlusconi and Others* EU:C:2004:624, Opinion of AG Kokott, para 156 (the UK and Ireland were, at that time, the only exceptions).

[104] *Coker v Georgia* 433 US 584, 596 (1977).

B. The Existence of Divergences among Member State Legal Systems

In the absence of a consensus, it appears that both courts would act with caution so as to avoid making choices of a moral or ethical nature that do not find support in the societies of European and American states.

i. *Judicial Prudence*

Where there are important divergences among Member State legal systems, the ECJ will not make general statements of a medical or ethical nature, but limit itself to interpreting the EU provision in question.

In *Mayr*,[105] a female worker was dismissed whilst she was undergoing *in vitro* fertilisation treatment. As a result of that treatment, she was feeling sick and could not come to work. At the time of the dismissal, her ova had already been fertilised by her partner's sperm cells, but those ova had not yet been transferred to her uterus. Thus, the ECJ was called upon to determine whether that female worker was dismissed at a time when she was pregnant. In carrying out its analysis, the ECJ stressed that it did not intend to solve questions of a medical or ethical nature, but merely to interpret the relevant provisions of Directive 92/85.[106]

It noted that the objective of the prohibition of dismissal provided for in Directive 92/85 is to avoid the risk of a dismissal, for reasons linked to the pregnancy, having harmful effects on the physical and mental state of pregnant workers. This means that it is the earliest possible date in a pregnancy which must be chosen to ensure the safety and protection of pregnant workers. However, compliance with the principle of legal certainty prevents pregnancy from beginning before the ova were transferred to the uterus. Since it was both legally and medically possible to keep the fertilised ova outside the uterus for many years, applying the protection against dismissal laid down in Directive 92/85 in favour of a female worker before the transfer of the fertilised ova could have the effect of granting the benefit of that protection even where that transfer is postponed, for whatever reason, for a number of years or even where such transfer is definitively abandoned, the in vitro fertilisation having been carried out merely by way of a precaution. That being said, the ECJ decided to examine the dismissal at issue in the main proceedings in the light of the principle of equal treatment for men and women which was at the time, as regards working conditions, implemented by Directive 76/207 (now Directive 2006/54).[107] It held that if a female worker is dismissed on

---

[105] Case C-506/06 *Mayr* EU:C:2008:119.

[106] Council Dir 92/85/EEC of 19 October 1992 on the introduction of measures to encourage improvements in the safety and health at work of pregnant workers and workers who have recently given birth or are breastfeeding [1992] OJ L 348/1.

[107] Dir 2006/54/EC of the European Parliament and of the Council of 5 July 2006 on the implementation of the principle of equal opportunities and equal treatment of men and women in matters of employment and occupation [2006] OJ L 204/23.

account of absence due to illness brought about by the *in vitro* fertilisation treatment that she is undergoing, then such dismissal constitutes direct discrimination on grounds of sex.

Similarly, in the *CD* case,[108] the ECJ was asked to determine whether a female worker was, as a commissioning mother who had a baby through a surrogacy arrangement, entitled to maternity leave as provided for by Directive 92/85. In other words, could such a worker fall within the scope of application of that Directive? It is worth recalling that Directive 92/85 applies, *ratione personae*, to female workers who are pregnant, have recently given birth, and are breastfeeding.[109] The Member State court also asked whether an employer's refusal to provide maternity leave to a commissioning mother who had a baby through a surrogacy arrangement constituted discrimination on grounds of sex within the meaning of Directive 2006/54. In the *Z* case,[110] involving a similar factual setting, a different Member State court asked, in addition, whether a refusal to provide paid leave equivalent to maternity leave or adoptive leave to a female worker who was unable to bear a child and who had availed herself of a surrogacy arrangement constituted discrimination on the ground of disability within the meaning of Directive 2000/78.

In *Z*, AG Wahl observed that

> the legislative landscape is varied in the Member States: surrogacy ranges from being legal and specifically regulated, to illegal or … unregulated, and there is considerable disparity between Member States as to how surrogacy arrangements and, in particular, the processes involved therein ought to be regulated.[111]

In *CD*, AG Kokott made the same observation.[112] In addition, both Advocates General agreed that Directive 92/85 pursues two different, albeit interconnected, objectives, ie, first, to protect the health of the mother of the child in the especially vulnerable situation arising from her pregnancy and, second, to ensure that the special relationship between a woman and her child is protected.[113] Nevertheless, AG Wahl and AG Kokott took different views as to whether Directive 92/85 applied to commissioning mothers.

On the one hand, AG Wahl posited that the objective of protecting the special relationship between a woman and her child was a logical corollary of childbirth, so that it lacked independent significance.[114] Accordingly, since commissioning mothers were not in 'an especially vulnerable situation' arising from childbirth, Directive 92/85 did not apply to them.

---

[108] Case C-167/12 *CD* EU:C:2014:169; and Case C-363/12 *Z* EU:C:2014:159.
[109] See Art 2 of Dir 92/85.
[110] *Z* (n 108).
[111] Case C-363/12 *Z* EU:C:2013:604, Opinion of AG Wahl, para 1.
[112] Case C-167/12 *CD* EU:C:2013:600, Opinion of AG Kokott, para 3.
[113] See Opinions of AG Wahl in *Z* (n 111) para 45; and AG Kokott in *CD* (n 112) para 45.
[114] See Opinion of AG Wahl in *Z* (n 111) para 47.

On the other hand, AG Kokott reasoned that the special relationship between a woman and her child was of primary importance for the purposes of Directive 92/85. Thus, in order to ensure the unhindered development of that relationship,[115] that Directive applied to a commissioning mother who takes the child into her care after she or he is born.[116] Admittedly, her reading of Directive 92/85 was not entirely consistent with that Directive's structure and general scheme. In her view, this was because when the EU legislator adopted Directive 92/85, it did not consider the question whether pregnant and breast-feeding workers could be different persons. Indeed, since '[in] the early 1990s the practice of surrogacy was not as widespread as it is today', '[it was] thus not surprising that the normative structure of Directive 92/85 is based on an approach which takes biological motherhood as the norm'.[117] However, in the light of the objectives pursued by Directive 92/85, AG Kokott stressed the fact that that Directive was open to a 'dynamic' interpretation that would better reflect the times in which we live.

Despite the fact that surrogacy is more common today than it was 20 years ago, one could, however, argue that the lack of consensus among the laws of the Member States showed that the passage of time had not set aside a biological understanding of motherhood. Arguably, that lack of consensus advised judicial prudence before departing from the historical context in which that Directive was adopted. In that regard, the ECJ followed, in essence, the Opinion of AG Wahl: Directive 92/85 only applies to female workers who have been pregnant and have given birth to a child.[118] That said, the ECJ pointed out that Directive 92/85 did not oppose value diversity in the Member States. As Directive 92/85 only establishes certain minimum requirements, nothing prevents Member States from granting maternity leave to commissioning mothers.[119]

As to Directive 2006/54, the ECJ held that an employer's refusal to provide maternity leave (or paid leave equivalent to maternity leave) to a commissioning mother did not constitute discrimination on grounds of sex within the meaning of that Directive. First, there was no direct discrimination given that 'a commissioning father who [had] a baby through a surrogacy arrangement [was] treated in the same way as a commissioning mother in a comparable situation, in that he [was] not entitled to paid leave equivalent to maternity leave either'.[120] Second, there was no indirect discrimination either, since there was nothing in the file in those two cases to establish that the refusal of leave at issue put female workers at a particular disadvantage compared with male workers.[121] Third and last, although

---

[115] See Opinion of AG Kokott in *CD* (n 112) para 62.
[116] ibid para 68.
[117] ibid para 39.
[118] *CD* (n 108) para 36; and *Z* (n 108) para 58.
[119] *CD* (n 108) paras 41 and 42.
[120] ibid para 47; and *Z* (n 108) para 52.
[121] *CD* (n 108) para 49 ; and *Z* (n 108) para 54.

Directive 2006/54 also prohibits 'any less favourable treatment of a woman that is related to pregnancy or maternity leave within the meaning of Directive 92/85',[122] 'a commissioning mother who has had a baby through a surrogacy arrangement cannot, by definition, be subject to less favourable treatment related to her pregnancy, given that she has not been pregnant with that baby'.[123]

Regarding Directive 2000/78, the ECJ held that the inability to have a child by conventional means does not constitute a 'disability' within the meaning of that Directive, where such inability neither makes it impossible for the female worker to carry out her work nor constitutes a hindrance to the exercise of her professional activity.[124]

Furthermore, outside the scope of EU social law, the ECJ can also be confronted with questions of a medical or ethical nature. Those questions may, for example, arise in the realm of the internal market. The judgment of the ECJ in the *Brüstle* case illustrates this point.[125] In that case, the ECJ was asked to interpret the concept of 'human embryo' for the purposes of Directive 98/44 which provides that the 'use of human embryos for industrial or commercial purposes' may not be patented.[126] However, the EU legislator did not define the concept of 'human embryo', leaving that question to judicial interpretation.

This was a delicate task for the ECJ given that it was, in fact, asked to define when human life begins. At the outset, the ECJ noted that, since the relevant provisions of Directive 98/44 did not make reference to the laws of the Member States, that concept had to be interpreted in a uniform manner throughout the territory of the Union.[127]

Next, the ECJ made clear that

> although the definition of human embryo is a very sensitive social issue in many Member States, marked by their multiple traditions and value systems, [it was] not called upon, by the present order for reference, to broach questions of a medical or ethical nature, but [had to] restrict itself to a legal interpretation of the relevant provisions of [Directive 98/44].[128]

In that regard, it ruled that that concept had to be interpreted in the light of the dignity and integrity of the person, a fundamental right which is recognised by the constitutional traditions common to the Member States and which is now enshrined in Article 1 of the Charter.[129] This meant that the concept of 'human

---

[122] See Art 2(2)(c) of Dir 2006/54.
[123] *CD* (n 108) para 52; and *Z* (n 108) para 57. In the *Z* case, the ECJ also held, in the light of Art 16 and recital 27 of Dir 2006/54, that 'the situation of a commissioning mother as regards the grant of maternity leave or adoptive leave is not within the scope of [that Directive]'. *Z* (n 108) para 65.
[124] *Z* (n 108) paras 81 and 82.
[125] Case C-34/10 *Brüstle* EU:C:2011:669.
[126] Dir 98/44/EC of the European Parliament and of the Council of 6 July 1998 on the legal protection of biotechnological inventions [1998] OJ L 213/13.
[127] *Brüstle* (n 125) paras 26–29.
[128] ibid para 30 (referring to *Mayr* (n 105) para 38).
[129] ibid para 32.

embryo' had to be 'understood in a wide sense'[130] so as to include 'a non-fertilised human ovum that has the inherent capacity of developing into a human being'.[131] Conversely, as the ECJ subsequently pointed out in the *International Stem Cell Corporation* case,

> where a non-fertilised human ovum [lacks that capacity], the mere fact that that organism commences a process of development is not sufficient for it to be regarded as a 'human embryo', within the meaning and for the purposes of the application of Directive 98/44.[132]

Mayr, CD, Z and *Brüstle* are four important judgments illustrating the fact that the ECJ may be called upon to define concepts of a moral, social and even philosophical nature. In so doing, the ECJ acts circumspectly. When defining concepts such as 'pregnancy', 'motherhood' or 'human embryo', the ECJ restricts itself to interpreting those concepts for the sole purposes of the EU measure in question. Hence, it does not seek to provide a general definition of those concepts which would amount to imposing a uniform notion of public morality on all the Member States as this would be contrary to the pluralism on which the EU is founded.

On the other side of the Atlantic, the same applies. For example, in *Washington v Glucksberg*, the US Supreme Court ruled out the existence of a right to physician-assisted suicide under the Due Process Clause of the US Constitution. In so doing, the US Supreme Court observed that there was 'a consistent and almost universal tradition that has long rejected [such a] right, and continues explicitly to reject it today, even for terminally ill, mentally competent adults'. If that right were to be recognised, Chief Justice Rehnquist observed, the US Supreme Court would be obliged 'to reverse centuries of legal doctrine and practice, and strike down the considered policy choice of almost every State'.[133] Accordingly, that right was not 'deeply rooted in this Nation's history and tradition'.

---

[130] ibid para 34.

[131] Case C-364/13 *International Stem Cell Corporation* EU:C:2014:245128, para 28.

[132] ibid para 29. It is worth noting that a joint reading of the judgments in *Brüstle* and *International Stem Cell Corporation* provides a perfect illustration of the fact that where the approach adopted by the ECJ does not achieve the outcome expected, Member State courts may invite the ECJ to reconsider its approach. Indeed, in *Brüstle*, the ECJ held that the term 'human embryo' applies to a human parthenote—eg an unfertilised human ovum whose division and further development have been stimulated by parthenogenesis—since the latter had, according to the written observations presented to it, the capacity of commencing the process of development which leads to a human being. See *Brüstle* (n 125) para 36. Subsequently, in *International Stem Cell Corporation*, a different Member State court drew the attention of the ECJ to the fact that 'according to current scientific knowledge, a human parthenote, due to the effect of the technique used to obtain it, [lacks the inherent capacity of developing into a human being]'. Thus, this led the ECJ to reconsider its approach by ruling that 'Directive 98/44 must be interpreted as meaning that [a human parthenote] does not constitute a "human embryo", within the meaning of that [Directive], if, in the light of current scientific knowledge, that ovum does not, in itself, have the inherent capacity of developing into a human being, this being a matter for the [Member State] court to determine.' See *International Stem Cell Corporation*, ibid paras 31 to 38.

[133] *Washington v Glucksberg* 521 US 702, 723 (1997).

ii. The Teleological Thrust of the Comparative Law Method

However, the existence of divergences among Member State legal systems may not *automatically* rule out the incorporation, into the EU legal order, of a legal principle which is recognised in only a minority of Member States.

As applied by the ECJ, the comparative law method is not tantamount to finding the 'lowest common denominator'. As AG Lagrange observed in *Hoogovens v High Authority*,

> the case law of the [ECJ], in so far as it invokes Member State laws (as it does to a large extent) to define the rules of law relating to the application of the Treaty, is not content to draw on more or less arithmetical 'common denominators' between the different Member State solutions, but chooses from each of the Member States those solutions which, having regard to the objects of the Treaty, appear to it to be the best or, if one may use the expression, the most progressive. That is the spirit, moreover, which has guided the [ECJ] hitherto.[134]

It follows from the comments of AG Lagrange that the comparative law method and teleological interpretation are deeply intertwined. With a view to ascertaining the different interpretative options available in Member State legal systems, the ECJ will at first have recourse to the comparative law method in order to identify them. Next, the ECJ will choose the option which is best suited to the attainment of the objectives pursued by the EU.

The way in which this operates may be illustrated by contrasting *Mangold*[135] with *Akzo*.[136] In the first case, the ECJ recognised, for the first time, that the principle of non-discrimination on grounds of age constitutes a general principle of EU law. That was so despite the fact that only two Member States had, when *Mangold* was delivered, conferred constitutional status on that principle. Conversely, in *Akzo*, by opting for the approach followed in the majority of Member States, the ECJ held that legal professional privilege could not cover exchanges within a company or group with in-house lawyers.[137]

Logically, the question is how those two different outcomes may be reconciled. The Opinion of AG Kokott in *Akzo* sheds light on the matter. In *Mangold*, she observes, '[the] principle [on non-discrimination on grounds of age] was consistent with a specific task incumbent on the [EU] in combating discrimination

---

[134] See Case 14/61 *Koninklijke Nederlandsche Hoogovens en Staalfabrieken v High Authority* EU:C:1962:19, Opinion of AG Lagrange, 283–84. See also Case 5/71 *Zuckerfabrik Schöppenstedt v Council* EU:C:1971:81, Opinion of AG Roemer, 989. More recently, see Joined Cases C-120/06 P and C-121/06 P *FIAMM and FIAMM Technologies v Council and Commission* EU:C:2008:98, Opinion of AG Poiares Maduro, paras 55 and 56; and Case C-282/10 *Dominguez* EU:C:2011:559, Opinion of AG Trstenjak, para 94.

[135] Case C-144/04 *Mangold* EU:C:2005:709.

[136] Case C-550/07 P *Akzo Nobel Chemicals and Akcros Chemicals v Commission* EU:C:2010:512.

[137] ibid para 44. Previously, in Case 155/79 *AM & S Europe v Commission* EU:C:1982:157, the ECJ, taking account of the common criteria and similar circumstances existing at the time in the laws of the Member States, held that the confidentiality of written communications between lawyers and clients should be protected at Community level.

(Article 19 TFEU) and had also been given specific expression by the [EU] legislature in the form of a directive',[138] namely Directive 2000/78.[139] In addition, that principle mirrored a recent trend in the protection of fundamental rights, which was given concrete expression in the Charter.[140] Accordingly, for the Advocate General, even if a principle is only recognised in a minority of Member States, it may still constitute a general principle of EU law in so far as it reflects a mission with which the authors of the Treaties have entrusted the EU, or mirrors a trend in the protection of fundamental rights.

AG Kokott found that those two elements were missing in *Akzo*. She thus posited that

> [t]he extension of the protection afforded by legal professional privilege to internal company or group communications with enrolled in-house lawyers is not justified on grounds of any special characteristics exhibited by the tasks and activities of the European Commission as competition authority [[141]] and it does not currently constitute a growing trend among the Member States, be it in the area of competition law or in any other field.[142]

Similarly, in the US, not only a majority, but also a 'growing trend' in the American states may serve to determine the existence of 'evolving standards of decency'.[143] The ruling of the US Supreme Court in *Atkins v Virginia* illustrates this point. In that case, the US Supreme Court held that the Eighth Amendment opposes the imposition of the death penalty on a mentally retarded person. In so doing, it overruled its previous decision in *Penry v Lynaugh*, a case in which the US Supreme Court upheld the death penalty for mentally retarded offenders.[144] Writing for the Court, Justice Stevens observed that the public reaction to the execution of a mentally retarded murderer in Georgia[145] and the US Supreme Court's decision in *Penry v Lynaugh* had triggered a dramatic shift in the state legislative landscape: from 1990 to 2001, 18 of the 38 states that, at that time, permitted capital punishment enacted legislation prohibiting the execution of

---

[138] Case C-550/07 P *Akzo Nobel Chemicals and Akcros Chemicals v Commission* EU:C:2010:229, Opinion of AG Kokott, para 96.

[139] Dir 2000/78/EC (n 40).

[140] Opinion of AG Kokott (n 138) para 96.

[141] She also observed that, in the course of antitrust proceedings, the powers of the Commission are similar to those of Member State competition authorities. Hence, 'if the vast majority of the Member States have no need to deny the competition authorities access to communications between an undertaking and its enrolled in-house lawyers, it is safe to assume that there is no compelling need to extend the scope of legal professional privilege at European Union level either', ibid para 99.

[142] ibid para 98.

[143] B Petkova, 'The Notion of Consensus as a Route to Democratic Adjudication?' (2011–12) 14 *Cambridge Yearbook of European Legal Studies* 663, 666.

[144] *Penry v Lynaugh* 492 US 302, 335 (1989) (holding that 'there is insufficient evidence of a national consensus against executing mentally retarded people convicted of capital offenses for us to conclude that it is categorically prohibited by the Eighth Amendment').

[145] ibid 313–14 (holding that '[in 1986], the public reaction to the execution of a mentally retarded murderer in Georgia ... apparently led to the enactment of the first state statute prohibiting such executions [in that state]').

mentally retarded persons.[146] Despite the fact that those 18 states represented *less than half* of the states that permitted capital punishment,[147] Justice Stevens posited that '[it was] not so much the number of [the] States that [was] significant, but the consistency of the direction of change'.[148] Accordingly, he found that the execution of mentally retarded persons was at odds with the nation's 'evolving standards of decency'.

In addition, that finding was consistent with the US Supreme Court's death penalty jurisprudence.[149] First, the execution of mentally retarded persons did not serve the social purposes of retribution and deterrence. With respect to retribution, he posited that the cognitive and behavioural impairments of mentally retarded offenders make them less morally culpable and thus, unfit for the maximum punishment. As to deterrence, Justice Stevens found that those same impairments would also prevent them from controlling their conduct upon being informed of the possibility of execution as a penalty. Second, because of those impairments, mentally retarded offenders also faced a special risk of wrongful execution.

The approach developed by the US Supreme Court in *Atkins* was confirmed in *Roper v Simmons*, where it held that the Eighth Amendment opposed the imposition of a death penalty on a juvenile offender younger than 18 when committing a capital crime.[150]

In *Atkins* and *Roper*, the US Supreme Court stressed the fact that, whilst the national consensus doctrine serves to gather objective evidence from state legislatures, it is ultimately the Court's 'own judgment [that] will be brought to bear on the question of the acceptability of the death penalty under the Eighth Amendment'.[151] 'Consensus is not dispositive', wrote Justice Kennedy for the majority in *Kennedy v Louisiana*. 'Whether the death penalty is disproportionate to the crime committed depends as well upon the standards elaborated by controlling precedents and by the Court's own understanding and interpretation of the Eighth Amendment's text, history, meaning, and purpose'.[152] In *Atkins*, for example, this would mean, in essence, that the US Supreme Court gave more weight to its death penalty jurisprudence than to the existence of a national consensus.

Despite those formal statements, the fact remains that the US Supreme Court has not yet been confronted with a case in which the national consensus doctrine and its own independent judgment point towards opposite solutions.[153] Arguably, it is still unclear which rationale should prevail in the event of a conflict.

---

[146] *Atkins v Virginia* 536 US 304, 314–15 (2002).
[147] ibid 342 (J Scalia, dissenting).
[148] ibid 315.
[149] ibid 318.
[150] *Roper v Simmons* 543 US 551 (2005).
[151] *Atkins v Virginia* 536 US 304, 312–13 (2002).
[152] *Kennedy v Louisiana* 554 US 407 (2008).
[153] Smith, Sarma and Cuilt (n 95) 2417 (observing that '[t]he [US Supreme] Court has never exercised its independent judgment in a way that conflicts with the results of its search for a national consensus').

In that regard, US scholars seem to be divided into two camps. According to some scholars, the meaning of a constitutional provision, such as the Eighth Amendment, that seeks to protect individuals against the use of arbitrary public power should not be left in the hands of state legislatures.[154] Conversely, other scholars opine that the US Supreme Court should refrain from relying on its own independent judgment where that judgment is inconsistent with a national consensus.[155] Only where there is no national consensus should the US Supreme Court rely on other methods of interpretation. In their view, the national consensus doctrine aims primarily to protect the US Supreme Court against 'a national popular backlash'.[156]

If that latter reading of the Eighth Amendment were to prevail, this would constitute a major difference from the ECJ's evaluative approach. That said, when considering a particular case, the ECJ will want to avoid 'going too far' and may therefore opt for a solution which is not necessarily the most ambitious, considered from the exclusive angle of EU law, but which has the advantage of being 'compatible' with the traditions of the Member States and of not hurting special sensitivities in certain Member States.[157] In the same way, when examining the compatibility of a Member State measure with EU law, the ECJ will 'gauge the temperature' of the Member State legal systems in order to ascertain the credibility and 'acceptability' of its decision for the whole of the EU.[158] It follows that, in so far as there is no EU harmonisation and Member State diversity does not call into question one of the principles on which the EU is founded, the lack of consensus militates in favour of finding a solution that does not risk encountering incomprehension or resistance in some Member States, which could undermine the effectiveness and the uniform application of EU law.

This point is illustrated by the case law of the ECJ relating to online gambling. In *Liga Portuguesa de Futebol Profissional*, for example, the question was whether the host Member State could prohibit a service provider established in another Member State from offering games of chance via the internet within the territory of the first Member State. In that regard, the ECJ held that such prohibition constituted a restriction on the freedom to provide services that needed to be justified by overriding reasons in the public interest, such as the objectives of consumer protection and the prevention of both fraud and incitement to squander money on gambling, as well as the general need to preserve public order.[159] In addition,

---

[154] See, eg, K White, 'The Constitutional Limits of the "National Consensus" Doctrine in Eighth Amendment Jurisprudence' (2012) *BUY Law Review* 1367.

[155] RM Ré, 'Can Congress Overturn *Graham v Florida*?' (2011) 34 *Harvard Journal of Law & Public Policy* 367.

[156] Hills (n 89) 22–23.

[157] Lenaerts (n 86) 879.

[158] ibid 896.

[159] See, eg, Case C-42/07 *Liga Portuguesa de Futebol Profissional and Baw International* EU:C:2009:519, para 56.

that prohibition had to comply with the principle of proportionality. In that context, the ECJ noted that

> the legislation on games of chance is one of the areas in which there are significant moral, religious and cultural differences between the Member States. In the absence of harmonisation in the field at EU level, it is for each Member State to determine in those areas, in accordance with its own scale of values, what is required in order to ensure that the interests in question are protected.[160]

This meant, in essence, that 'the mere fact that a Member State has opted for a system of protection which differs from that adopted by another Member State cannot affect the assessment of the need for, and proportionality of, the provisions enacted to that end'.[161] Accordingly, just as it did in *Omega* and *Sayn-Wittgenstein*, the ECJ applied a version of the principle of proportionality that allowed room for value diversity. The ECJ did not look for the least restrictive alternative to the freedom to provide services that it could think of, but examined the compatibility of the Member State measure in question with the principle of proportionality by reference to the objectives pursued by the competent authorities of the Member State concerned and the degree of protection which they seek to ensure.

III. Concluding Remarks

Drawing the line between law and politics in a system of multilevel governance such as the EU or the US is a complex endeavour. This is because judges do not operate in a vacuum, but must give meaningful solutions to the cases before them, whilst upholding the structural and substantive principles of the legal order to which they belong.

Although, in the EU, consensus 'is only a complementary element to judicial reasoning and is thus not an independent logical structure on which the courts rely', it 'provides the [ECJ] with a link to popular opinion and the empirical realities of the extrajudicial environment'.[162] This helps EU citizens to identify themselves with the values promoted by the EU.

The evaluative approach followed by the ECJ favours a dynamic interpretation of EU law. Where societal change brings about a high degree of convergence in the laws of the Member States, the evaluative approach enables the EU legal order to cope with those changes, thereby aligning the EU's legal culture with those of its Member States. As the US Supreme Court's case law demonstrates, a consensus-based analysis enables an evolutive interpretation of EU law: the emergence of a

---

[160] ibid para 57. See Joined Cases C-186/11 and C-209/11 *Stanleybet International and Others* EU:C:2013:33, para 24; and Case C-156/13 *Digibet and Albers* EU:C:2014:1756, para 24.

[161] Case C-42/07 *Liga Portuguesa de Futebol Profissional and Baw International* EU:C:2009:519, para 58.

[162] Petkova (n 143) 693 and 695.

consensus may militate in favour of departing from existing case law that has, with the passage of time, become inconsistent with contemporary societal values.

Of course, in order for that method not to become a 'Trojan horse' of judges' own ideological preferences, the existence or absence of consensus must be based on objective evidence. This means that EU judges and Advocates General must make sure that the comparative law method is based exclusively on reliable indicators such as Member State laws.

However, just like in the US, in the EU 'consensus is not dispositive', as Justice Kennedy wrote. The evaluative approach indeed enables the EU legal order to preserve its autonomy. Admittedly, the existence of consensus among the Member States plays an important role in supplying the content of EU law, notably in discovering general principles of EU law. The same applies when the ECJ engages in federal common law-making. But the incorporation into EU law of a norm based on consensus at Member State level must always be made subject to its consistency with the founding principles of that law. Indeed, whilst the 'migration of constitutional ideas' may facilitate a mutual understanding among different levels of governance, it is important to determine the way in which such migration is to take place. Otherwise, there is a risk that a constitutional idea that originated at Member State level may fail to work in practice or that it may have unintended consequences at EU level.[163] In the same way, the absence of such a consensus does not prevent the ECJ from having recourse to other sources of law, such as international law, or from applying other methods of interpretation. That said, as the *Mayr*, *CD*, *Z* and *Brüstle* cases demonstrate, the absence of a consensus counsels the ECJ to act with caution.

In addition, the evaluative approach may give rise to a 'spill-over effect' triggering public debate in the Member States in which the solution advocated by the ECJ is not present in their law. That approach produces cross-fertilisation and mutual influence between the EU and Member State legal orders, thereby creating a 'common constitutional space'.

---

[163] N Walker, 'The Migration of Constitutional Ideas and the Migration of the Constitutional Idea: The Case of the EU' (2005) EUI Working Paper Law, No 4. Available at http://cadmus.eui.eu/bitstream/handle/1814/3324/law05-04.pdf.

5

Ideology and Legal Reasoning at the European Court of Justice

I. Introduction

The Zagreb Conference, which inspired the publication of this book, included a discussion on ideology in the courts. Judge Lenaerts, President of the European Court of Justice (ECJ), defended the position that ideology does not affect the work of his court. His contribution to the conference and to this volume explains that the comparative method is one of the tools that the Court uses to prevent ideology from influencing its decisions. In the opening part of his contribution, he claims: '[w]hen called upon to resolve particular gaps, conflicts and ambiguities in the existing regime, judges should have a sincere feeling of constraint that inhibits them from engaging in strategic behaviour to dispose ideological stakes'.[1]

Thus, Judge Lenaerts accepts the proposition that the law is not determinate and leaves 'gaps, conflicts and ambiguities' that judges are called upon to clarify by interpretation. However, he is eager to stress that judges should not and do not involve their personal politics (or ideology) in interpretation.

On the other hand, the Critical Legal Studies (CLS) movement, and in particular Duncan Kennedy in his work, claims that 'ideology influences adjudication, by structuring legal discourse and through strategic choice in interpretation'.[2] This is so, he claims, notwithstanding denial by judges.

[*] Tamara Ćapeta is Professor of EU Law at the Faculty of Law of the University of Zagreb. I wish to thank Luka Burazin, Daniela Caruso, Zdenek Kühn, Siniša Rodin, Tuan Samahon and Martijn van den Brink for their valuable comments. The research for this paper was conducted under the research project 'Novi hrvatski pravni sustav' of the Faculty of Law in Zagreb.
[1] K Lenaerts, 'Discovering the Law of the EU: The European Court of Justice and the Comparative Law Method' (in this volume).
[2] D Kennedy, *A Critique of Adjudication (fin de siècle)* (Cambridge, Harvard University Press, 1997) 19.

The question with which I left the Conference was not whether ideology finds its way into adjudication. I am convinced it does, even though this is difficult to prove (section III.B). I was also persuaded by the sincerity of Lenaerts' effort to try to keep ideology out of the ECJ, even though I am not convinced that this is what always happens (section III.A). However, the question which has stayed with me, and which has inspired this contribution, is why judges so eagerly try to convince us of the absence of ideology in adjudication. The question might seem irrelevant—if publicly judges can offer convincing legal arguments for their decisions which do not include ideology, why does it matter what really influenced them? However, if Kennedy's argument that 'denial of the presence of ideology in adjudication leads to political results different from those that would occur in a situation of transparency' is right,[3] then my question becomes relevant.

Before engaging in further discussion, I need to clarify an issue. When one reads ECJ decisions, there is no mention of any political/ideological positions of the Court or its individual judges. How can I then claim that ideology influences adjudication? Legal philosophers tend to divide the adjudication process into the process of discovery and the process of justification.[4] The process of discovery relates to everything that is really happening (in the judge's mind, in chambers or among judges in collegiate courts) which contributes to a decision, whereas the process of justification denotes finding appropriate legal reasoning to justify a decision publicly. It is quite clear to anyone who reads the ECJ's decision that ideology is never mentioned in the judgments as published. Thus, my claim obviously does not relate to the process of justification. Rather, my claim that ideology is present in adjudication at the ECJ refers to the process of discovery. My position is that ideology influences the desired outcome of a case, and with it also the choice of the legal rule(s) to be applied as justification, as well as the 'proper' meaning or scope of that rule, even if this is not visible in the justification. The valid question, then, is why is what happened in discovery hidden in the Court's reasoning which is made public?

It seems that in Europe, not only judges but also scholars avoid discussing ideology in the ECJ. Books devoted to judicial reasoning in the ECJ, and there have been several published lately,[5] either completely ignore the presence of ideology in judging or they admit it, but pay little attention to it. The reasons may differ. For one, it is difficult to discover what is attributable to an individual judge in collective judgments decided behind closed doors. It is much easier to research what is available—publicly disclosed legal reasoning. But another possible

---

[3] ibid.

[4] For instance, L Silveira, 'Discovery and Justification of Judicial Decisions: Towards More Precise Distinctions in Legal Decision-Making' (2014) *Law and Method* www.lawandmethod.nl/tijdschrift/lawandmethod/2014/09/RENM-D-14-00003.

[5] G Beck, *The Legal Reasoning of the Court of Justice of the EU* (Oxford, Hart Publishing, 2012); G Conway, *The Limits of Legal Reasoning and the European Court of Justice* (Cambridge, Cambridge University Press, 2012); S Sankari, *European Court of Justice Legal Reasoning in Context* (Groningen, Europa Law Publishing, 2013).

explanation for not even trying to look into the presence of ideology is the view about what judging should look like—and for most Europeans, it should not be personal. Most Europeans, lawyers and non-lawyers alike, want to believe that judges find solutions only by the application of legal reasoning. Thus, scholars possibly believe that what is described in justification, ie the legal reasoning underpinning a decision, is all that was happening in the discovery phase as well, or at least, all that is important. This, I claim, is not so. However, my claim is not a normative one— I am neutral towards whether ideology should influence adjudication or not.

The claim on which this contribution is based is purely descriptive: ideology does influence the process of adjudication. Even if rarely, judges sometimes admit this. In one of the few articles in which a judge talks about his personal experience of judging, Judge Koopmans, former judge of the ECJ, asked the following question:

> [I]s the lawyer's reasoning deductive or regressive? In other words, does he start by looking at precedents and legislative provisions, adjusting them to the case at hand by longer or shorter chains of reasoning, or does he first try to find a good solution, trying thereafter to build a bridge between the solution and the applicable case-law and legal provisions? The real question here is whether legal reasoning serves for finding the solution to a legal problem or for justifying it.[6]

He then admits that in his personal experience both methods were present. Especially when 'faced with a difficult case', he tended to look at both—'the deductive reasoning and at just solution in turn'.[7]

Looking for a good or just solution is, therefore, something that judges do in their decision-making. What is good for one person is not necessarily good for another. This depends on that person's subjective personal beliefs and values, or their ideology. For the purposes of this contribution, the word 'ideology' is used in a very general sense—to describe one's personal beliefs about how society should best be organised, the same belief being at the same time universalised, or shared by other people having a similar ideology and being publicly perceived as reflecting that ideology.[8] Ideology necessarily entails value judgments about what is good for society and its members. Different judges have different ideologies. Different value judgments of 'good' may lead to different judgments about how benefits and burdens in society should be distributed.

This being said, in this contribution I explore two questions: first, how can one prove and discuss ideology in adjudication at the ECJ? (sections III and IV); and second, why do European judges deny ideological influence (section V)? While looking into these questions, I will use the opportunity to deconstruct some

---

[6] T Koopmans, 'Judicial Decision-making' in AIL Campbell and M Voyatzi (eds), *Legal Reasoning and Judicial Interpretation of European Law: Essays in Honour of Lord Mackenzie-Stuart* (London, Trenton Publishing, 1996) 93, 96.

[7] ibid.

[8] Duncan Kennedy describes ideology as the universalisation of group interests. Kennedy (n 2) 41.

judgments that have puzzled me for a long time, or to retell certain EU judicial stories through different narratives. Before examining these questions, I will first offer a few preliminary observations about the Court of Justice, necessary for further discussion (section II).

II. About the European Court of Justice

A. Law Interpretation versus Law Application in the ECJ

The European Court of Justice is the Court having, among other things, the constitutional task of interpreting EU law for other courts in the system, such interpretations having for those courts final authority. Other courts, consisting of lower EU courts[9] and all courts of the EU Member States, must follow the interpretations that the ECJ gives to EU legal norms. National courts were co-opted into the EU judicial system by the Court of Justice which turned them into primary courts of EU law via doctrines of direct effect and supremacy. When national courts adjudicate in the function of EU law, the ECJ tries to influence and shape their powers. Some of the obligations imposed by the ECJ on national courts will be part of this story.

Most cases that are solved by the application of EU rules take place in national courts. The ECJ becomes involved in such cases via the so-called preliminary ruling mechanism.[10] These types of cases represent the majority of the ECJ's work today.[11] In preliminary rulings, the ECJ is asked only to interpret the law, but not to apply it. The division of labour between the ECJ and national courts in this procedure is that the ECJ interprets, and national courts apply that interpretation to the facts of the case.[12] The ECJ has stressed this in its recommendations for national courts in the preliminary ruling procedure.[13]

---

[9] At the moment when I handed in the final version of this contribution, there was only one lower European Court—the General Court. The other lower court—the Civil Service Tribunal—was dismantled on 1 September 2016 as a result of judicial reform at the CJEU.

[10] This procedure is regulated today by Art 267 TFEU. For a detailed description of how the procedure has evolved in practice, see MP Broberg and N Fenger, *Preliminary References to the European Court of Justice* (Oxford, Oxford University Press, 2010).

[11] In 2015, preliminary references constituted 65.58 per cent of the Court's workload. Annual Report of the Court http://curia.europa.eu/jcms/jcms/Jo2_7000/en/.

[12] The ECJ has emphasised such a division of functions since its early case law, including Case 26/62 *Van Gend en Loos* EU:C:1963:1 and Case 6/64 *Costa v ENEL* EU:C:1964:66.

[13] Recommendations to national courts and tribunals, in relation to the initiation of preliminary ruling proceedings, Official Journal of the European Union, C 439, 25 November 2016, point 11: '[l]astly, although, in order to deliver its decision, the Court necessarily takes into account the legal and factual context of the dispute in the main proceedings, as defined by the referring court or tribunal in its request for a preliminary ruling, it does not itself apply EU law to that dispute'.

I understand the term 'interpretation' as a decision-making activity of choosing between multiple potentially applicable legal rules as well as choosing between multiple possible meanings of the applicable legal rules. Such a view presupposes certain 'rule-scepticism', ie the acceptance of the position that law is indeterminate. This does not, however, necessarily mean that law has no meaning whatsoever prior to interpretation. I stand by rule-scepticism as described by Riccardo Guastini:

> [R]ule- scepticism has no need of such a bold assumption as the no- previous- meaning thesis. The very ground of rule- scepticism is the simple acknowledgement that a plurality of interpretations (of one and the same text) are almost always possible, coupled with the thesis that no persuasive criterion of truth exists for interpretive sentences.[14]

Many would object that under such a view the activity of choosing between multiple meanings amounts to judicial legislation, as it is the Court that in the end shapes the rule that is applicable to the case at issue. The Court 'legislates' for the purposes of the facts of the case at hand, but the created rule does not end its existence there, but is carried on to future cases. How this happens differs from system to system, but it happens both in common law and civil law systems, and in the EU system. In my opinion, interpretation is necessary in all cases, both hard and easy. The distinction between the two, if there is one in advance of adjudication, might be that in easy cases most persons would come to the same conclusion, whereas in hard cases there is great likelihood that different interpreters would arrive at different conclusions. In any case, the majority of questions that arrive at the ECJ in the preliminary ruling procedure come from disputes in which precisely either the question of the applicability or the possibility of the different meaning or effect of EU rules is the reason for referring the issue to the Court.[15]

The result of adjudication in a preliminary ruling is the clarification of the meaning of an EU legal rule in a given context. This clarification is public. It is often referred to as 'interpretation' given by the Court. In this sense (different from how I use it in this text), the word 'interpretation' denotes not only the process of choosing the meaning, but also the end result of that process. This 'end result' is published and sent back to the referring national court to apply. However, the legal reasoning offered for the chosen clarification does not necessarily reveal what happened in the process of discovery. It is worth noting here that this non-transparency opens the possibility of different interpretations

---

[14] R Guastini, 'Rule-Scepticism Restated' in L Green and B Leiter (eds), *Oxford Studies in Philosophy of Law* Vol 1 (Oxford, Oxford University Press, 2011) 158–59.

[15] However, national courts often use the preliminary ruling procedure not because of their doubt in the meaning of an EU rule, but rather in order to obtain the ECJ's support for a decision to set aside a contrary rule of national law. Arguably, in such cases, there is no doubt about the meaning of applicable EU rule. However, even in such situations, it will often still be in the interest of one party to dispute the apparently clear meaning of the relevant EU rule, or, failing that, its applicability. Consequently, the task of the Court would be either to choose the meaning desired by the referring court (and in most situations one of the parties to a dispute) or a different meaning, leading to a result different from that sought by the national court.

of a given ECJ 'interpretation', be it by the national courts that apply it, or by the academic community or by political institutions.

Interestingly and different from the normal description of the task of the courts, which is to interpret the law in the function of applying it, in the EU system, the ECJ only interprets EU law, whereas the application of such interpretation is left for the referring national courts. At odds with the efforts of those political philosophers who argued that the application and the interpretation of law do not differ,[16] the EU founding Treaties prescribed the difference. In view of classical legal positivism, according to which what is not law application is necessarily judicial legislation,[17] the ECJ must be seen as a political court endowed with law-making powers.

Detaching interpretation from application arguably makes the ECJ more a legislator than a court. However, the ECJ is and wants to be seen as a court. Relatively early on, therefore, it decided to give its interpretations in close connection to the factual and legal context of the case from which it received the question of interpretation. It has developed this so far that it sometimes refuses to answer, declining its jurisdiction, if the referring court does not explain to a satisfactory level the context within which the question of interpretation arose.[18] Thus, the ECJ has interpreted the preliminary ruling mechanism as a procedure that aims to provide national courts with concrete aid in resolving specific cases that involve an issue of EU law[19] rather than a procedure endowing the Court with the abstract power of creating or explaining legal rules. This has resulted in formulae that are linguistically difficult to understand and by which the Court pronounces its interpretation, attempting at the same time not to apply it to solve the case (as this is the task for national courts), but at the same time also applying it to the facts of the case (as, otherwise, the Court risks being seen as a legislator).[20] If the aesthetics

---

[16] See, in this respect, Kennedy's description of five different approaches to this issue in *Critique of Adjudication* (n 2) 30–38.

[17] ibid 31.

[18] The ECJ for the first time denied its jurisdiction to answer the referred question because the reference lacked an explanation of the facts relevant for understanding the case in Case C-320-322/90 *Telemarsicabruzzo*, EU:C:1993:26. It continued this practice afterwards, even if it has sometimes decided to answer notwithstanding the insufficiently explained reference (eg Case C-316/93 *Veneetveld* EU:C:1994:82). Such an interpretation of a preliminary ruling is today embodied in Art 94 of the Court's Rules of Procedure, which describe the necessary content of a preliminary reference, including, among these requirements, an explanation of the facts and context of the case from which the question is referred.

[19] Ever since Case 244/80 *Foglia v Novello (No 2)* EU:C:1981:302 (see especially para 18).

[20] The formula is originally written in French and then translated into other languages. From my personal experience, I am aware of the difficulties the translation of the formula causes to lawyer linguists of different EU languages. In English, it goes more or less like this: 'Article 5(2)(b) of Directive 2001/29/EC of the European Parliament and of the Council of 22 May 2001 on the harmonisation of certain aspects of copyright and related rights in the information society must be interpreted as precluding a scheme for fair compensation for private copying which, like the one at issue in the main proceedings, is financed from the General State Budget in such a way that it is not possible to ensure that the cost of that compensation is borne by the users of private copies', taken from the judgment in Case C-470/14 *EGEDA and others* EU:C:2016:418.

of judgments contribute to the legitimacy of the courts,[21] this is certainly not helpful to the ECJ.

The most plausible explanation of the Court's choice to interpret the preliminary ruling procedure in the way just described is the Court's own vision of the proper role of the courts. If it only interpreted the law, it would cease being the Court. If it interpreted the law for the purpose of applying it, it would do what courts are meant to do. Thus, the ECJ was only defending its existence in the new legal system.

B. Dworkin at the ECJ

European lawyers, including judges, no longer deny the indeterminacy of law. This necessarily demands that judges make choices about the proper meaning of a rule. The question is, then, what informs the judges in looking for the meaning, or in finding the proper interpretation to be applied to a case. The prevailing belief is that such a choice has nothing to do with the judges' personal political preferences, and neither should it. EU judges, so it is claimed, are not guided by their values, but by something else. What is this something else?

The usual narrative is that judges are guided by the objective purpose of the rules placed in the context of the legal system as a coherent whole, which has its own underlying objective. The Treaties aim at 'integration', and therefore the Court is able to extrapolate 'political theory/philosophy'[22] and 'principles'[23] which fit the legal order the Treaties have created. The following citation from former ECJ Advocate General Poiares Maduro illustrates the point:

> In this sense, all courts (and their members) have a judicial philosophy, be it publicly articulated or not. Such a judicial philosophy is however, to a large extent, a product of the system of law in which those courts operate. The methods of interpretation used by courts as well as their institutional and value choices reflect (or ought to reflect) a certain systemic understanding of the normative preferences and institutional constraints of the legal order in which those courts operate. Only such an approach is capable of securing the coherence as well as the integrity of that legal order (by fitting individual decisions into a coherent whole) and judicial accountability (by constraining the power of courts in individual decisions and subjecting them to a normative, and not political, scrutiny with regard to the normative preferences they attribute to their legal order). Understood in this way, a theory of judicial adjudication or a judicial philosophy (which ought not to be confused with a judicial ideology or, even less so, with political ideology) serves not only to objectivise and constrain the subjective preferences of

---

[21] S Rodin, 'Elegant Jurisprudence', Talk at the Mentor Group dinner, Brussels, 11 April 2016 (in author's possession).

[22] R Dworkin, 'Hard Cases' (1975) 88 *Harvard Law Review* 1057, see especially 1084ff.

[23] ibid.

judges, but also to define and legitimate the proper role of courts in a given political community.[24]

Thus, the usual narrative would continue, as the system has its underlying reason and purpose, for as long as the judges' choices fit that purpose, they cannot be blamed for imposing their own ideology. If the law does not give a clear answer to a particular question, a judge will always be able to find a proper legal solution by creating a rule which corresponds to the integrationist 'preference implicit in legal materials', to use Kennedy's terminology.[25] If a judge does so, he is not imposing his personal preferences, and his action is therefore not illegitimate.

EU legal actors, therefore, accept that judges make law, ie make choices about applicable rules and their meaning. This is legitimate if they retain interpretive fidelity, which is achieved if their decisions are principled (and not personal) and coherent with the underlying objectives of the system. These guide judges in finding the 'right answer'. And there is always a right answer, at least this is how the ECJ frames its decisions. Thus, the ECJ is the Hercules of a Dworkinian legal world.[26]

But is this really possible? Can judges really decide on the basis of some recognisable politics built in the system in every particular case?

III. There Must be Ideology behind the ECJ's Decisions

A. Working with Legal Materials

A claim that ideology is present in adjudication does not mean that judges decide exclusively in accordance with their personal preferences. The rule of law, as explained by Kennedy, requires 'that judges understand themselves to be bound by a norm of interpretive fidelity to the body of legal materials that are relevant to whatever dispute is before them'.[27] This norm, in short, means that judges cannot ignore the existence of a legal text (be it a Constitution, legislation or previous case law). Thus, admitting the presence of ideology in judicial decision-making is not equivalent to saying that judges are unconstrained in their decisions by the

---

[24] M Maduro, 'Interpreting European Law—On Why and How Law and Policy Meet at the European Court of Justice' in H Koch, K Hagel-Sorensen, U Haltern and JHH Weiler (eds), *Europe. The New Legal Realism*, (Copenhagen, DJØF Publishing, 2010) 457, 460.

[25] Kennedy (n 2) 35.

[26] Dworkin (n 22) 1083, introducing Hercules; see also R Dworkin, *Law's Empire* (Cambridge, Harvard University Press, 1988); R Dworkin, *A Matter of Principle* (Cambridge, Harvard University Press, 1986). cf J Bengoetxea, *The Legal Reasoning of the European Court of Justice* (Oxford, Clarendon Press, 1993) vi.

[27] Kennedy (n 2) 13.

existing legal rules. However, if judges cannot neglect legal materials, they may still 'work' with them. The ECJ is, I believe, aware of this.

Good proof that ECJ judges recognise that it is possible to work with legal materials towards achieving a certain adjudicative outcome is the obligation of conforming interpretation that the ECJ imposes on national judges. This so-called 'indirect' or 'interpretive' effect of EU law, which the ECJ found inherent in the Treaties,[28] creates an obligation for a national judge to interpret national law, as far as possible, 'in the light of the wording and purpose' of relevant EU law in order to achieve the result sought by that law.[29] National judges are supposed to look into their entire domestic legal system, and work with it, to find a solution that is in accordance with EU law. As stated by the ECJ:

> Although the principle that national law must be interpreted in conformity with Community law concerns chiefly domestic provisions enacted in order to implement the directive in question, it does not entail an interpretation merely of those provisions but requires the national court to consider national law as a whole in order to assess to what extent it may be applied so as not to produce a result contrary to that sought by the directive.[30]

The obligation of conforming interpretation puts an important constraint on national judges. Their interpretative strategy has to be oriented towards achieving results imposed by EU law. And the results required are not interpreted by national judges, but rather by the ECJ. Research on whether national judges really follow this instruction of the ECJ hardly exists. It is therefore a highly interesting and relevant topic, although it is not the subject of this contribution. For the purposes of this chapter, it suffices to observe that the ECJ accepts that judges can work with legal materials and can do so strategically, with a view to achieving certain desired outcomes.

If this is true for national judges, why would it not also be true for European judges? But ECJ judges never admit any strategy in their interpretive choices, except possibly working toward achieving certain meta-teleological aims, usually the effectiveness or uniformity of EU law.[31] They also never admit that they are 'working' with the legal materials, and that different outcomes are possible. They present their outcome as if it is the only possible one. Even if other outcomes, or different reasoning ending in the same judgment, were discussed during the procedure before the Court, this is never revealed in the text of the judicial decision. Only by reading the Advocate General's opinion can an outsider learn that

---

[28] Joined Cases C-397—403/01 *Pfeiffer* EU:C:2004:584 para 114.

[29] Case 14/83 *Von Colson and Kamman* EU:C:1984:153 para 26. This was the first case in which the Court developed interpretive obligation. The requirement on national courts has been repeated on numerous occasions since then. One of the recent cases repeating this requirement in strong words was Case C-282/10 *Dominguez* EU:C:2012:33.

[30] *Pfeiffer* (n 28) para 115.

[31] M Lasser, *Judicial Deliberations—A Comparative Analysis of Judicial Transparency and Legitimacy* (Oxford, Oxford University Press, 2004) 212ff.

there were different options and that they were discussed—and this only if the AG indeed discussed different options, or offered her different opinion. Additionally, ECJ decisions leave the decision-making procedure as the (apparently) unanimous positions of the deciding chamber. Even if the judges voted, which is an option under the Rules of Procedure,[32] outside readers will never know.[33]

One very good example that there must have been issues discussed by the Court, but that were completely omitted in the final decision as published, is the *Dominguez* case.[34] There, the ECJ was asked about whether the application of a directive that fulfilled the conditions for direct effect could lead to the disapplication of domestic law in a horizontal situation. Settled case law has it that in horizontal situations, as was the one in the case at hand, directives cannot be invoked directly, either in order to cause the non-applicability of a domestic legal rule,[35] or to create a right for an individual.[36] It is quite unlikely that the French Cour de Cassation, which referred the question to the ECJ, did not know this. The possible reason why the French Court posed such a question was the recent controversial (*Mangold/Kücükdeveci*) case law[37] preceding *Dominguez*, in which the ECJ allowed for the application of a directive in a horizontal case in a situation where the right a directive granted to individuals was in fact already granted on the basis of a general principle of EU law (in the cases at issue, by the principle prohibiting discrimination on the ground of age, disputed in itself). Thus, a directive was seen only as working out the right contained in another, more general rule—a general principle of EU law.

It seems that in *Dominguez*, and one may learn this only by reading the opinion of the Advocate General,[38] some time was spent on discussing whether the *Mangold/Kücükdeveci* reasoning could be transposed to this case. The difference was that the fundamental right that a directive further developed was not equality, but rather one of social rights, in this case the right to paid annual leave. As the previous two cases were heavily criticised and the ECJ judges obviously could not agree on how to proceed, they chose to entirely ignore that issue in the

---

[32] Art 32(4) of the Rules of Procedure provides: 'The conclusions reached by the majority of the Judges after final discussion shall determine the decision of the Court'. The Rules of Procedure of the ECJ are published on the website of the ECJ: http://curia.europa.eu/jcms/upload/docs/application/pdf/2012-10/rp_en.pdf.

[33] On occasions, however, an historical analysis of case law might reveal some details. Thus, it is today clear that the influence of two judges, Judge Robert Lecourt and Judge Alberto Trabucchi, changed the majority in the historical *Van Gend en Loos* case. See Morten Rasmussen, 'Law Meets History: Interpreting the Van Gend en Loos Judgment' in B Davies and F Nicola (eds), *EU Law Stories* (Cambridge, Cambridge University Press, forthcoming) 115–16.

[34] *Dominguez* (n 29).

[35] Even if this aspect of horizontal effects of a directive still cannot be said to be settled for good, as Case C-194/94 *CIA v Signalson and Securitel* EU:C:1996:172 and Case C-443/98 *Unilever v Central Food* EU:C:2000:496 were never revisited and explained by the ECJ.

[36] Case C-91/92 *Faccini Dori* EU:C:1994:292.

[37] I am referring to Case C-144/04 *Mangold* EU:C:2005:709 and Case C-555/07 *Kücükdeveci* EU:C:2010:21.

[38] See the Opinion of AG Trstenjak in *Dominguez* (n 29).

final judgment. If one reads only a judgment, and not the AG's opinion, the Court's answer, relying on the classical interpretive/direct effect/liability logic, would not be surprising. It was one of the possible solutions in this case. But behind it is the strategy of the ECJ to turn a hard case into a seemingly easy one. What the ECJ did is what the courts do all the time—it chose one set of rules as applicable to the case at hand. It has, thus, in Kennedy's words, constituted the field in the way it wished the case to proceed.[39] However, the decision entirely hides the fact that there was a different set of rules that could have also been applied in this case and which was discussed by the parties and the AG. The strategic goal of this choice was probably the desire to postpone a difficult decision about the legal effects of fundamental rights in the EU legal order.[40] The ECJ obviously worked with the legal materials, but the entire process was hidden from the public. Thus, it is not possible to know whether there were any value judgments, and perhaps even disagreements between the judges in the deciding chamber. Did the judges, for example, consider that equality was more important in EU society than certain social rights, which is why the former right was to be recognised as having direct effect whereas the latter was not? Additionally, the Court did not seem to answer the question of the French Court which, in the very end, had to decide the case.

B. Value Judgments

In certain situations, it is clear that nothing but the Court's value judgment is able to resolve the case. I will take as an example one of the cases which Judge Lenaerts describes in his contribution to this book—the *Reed* case.[41] He uses this case to show that the ECJ employs comparative research of national legal systems in order to find a solution for a question that is not clearly settled at the EU level. The comparative method is, he claims, one of the means to prevent the Court from imposing its personal views in particular cases.[42] In *Reed*, the question was whether the term 'spouse' in an EU Regulation[43] should include an unmarried partner of a Union citizen residing in a Member State different from his state of origin. If so, unmarried partners would have the right to reside in the Member State in which their partner resides on the basis of the Regulation at issue. Comparative analysis showed that the legislation of some Member States equalised married and unmarried couples, and some did not. Thus, comparative analysis did not help the Court

---

[39] Kennedy (n 2) 140.

[40] Some light, although quite dim, was shed later in Case C-176/12 *AMS* EU:C:2014:2.

[41] Case 59/85 *Reed* EU:C:1986:157.

[42] Lenaerts, 'Discovering the Law of the EU' (in this volume).

[43] Reg (EEC) No 1612/68 of the Council of 15 October 1968 on freedom of movement for workers within the Community [1968] OJ L 257/2, which was repealed by Reg (EU) No 492/2011 of the European Parliament and of the Council of 5 April 2011 on freedom of movement for workers within the Union Text with EEA relevance [2011] OJ L 141/1.

in finding a uniform solution in all Member States. It allowed for both choices—to subsume unmarried couples under the term 'spouse' or to reserve the expression only for married couples. As the comparative method did not resolve the issue, the Court obviously had to make a choice on another basis. It decided that the term 'spouse' contained in the relevant EU Regulation does not include unmarried stable couples. One may argue that such a decision of the Court was founded on conservative ideology. As the Court explained:

> In the absence of any indication of a general social development which would justify a broad construction, and in the absence of any indication to the contrary in the Regulation, it must be held that the term 'spouse' in Article 10 of the Regulation refers to a marital relationship only.[44]

Thus, the Court read the non-expressed 'objective policy' in the Regulation as corresponding to the policy choices of more conservative national solutions. It decided to preserve the situation as it was in those states in which married and unmarried couples were not equalised. One may, however, imagine the Court arguing that precisely because the move towards recognising the same status of unmarried couples had been made in several states, such a trend should be reflected in EU legislation. The quoted justification of the Court could easily be replaced by the following:

> In view of the trend in social developments in certain Member States, and in the absence of any indication to the contrary in the Regulation, it must be held that the term 'spouse' in Article 10 of the Regulation refers also to a non-marital relationship.

This could be further justified by the statement that such reading enhances the possibilities of movement for EU citizens, which is one of the integrationist aims of the Treaties. The Court could have backed a more liberal view by arguing that free movement of people, as one of the fundamental freedoms in the EU, demands that situations allowing for movement are construed as broadly as possible under the Regulation. The Court did, in the end, find in favour of Miss Reed, but it based its justification on the prohibition of discrimination on the basis of nationality, given that the law in the Netherlands enabled the residence of the unmarried partners of Dutch citizens. To do this, however, the Court had to stretch the interpretation of another term, the term 'social advantage', in the same Regulation, which provided that workers from other Member States must 'enjoy the same social and tax advantages as national workers'. Thus, the Court opted to treat the possibility to live together with an unmarried partner as 'social advantage' rather than to treat an unmarried partner as a 'spouse'. The choice made by the ECJ might be understood as reflecting the Court's understanding of the proper vertical division of powers between the EU and the Member States. It can, thus, also be seen as the ECJ's belief that regulation of family life is better left to Member States. However, such a choice is not expressed anywhere in the judgment and it might have

---

[44] *Reed* (n 41) para 15.

motivated the decision, just as much as ideology could also have been its real reason.

As the option to read the term 'spouse' as including unmarried partners was available to the Court, and neither of the two possible readings was true or untrue in itself, and since such an interpretation would be in line with the prointegration underlying purpose of the Treaties, it is likely that the personal beliefs of the judges (or the majority of them) influenced the choice the Court made in the end. Another possible influence would be reluctance to expose the Court to attacks for activism by conservative parts of society (which may also be seen as the ideological choice Kennedy would attribute to the difference-splitting judge).[45]

The same, I would argue, can be said in other situations described by Lenaerts,[46] where a comparison of Member States' systems point to more than one solution. If the comparative method which 'serves as a crucial interpretative tool that enables the ECJ to resolve particular gaps, conflicts and ambiguities without embarking on judicial legislation'[47] did not offer a solution, something else did. Lacking any explanation as to what else has guided the Court, ideology seems, if not the only explanation, then at least a possible and convincing one.

IV. Difficulties of Discovering Ideology in Adjudication

While legal scholars often comment on the Court's decisions by taking into consideration their policy outcomes, and even compare these outcomes to their own ideological preferences, they do not, with few exceptions,[48] engage in reading the Court's decisions as hiding the ideological choices of judges.

One reason for this might be that, due to the organisation and decision-making methods at the ECJ, it is difficult to discover the individual position of judges.

A. Decision-making Method of the ECJ

The ECJ functions on the basis of what judges usually call the principle of collegiality. This is understood not only as the fact that the decision is almost always one

---

[45] Kennedy (n 2) 184–85.
[46] Case C-120/06 P and C-121/06 P *FIAMM and Others v Council and Commission* EU:C:2008:476; Case C-58/12 P *Groupe Gascogne v Commission* EU:C:2013:770; Joined Cases C-122/99 P and C-125/99 P *D and Sweden v Council* EU:C:2001:304.
[47] Lenaerts, 'Discovering the Law of the EU' (in this volume).
[48] For example, C Kaupa, 'Maybe Not Activist Enough? On the Court's Alleged Neoliberal Bias in Recent Labour Cases' in M Dawson, B De Witte and E Muir (eds), *Judicial Activism at the European Court of Justice* (Cheltenham, Edward Elgar, 2013); C McGlynn, 'Ideologies of Motherhood in European Community Sex Equality Law' (2000) *European Law Journal* 29.

of the judicial chamber rather than of an individual judge, but also as demanding that all judges need to agree on the final text as it will be publicly presented. In the words of Judge Lenaerts: 'the CoJ operates under the principle of collegiality. In light of the latter principle, reaching an outcome based on consensus is of paramount importance for the daily inner workings of the CoJ'.[49] Therefore, any possible disagreements among the judges that were present during deliberations are not revealed in the decision.

The decision is arrived at in what Judge Rodin called a pyramidal way.[50] This means that the direction in which the decision goes is constantly narrowed down at all stages of decision-making. When a new case arrives at the Court, the President allocates it to a judge who serves as reporting judge (*juge rapporteur*) for that case. The reporting judge at first prepares a preliminary report, outlining the main legal problems he finds in the case, assessing the difficulty of the case and proposing the appropriate decision-making chamber. All judges and advocates general meet every Tuesday at a general meeting (*reunion général*) where they discuss the preliminary report. On that occasion cases are allocated to appropriate chambers (of three or five judges or to a grand chamber) and a decision is made on whether an AG will give an opinion in the case. At this stage, the case can still go 'backwards' in a way that it is, for instance, allocated to a bigger formation of the Court if it is found that it poses more difficult issues than originally assessed. Once settled, however, this issue is not revisited. Thus, this first step already influences the decision whether the case will be treated as one that is harder or less hard. The next stage is when the judge rapporteur presents his first draft decision, which is circulated among judges. Other judges of the deciding chamber may react to the draft with a note, disagreeing with some proposals, or proposing alternative routes. If this happens, judges meet at the so-called '*tour de table*'. At this meeting the judges agree on one direction in which the judge rapporteur is to draft the proposal of a decision, which he has to take even if this is not the way that the particular judge would have preferred to have taken. Other possible directions are thus left behind and are not revisited in any further step of decision-making. The draft judgment is finally discussed by the judges at deliberations, behind closed doors. In principle, there is only one round of deliberation. Only rarely is the judge rapporteur requested to draft a new proposal, based on an even narrower number of arguments, which then goes for a second round of deliberations. The public version of the Court's decision is based only on the arguments that were acceptable to all deciding judges.

The documents described in this process—the preliminary report, the first version of the draft judgment, notes, the draft on the basis of which the judges

---

[49] K Lenaerts, 'The Court's Outer and Inner Selves: Exploring the External and Internal Legitimacy of the European Court of Justice' in M Adams et al (eds), *Judging Europe's Judges: The Legitimacy of the Case Law of the European Court of Justice* (Oxford, Hart Publishing, 2013) 46.

[50] See the more detailed description of the process in S Rodin, 'A Metacritique of the Court of Justice of the European Union' (2016) 2 *Il Diritto dell'Unione Europea* 191, 196ff.

deliberate—are not public. The final version of the judgment does not describe the process of how the judges arrived at the decision, nor does it reveal other possible directions or give reasons why they were not taken. For the public outside of the Court, it looks as if the decision represents the preferred (or indeed the only possible) outcome of the entire Court (or at least of the deciding chamber). Thus, if one is to seek the ideology behind the judgment from what is public, one may only discuss the ideology of the Court, not of individual judges.

Even if this system often results in the poor quality of judgments,[51] and a loss of the Court's authority, the Court insists on preserving it. The system, however, is not prescribed by any written rule. Quite the contrary, the Court's Rules of Procedure do not provide for unanimous judgment, but rather judgment by the majority.[52] A change of the decision-making method, thus, does not demand any change in law, but only the willingness of the Court to change the method.[53] It would be perfectly possible for the final text of the judgment to reflect only the majority view, and for the fact that there were judges opposing to be revealed to the public. It is even possible for the majority judgment to describe the minority view and to defend the majority view against the former. For this, it is not necessary for dissenting opinions to be introduced in decision-making at the ECJ, as sometimes suggested.[54] Indeed, there are reasons against allowing them, the most persuasive being the difficulty and cost (both in money and in time) of translating such judgments which would necessarily be much longer than at present. The EU is a multilingual community and all judgments are translated into every one of its 24 official languages.[55]

Revealing to the public the individual position of judges is usually seen as damaging for the independence of the ECJ justices. This is so because the six-year term of office is renewable and reappointment is made by the judge's Member State of origin, even though formally a common decision of all Member States is necessary.[56] In order to please their states, the judges might thus be constrained in the choices they are willing to reveal publicly. As far as this is convincing as an argument, there are at least two ways out: the term of office of judges can be turned into a non-renewable one;[57] or even nothing has to be modified, since

---

[51] 'The Court of Justice in the Limelight—Again', Editorial Comments (2008) 45 *CML Rev* 1571.

[52] Art 32 of the Rules of Procedure, entitled 'Deliberations', envisages in its fourth paragraph that '[t]he conclusions reached by the majority of the Judges after final discussion shall determine the decision of the Court'.

[53] T Ćapeta, 'EU Judiciary in Need of Reform?' in A Lazowski and S Blockmans (eds), *Research Handbook on EU Institutional Law* (Cheltenham, Edward Elgar Publishing, 2016) 276ff.

[54] J Laffranque, 'Dissenting Opinion in the European Court of Justice: Estonia's Possible Contribution to the Democratisation of the European Union Juridical System' www.juridicainternational.eu/public/pdf/ji_2004_1_14.pdf; V Perju, 'Reason and Authority in the European Court of Justice' (2009) 49 *Virginia Journal of International Law* 307.

[55] In practice, not all judgments are translated into Gaelic.

[56] Art 253 TFEU.

[57] This solution has been proposed and discussed on several occasions. Most importantly, it was part of the discussions on the organisation of the Court conducted during the work of the Convention leading to the ultimately unsuccessful proposal for the Constitutional Treaty for Europe.

the final decision can reveal different positions and results of voting, without the names of individual judges being given.

The stubborn defence by the judges of the Court of collegiality understood as unanimity may be motivated by the strategy of the judges to conceal the fact that ideology is involved in decision-making. It also hides the other 'possible truth' which ought to remain unrevealed under the current fiction of how democratic legal systems work. This is the fiction that there is always a right legal answer and that legal reasoning always leads to interpretive closure. Even if judges might today agree that, due to the indeterminacy of legal rules, there are more possible answers to, at least, certain problems which reach the courts, they still insist that by the application of the proper legal method they always find the right answer. Any disagreements among judges during deliberations are just part of discovering the right answer, and need not be presented publicly. Admitting this publicly could give the impression that something other than the law has led the judges to a judgment. If stated in the terms of Pieter-Augustijn Van Malleghem's contribution to this volume, this would describe the ECJ as a cynical formalist court.[58] Formalist, because publicly it insists on the possibility of one interpretive closure. Cynical, because its judges are aware of a multiplicity of equally correct closures.

To conclude this section, at least part of the explanation of why it is difficult to discover the personal standing of the ECJ judges can be found in their own choice of the decision-making method which is suitable to hide any ideology. This significantly restricts research efforts to find the personal positions that lie behind judgments. A possible solution to this problem is to pay more attention to the outcome of the cases depending on the reporting judge, and to enter into the minds of judges by researching their extra-judicial work.

B. Is 'Prointegrationism' an Ideology?

Many scholars claim that if the Court is to be characterised in terms of the values it stands for, it is best described as (pro)integrationist. The question connected to this is whether attributing to the ECJ the quality of a prointegrationist court is an ideological characterisation.

The meaning of the term is not clear, nor is it used in a uniform way. Sometimes, often in discussions about competences, it is seen as a goal the Court is trying to achieve. In this sense, it is used both to criticise and defend the Court. The critics argue that, under the cover of integration, the Court is centralising regulatory powers at the EU level and attributes new competences on the EU which were, according to the critics, not envisaged by the Member States as masters of

---

[58] Pieter-Augustijn Van Malleghem, 'Reflections on European Legal Formalism' (in this volume).

the Treaties.[59] For those defending the Court's choices, a generous reading of EU competences is consistent with the goals of European integration, which is to build an 'ever closer Union'.[60]

Some do not see prointegrationism as the *telos*, but rather as the essence (*ontos*) of the EU, and it is this essence that informs judges when they interpret EU law. Thus, Rodin explains:

> [t]o my mind it is not τέλος but ὄντος—the authentic essence of the EU and its law—that informs interpretation of EU law and constitutes its specific identity as distinguished from identity of national and international law. Understood in this, existential, way, ontology, unlike teleology, does not insist on reaching a certain result, but on justification of assumptions that are essential for its existence.[61]

One of such 'ontological identities', Rodin explains further,

> is Art 1 of the TEU which speaks about the 'process of creating an ever closer union among the peoples of Europe.' This process can indeed be understood as a basic ontological identity of the EU having in mind that it is inextricable from fundamental values of the EU. In other words, the process of creating an ever closer union existentially depends on respect for the same value framework which has to be interpreted uniformly.[62]

However, be it *telos* or *ontos* 'an ever closer union' can mean whatever the Court will construe it to mean. People of Europe can get closer by removing borders to trade and movement, or they can get closer by sharing the costs of a social Europe. Integration as a term does not mean anything in itself. I imagine everyone can agree that the ECJ is a prointegrationist Court to the extent that it is difficult to imagine that it would work towards the disintegration of the EU[63] (if for no other reason than to secure its own existence). An 'ever closer union' or furthering integration as the meta-teleological goal which the ECJ allegedly prefers requires a certain ending that the integration is aiming at in order to acquire meaning.[64] Is the ECJ furthering integration in order to arrive at a sort of federal state, and thus overcome existing societies based on nation-states; or is the ECJ, through the creation of an 'ever closer union', aiming at maintaining a multi-level system of governance in which both the EU and Member States share powers but which,

---

[59] D Wyatt, 'Does the European Court of Justice Need a New Judicial Approach for the 21st Century', presentation at the Conference: 'A More Literal and Predictable Approach for the Court of Justice of the EU?' 2 November 2015, point 41, www.biicl.org/documents/760_derrick_wyatts_paper.pdf.

[60] Art 1 TEU.

[61] Rodin (n 50) 209.

[62] ibid 204, fn 44.

[63] However, I have to admit that this statement does not necessarily seem so obvious today. Imagine that the question of the reversibility of the Brexit notification comes to the ECJ. Would prointegrationism demand a search for solutions to help keep the UK in the EU, arguing for reversibility, or would it suggest a contrary reading?

[64] C Eckes, 'European Union Legal Method—Moving Away from Integration' in Ulla Neergaard and Ruth Nielsen (eds), *European Legal Method—Towards a New European Legal Realism?* (Copenhagen, DJØF Publishing, 2013) 188.

however, does not lead to the dismantling of the existing nation-states? An 'ever closer union' requires some meaning also if understood as the very raison d'être of the EU which can explain the interpretative choices of the Court.

There are, indeed, different competing visions of an 'integrated Europe' which the Court can endorse. The EU can be seen as a predominantly economic integration project,[65] or an identity-building one, which goes beyond mere economic cooperation.[66] All these visions are based on some sort of integration among the European nations. Depending on the commentator's vision of a united Europe, the ECJ's case law may be read as integrationist, or not integrationist enough, at the same time. The refugee crisis and Brexit which were happening while I was finalising this contribution opened new questions and visions, for both the right and the left.[67] I would argue that already at this macro-level it is difficult to find consensus among the 28 ECJ judges.

However, and more importantly, whichever of these macro-ends of integration the Court or its judges believes in, the real question is why they want such an 'ending', or why they read such a 'reason' for the integration process. Is the ECJ pushing for a supranational, federal-state or intergovernmental EU in order to preserve existing power relations, which would make it a conservative court? Or is the ECJ 'furthering integration' in order to create a liberal, largely non-interventionist Europe, because of its belief that the market will find the best solution? Or, is the ECJ possibly liberal-left, building society around market powers, but trying at the same time to correct the outcomes of the market in the name of social justice and a more equitable society? All of this can from time to time be concluded from the ECJ's case law. But any of these strategies may be justified by prointegrationism. Prointegrationism, thus, even if it could be described as the macro-level ideology of the Court, cannot be understood as the ECJ's ideology in the sense this word was usually used in American CLS discussions. It is neutral as to whether the Court is right or left, conservative or liberal, as long as it furthers integration. This brings into question whether CLS-type legal critique is at all appropriate within the contemporary EU legal framework.

Another problem worth repeating is that ideology cannot easily be attached to the Court as an institution, but can meaningfully be discussed only in relation to individual judges, taking into account their interaction with the Court's other judges. As explained, however, due to the ECJ's decision-making methods, it is difficult to find out about the political preferences of individual judges.[68]

---

[65] M Maduro, *We the Court: The European Court of Justice and the European Economic Constitution* (Oxford, Hart Publishing, 1998).

[66] See, for instance, articles published in the special issue of (2013) 14(5) *German Law Journal—Regeneration Europe*.

[67] For the left position, see the inspiring contribution by Alexander Somek, 'Four Impious Points on Brexit' (2016) 17 *German Law Journal*—Brexit Supplement http://static1.squarespace.com/static/56330ad3e4b0733dcc0c8495/t/5776e635579fb3bc18d94122/1467409973572/20+PDF_Vol_17_Brexit+_Somek.pdf.

[68] This is in sharp contrast to public knowledge about the ideology of the US Supreme Court justices. Reports such as those by B Woodward and S Armstrong, *The Brethren: Inside the Supreme Court*

Today's Court, with its 28 judges with different backgrounds and coming from very different domestic political cultures, can hardly have a common ideology. Already the macro-level common ideology of today's Court, understood as the finality of the integration process, seeing the EU's future as a federal state or not, does not seem possible. It is possible that at a certain point in the beginnings of the integration process, after Judge Lecourt joined the Court, the entire Court, that is, all of its judges (who were at first only seven and then nine) had a common macro ideology, or, as claimed by Judge Pescatore, a common idea of Europe ('*une certaine idée de l'Europe*').[69] But this can hardly be the situation today. Already the way in which judges are nominated to the Court argues to the contrary.[70] This is notwithstanding the inclusion of the 255 Committee in the appointment procedures, even though it is still too early to assess to what extent this new body may impose its own vision of Europe in deciding which candidates fit, and which do not, the requirements for a Court of Justice of the European Union (CJEU) judge. The different backgrounds of judges, coupled with the proliferation of EU policies, which today match all the issues the states commonly regulate, make it almost impossible for the 28 judges of the ECJ (not to mention the additional soon-to-be 56 judges of the General Court) to share the same political positions towards all the involved issues.

Saying that it is difficult to discover the ECJ judges' ideologies does not mean that ideology is not present during the adjudication process in that Court. It likewise does not mean that scholars could not put more effort into finding the ideology behind the Court's decisions (for example, by studying the differences in judgments of different chambers,[71] or by taking into consideration who the judge rapporteur was). But for scholars to start looking for ideology, they first have to admit that it is (or might be) there, and that this might make a difference in how the law develops.

V. Why do Courts Deny Ideology in Adjudication?

A. Public Expectations that Courts be Detached from Politics

If ideology is not always and even cannot be avoided in the Court, as I have tried to establish in the two previous parts, the question that follows is why judges are

---

(New York, Simon & Schuster, 1979) or J Toobin, *The Nine: Inside the Secret World of the Supreme Court* (New York, Anchor 2008) do not exist in Europe.

[69] P Pescatore, 'The Doctrine of "Direct Effect": An Infant Disease of Community Law' (1983) 8 *European Law Review* 155, 157.

[70] About the process of appointment of the ECJ justices, see M Lasser, 'Judicial Appointments, Judicial Independence and the European High Courts' (in this volume).

[71] M Malecki, 'Do ECJ Judges All Speak with the Same Voice? Evidence of Divergent Preferences from the Judgments of Chambers' (2012) 19 *Journal of European Public Policy* 59.

hiding this. Why cannot we find policy, or arguments of ideology, in the public justification for judicial outcomes?

The only possible answer seems to be that, due to the current paradigm of a good society, the expectation is created that courts do not decide on the basis of ideology. This is reserved, in a democratic society based on the separation of powers, for another institution—the legislator. Even if ideology is present in the adjudication, this should not be part of the story told of a good legal system. Thus, denying ideology in adjudication is part of the effort of maintaining the narrative of a society based on the separation of powers.

As brilliantly demonstrated by Harari,[72] the history of humankind is based and dependent on believing in socially construed stories as if they were real. It is precisely this human ability to believe in the same fiction that has pushed homo sapiens to the top of the food chain, as it has enabled us to function in big groups. Society will maintain the established and functioning myth for as long as it is not replaced by an alternative, equally functioning one. While a certain fiction is still the one which guides human behaviour, presenting its main features as true is important for the organisation of social life. Maintaining 'fictions' as real thus has its function.

Therefore, participants of the legal system do not admit ideology in adjudication even if it is there in order to maintain the fiction we live under. This is true for judges, but also for other participants in the 'legal game'—legislators and legal scholars.

From time to time, there have been outcries in the EU demonstrating that the emperor has no clothes. Politicians, as well as legal scholars, have from time to time attacked the ECJ for acting politically. Probably the most famous political attack on the Court was by Roman Herzog (the former German President and president of the Federal Constitutional Court of Germany) and Lüder Gerken, (Director of the Centre for European Policy),[73] which followed the ECJ's *Mangold* judgment.[74] The Court was criticised for acting ideologically also by academics. Probably the most famous academic attack was the one by Hjalte Rasmussen in 1986.[75]

Scholars have predominantly reacted to such attacks by defending the Court, not (or not only) for the outcomes of its 'activism' (thus by defending the Court's alleged ideology), but rather by trying to show that the Court did not act on the basis of its convictions, but rather on the basis of law seen as a coherent system with inbuilt purposes (thus, by denying the existence of the Court's ideology).

---

[72] YN Harari, *Sapiens—A Brief History of Humankind*, Kindle edition (New York, Harper Collins, 2015).

[73] R Herzog and L Gerken, 'Stop the European Court of Justice' (10 September 2008) *EUobserver* https://euobserver.com/opinion/26714.

[74] *Mangold* (n 37).

[75] H Rasmussen, *On Law and Policy in the European Court of Justice* (The Hague, Kluwer, 1986). See also Patrick Neill QC, 'The European Court of Justice—A Case Study in Judicial Activism' (1995) *European Policy Forum*.

The following quote illustrates this point: 'In short, in all the cases in which the Court has been criticized for "legislating", it was acting on clearly identifiable legal principles and not on extraneous considerations'.[76] Many legal scholars in Europe, therefore, deny that the Court acts ideologically.[77]

Another possible explanation why ideology in courts cannot be admitted might be the effort to justify law as a self-standing discipline,[78] both for lawyers and non-lawyers. For this, it is necessary to insist that the law has its own, 'legal' methodology for solving 'legal' questions (it, indeed, needs to insist that there are legal questions). If judges do not need legal method to find law, but can, rather, understand what the law is by applying existing rules understood according to one's own ideology and common sense, then insisting on having trained lawyers as judges becomes obsolete. It also becomes difficult to justify legal education as a whole.

Taking into consideration that legal actors and non-legal actors expect that the courts do not act politically, it seems reasonable that judges publicly, including in their decisions, deny the presence of any ideology in adjudication. This means that judges, in fact, act in bad faith. For now, I will leave aside the question whether I think this is justifiable or not (but see Duncan Kennedy's contribution in this volume).

B. Policy Arguments versus Legal Arguments in Justification

In the current paradigm of a good legal order, courts would lose their authority if they admitted publicly that the personal values of judges influenced the outcome of legal disputes. Judges are supposed to solve disputes by the application of legal rules. However, legal rules are not value-free. Therefore, when they apply legal rules, judges necessarily advance certain values. Therefore, judges cannot avoid involving values in the publicly announced judgments. Thus, as admitted by Judge Lenaerts in the introductory part to his contribution to this volume,[79] the ECJ sometimes uses policy arguments to justify its decisions. However, Judge Lenaerts prefers to call them non-deductive arguments.[80]

Policy that judges sometimes admit to is not presented as the personal policy of judges, but rather as a policy which is inbuilt in the rules and which justifies them within the wider policy built in the legal system as a whole (meta-policy).

---

[76] J Temple Lang, 'Has the European Court of Justice Been Involved in "Judicial Legislation"?' (2011) *Svensk Juristtidning* 307 http://svjt.se/svjt/2011/299.

[77] Many, but not all. See, for instance, O Lando, 'Some Remarks on Adjudicators' Reasons' in H Koch, K Hagel-Sorensen, U Haltern and JHH Weiler (eds), *Europe. The New Legal Realism* (Copenhagen, DJØF Publishing, 2010) 381.

[78] As to the impossibility to disprove the law as a separate discipline, a science, and this despite accepting its indeterminacy, see P Schlag, 'Phrenology and Law' (1997) 110 *Harvard Law Review* 877.

[79] Lenaerts, 'Discovering the Law of the EU' (in this volume).

[80] ibid.

By taking into consideration the 'system's preferences', the separation of powers requirement is resolved satisfactorily. The Court is not encroaching upon the legislator's or Treaty maker's domain, as it is not imposing its personal policy preferences, but follows the 'system's policy preferences'.

The way it is explained that the Court achieves this is by the use of the teleological (purposive) interpretation. Thus, it has become a truism, reproduced in all textbooks on EU law,[81] that the ECJ uses the teleological interpretative method as one of its main tools[82] for understanding the law. This is sometimes further explained as being easily achievable in the EU, as the *telos* of the rules is often clearly expressed. The following quotation of Judge Edwards, former judge of the ECJ, backs such a point; he stated that in the EU system '[t]he Community treaties set out very clearly what is their object and purpose'[83] and '[w]hen Community legislation is enacted in the form of regulations and directives, these will, unlike British Acts of Parliament, always contain a preamble which sets out the legislative purpose and is a guide to interpretation of the text'.[84]

Thus, the *telos* of the EU law is presented as given, not as being construed by judges, but rather as being found by judges as emanating from the system's policy. Teleological interpretation is, thus, seen not as an expression of the Court's choice, but as a method that maintains the Court's objectivity. This is nicely reflected in the following excerpt from Maduro:

> Teleological interpretation in EU law does not, therefore, refer exclusively to a purpose driven interpretation of the relevant legal rules. It refers to a particular systemic understanding of the EU legal order that permeates the interpretation of all its rules. In other words, the Court has not simply been concerned with ascertaining the aim of a particular provision. It also interprets that rule in light of the broader context provided by the EC (now EU) legal order and its 'constitutional telos'. There is a clear association between the systemic (context) and teleological elements of interpretation in the Court's reasoning. It is not simply the telos of the rules to be interpreted that matters, but also the telos of the legal context in which those rules exist. We can talk therefore of both a teleological and a meta-teleological reasoning in the Court.[85]

---

[81] A Arnull, *The European Union and its Court of Justice* 2nd edn (Oxford, Oxford University Press, 2006) 607; P Craig and G De Búrca, *EU Law—Text, Cases and Materials* 6th edn (Oxford, Oxford University Press, 2015) 63–64; A Dashwood, M Dougan, B Rodger, E Spaventa and D Wyatt, *Wyatt and Dashwood's European Union Law* 5th edn (Oxford, Hart Publishing, 2006) 404–05; J Fairhurst, *Law of the European Union* 5th edn (Harlow, Pearson/Longman, 2006) 161; TC Hartley, *The Foundations of European Union Law* 8th edn (Oxford, Oxford University Press, 2014) 66.

[82] It is not the only interpretative method used. A good example of other methods seen as important at the CJEU is given in Case T-18/10 *Inuit* EU:T:2011:419 as decided by the General Court. Faced with the constitutional question usually decided by the ECJ, the General Court tried to justify its position by using all of the interpretative methods it assessed as important in constitutional adjudication. These were, as explained by the General Court, a literal, a historical and a teleological interpretation. See para 40 of the judgment.

[83] D Edward, 'The European Court of Justice—Friend or Foe?' 69, www.law.du.edu/documents/judge-david-edward-oral-history/1996-the-european-court-of-justice.pdf.

[84] ibid 70.

[85] Maduro (n 24) 462.

Thus, the ECJ is a court which accepts that the law is not detached from politics. Rather, politics, as a necessary determinant of the goal that the rules are aiming to achieve (their *telos*), seems to be an inherent part of legal rules. But the politics at issue is the system's politics, not one personal to judges. The teleological approach, thus understood, is therefore not only democratically acceptable, but even desirable. It is what makes the ECJ a legitimate court and preserves the separation of powers.

Policy arguments, seen as systemic policy, thus become acceptable as justification of the ECJ's decisions. This is true to a certain degree, but still policy arguments cannot stand alone as justifications for a decision. Policy argument might be, as Kennedy states, 'a Trojan horse for the introduction of ideology into law'.[86] Such an argument is, therefore, a suspect whose presence in the judgment should be carefully weighed.

Therefore, there is an expectation that every choice of the Court is always based on legal arguments. If the Court does not justify its choices by legal arguments, but only by policy arguments, even if these are policy preferences of the system (or at least this is how the Court explains them), it risks that its decisions will not be followed. The ECJ learned this relatively early on, when it started to develop the doctrine of direct effect of directives.

The first case in which the Court found that directives might have direct effect was the case *Van Duyn*.[87] To introduce a reader unfamiliar with the issue, directives are described by the Treaty as acts 'binding, as to the result to be achieved, upon each Member State to which they are addressed, but leaving to the national authorities the choice of form and methods'.[88] Thus, directives are meant to be transposed into the national legal order of each Member State by appropriate domestic procedures and instruments. They normally produce legal effects by transposing national rules. In *Van Duyn*, however, the Court considered that even if a state did not transpose a directive into its domestic legal order, an individual could still rely on it in the national court. The only justification the Court offered for such a reading of the Treaty was useful effect ('*effet utile*'):[89] directives would be less effective as legal instruments in achieving the aims of integration if individuals could not rely on them in the case where states did not transpose them. Thus, the Court offered a convincing policy argument.

---

[86] Kennedy (n 2) 111.

[87] Case 41/74 *Van Duyn* EU:C:1974:133.

[88] Art 288 TFEU.

[89] *Van Duyn* (n 87) para 12. The Court explained: 'It would be incompatible with the binding effect attributed to a directive by article 189 to exclude, in principle, the possibility that the obligation which it imposes may be invoked by those concerned. In particular, where the Community authorities have, by directive, imposed on Member States the obligation to pursue a particular course of conduct, the useful effect of such an act would be weakened if individuals were prevented from relying on it before their national courts and if the latter were prevented from taking it into consideration as an element of Community law'.

However, for directives to really have direct effect, it was not enough for the Court to pronounce that this was so. It was also necessary for the Court's reading of the Treaty to be accepted by those who have to give life to direct effect—national courts of the Member States. And here is where the complications started. Namely, the justification offered in *Van Duyn* was only a policy justification—*effet utile*. The Court did not offer any classical legal argument; it did not rely on another rule of law in order to justify its conclusion that a directive may be invoked in the court. One important and influential national court—the French Conseil d'Etat— was not convinced by the Court's policy argument. In *Cohn-Bendit*,[90] the French court refused to follow the case law of the ECJ, refusing the direct effect of directives.

Thus, the Court had to find legal arguments in order to make its interpretation convincing for national judges.[91] The opportunity occurred in *Ratti*.[92] In this case, a company director was sued by the state for disrespecting domestic Italian law, with which, however, he would have been in compliance had the state adjusted the law to a directive. This gave the Court an opportunity to add a legal reason why an individual could invoke a directive against a state that failed to transpose it before the expiry of the transposition time limit. It established that the state cannot defend itself against an individual by claiming that it had failed to fulfil its obligation under EU law.[93] Thus, the argument, called in EU law the estoppel argument, became the main justification for the direct effect of directives. The rule estopping a state from pleading its own failure for its own benefit did not exist as a written rule anywhere in the EU legal order. However, it could have been seen as a legal principle underlying the European systems of law. Thus, it provided for the necessary 'legal' or principled justification for the direct effect of directives. Effectiveness remained one of the justificatory arguments, but was now coupled with a new legal argument.

This ultimately persuaded the resistant courts to accept the Court's view about the effect of directives. It has, at the same time, constrained the ECJ in the further development of law with regard to directives. In subsequent cases, limited by the new justification based on the obligation imposed by directives on states, the Court excluded the horizontal direct effect of directives, ie the possibility for a directive to be relied on in the court against an individual.[94] Namely, as individuals do not have an obligation to transpose a directive, direct effect cannot be based on their failure to fulfil an EU obligation. The denial of horizontal effect, in turn, diminished the *effet utile* of directives. Later case law was thus in conflict with the starting policy position of the Court expressed in *Van Duyn*, looking

---

[90] Arret du 22 décembre 1978—ministre de l'intérieur c/ Cohn-Bendit—Rec Lebon 524.

[91] cf D Chalmers, G Davies and G Monti, *European Union Law* 2nd edn (Cambridge, Cambridge University Press, 2010) 287.

[92] Case 148/78 *Ratti* EU:C:1979:110.

[93] ibid para 22.

[94] See Case 152/84 *Marshall* EU:C:1986:84 and Case 91/92 *Faccini Dori* (n 36).

for the most effective interpretation of the effect of directives. The case law that followed, through which the Court imposed an interpretative obligation on national courts[95] and developed the concept of the liability of states for damages,[96] might be interpreted as the Court's effort to compensate for the loss of effectiveness caused by the use of estoppel as a legal justification for the direct effect of directives.

The story of directives illustrates the difficulties of judicial law-making under the constraint imposed by the expectation that the Court decides exclusively on the basis of law. Even if a policy aim (effectiveness) motivated the Court to choose an interpretation, and even if this policy aim could be justified as inherent in the system, the necessary search for legal justification prevented the full achievement of the desired policy aim.

C. Arguments from Coherence

Arguments from the coherence of the system, unlike the arguments of effectiveness, are not seen as policy, but rather as legal arguments.[97] The coherence of the EU legal system is presented by the Court as a fact, not as an aim.[98] Thus, arguing from coherence makes the Court's choices credible as legal and not ideological or policy choices. Such justifications, it seems, are not questioned by national courts, or by legal scholars. One such example, which has always puzzled me, but has never (to my knowledge) been contested, is the centralisation of the judicial review of EU law by the ECJ, starting with the case *Foto-Frost*.[99]

Article 267 TFEU describes the preliminary ruling procedure, which represents, as already explained, a major part of the work of the ECJ today. Under this procedure, national courts may refer to the ECJ questions relating to either the interpretation or validity of EU law. This is prescribed in the first paragraph of Article 267. The subsequent two paragraphs then make a difference between two different groups of national courts, bestowing on the first the power, and on the second the obligation, to refer. Thus, any court may refer to the ECJ. However, the courts of last instance must refer if they are faced with the question described in the first paragraph, ie a question of interpretation or of validity of EU law. Textually, the distinction among the courts resulting in only empowerment or in bestowal of an obligation to refer is the same whether the question to be referred is a question of interpretation or of validity.

---

[95] Starting with *Von Colson and Kamman* (n 29).

[96] Starting with Joined Case C-6 and 9/90 *Francovich* EU:C:1991:428.

[97] Rodin describes coherence as an aesthetic argument. For him, as the law is an art rather than science, aesthetic arguments are important in both discovery and justificatory phases of adjudication. Rodin (n 21).

[98] Case 294/83 *Partie écologiste 'Les Verts'* EU:C:1986:166 para 23; Case C-50/00 P *Unión de Pequeños Agricultores (UPA)* EU:C:2002:462 para 40. K Lenaerts, 'The Rule of Law and the Coherence of the Judicial System of the European Union' (2007) 44 *CML Rev* 1625.

[99] Case 314/85 *Foto-Frost* EU:C:1987:452.

In *Foto-Frost*, the German financial court (*Finanzgericht*) from Hamburg questioned the validity of a Commission decision. Even if this court was not the last instance in the case at hand, it was not sure whether it was obliged or just empowered to refer. Thus, it referred to the ECJ three questions. The first one asked whether a national court which is not last instance may review on its own the validity of a Commission decision. The other two questions were asked alternatively dependent on the answer to the first question: if the German court at issue may review validity, the ECJ was asked for an interpretation of the pertinent parts of EU law; if, on the contrary, the German court could not assess the validity of the decision at issue, it asked the ECJ to assess it. In a judgment, which is part of all textbooks on EU law, the ECJ found that it is only for it to find an EU act invalid. Therefore, notwithstanding the mere empowerment of the lower-instance courts without the imposition of the obligation to refer in paragraph 2 of Article 267 TFEU, the ECJ considered that the text at issue 'did not settle the question whether those courts themselves may declare that acts of Community institutions are invalid'.[100] The same text, when the question is a question of interpretation of EU law, was interpreted differently. In such a case, a national court of lower instance was allowed to interpret EU law on its own, and thus possibly make a mistake (mistake being an interpretation different from the one that would be given by the ECJ). The ECJ considered that the threat to the uniformity of the EU legal order was much greater if a mistake relating to the validity of an EU act was allowed than if a mistake relating to interpretation was allowed.[101] I do not see why this is so,[102] but let us proceed as if the Court's conclusion on that matter is convincing. This then justifies the need to read the same text differently, as the context is different. So far so good. The ECJ in the end concluded that courts of lower instances may on their own reject claims of invalidity, but cannot on their own declare an EU act invalid.[103]

After introducing such a reading, the ECJ offered a justification for its decision: coherence of the EU legal system. It insisted that the Treaties 'established

---

[100] ibid para 13.

[101] ibid para 15.

[102] If a national court 'wrongly' holds an EU legal rule invalid in a case, the consequence would be the non-application of that legal rule in the case at issue. If a national court 'wrongly' interprets an EU legal rule in a case, the consequence would be the same—the non-application of the legal rule in its correct meaning in the case at issue; this is not much different from its non-application. If a losing party is unhappy with the court's interpretation, it may lodge an appeal, and reach the court of last instance, which would be under the obligation to refer the question to the ECJ. The same is true in cases of (in)validity. If a losing party thinks that a national court has wrongly held an EU act invalid, she/he may, by appeal, reach the instance which has an obligation to refer. The problem, however, arises sometimes because of the EU's constitutional choice of executive federalism, which came to the surface in *Foto-Frost*. Namely, as the German customs authority, which was one of the parties to the dispute, was acting as an EU executive organ, implementing the Commission's decision, but in fact not agreeing with that decision, the dispute about the substance was not real. If a national court decided that the Commission's decision was invalid, there was nobody to appeal, as both parties would be content with the outcome. This might be a powerful reason why judicial review of EU law should be centralised in the hands of the ECJ. However, this was not at all discussed in the *Foto-Frost* judgment.

[103] *Foto-Frost* (n 99) paras 14 and 15.

a complete system of legal remedies and procedures designed to permit the Court of Justice to review the legality of measures adopted by the institutions'.[104] Part of that coherent system is direct actions by which the annulment of an EU act may be claimed, and the other part is the indirect judicial review through a preliminary ruling procedure initiated by a national court. The ECJ then went on to conclude that since in direct annulment actions the Court has

> exclusive jurisdiction to declare void an act of a Community institution, the coherence of the system requires that where the validity of a Community act is challenged before a national court the power to declare the act invalid must also be reserved to the Court of Justice.[105]

The Court has never explained why the Treaties are to be read as establishing a coherent system of legal remedies. But even if this is so, coherence does not demand that the national courts be deprived of the possibility of excluding the application of an EU rule on the basis of a plea of illegality introduced by one party. Namely, the consequence of the decision of the ECJ, either in direct actions[106] or in a preliminary ruling,[107] is the invalidity of an EU act *ex tunc* and *erga omnes*. The consequence of holding an EU act invalid in a case before a national court is confined to the inapplicability of that act in that case. Outside the case, the act continues its legal life. Thus, coherence does not demand centralising the power of assessment of the validity of an EU act in the hands of the ECJ, as the Treaty envisaged exclusivity for the ECJ for the purpose of permanently invalidating an act.

'Coherence' as a justification for centralisation is even less convincing when one compares this to the decentralisation of judicial review in national legal systems introduced by the ECJ since the *Simmenthal* case.[108] In the name of direct effect and primacy of EU law, the ECJ empowered national courts to review the validity of domestic laws for their compatibility with EU law. Even if many domestic constitutional systems did not envisage such power for the courts, but rather centralised it in the hands of one (constitutional) court, often in the name of uniformity of the national legal order, the ECJ did not look into that argument of domestic legal orders. Rather, it explained that the power of a national court bestowed by EU law is not to invalidate domestic law, but only to disapply it in the case at hand.[109] The same was true in the parallel situation at the EU level, but the Court disregarded this altogether. How is that coherent?

Apart from coherence, the only other argument the ECJ offered in *Foto-Frost* was that it is in a better position to assess the validity of EU law than national courts, if for no other reason than because the enacting institution whose act's

---

[104] ibid para 16.
[105] ibid para 17.
[106] According to Art 231 TFEU.
[107] As explained in Case 66/80 *International Chemical Corporation* EU:C:1981:102 paras 12 and 13.
[108] Case 106/77 *Simmenthal* EU:C:1978:49.
[109] Case C-10 and 22/97 *IN.CO.GE* EU:C:1998:498 paras 18–21.

validity is at issue may intervene in a case before the ECJ.[110] As much as I find this quite a convincing reason, it is not a 'legal' argument. 'We think we can do it better' is, at best, a policy argument. Thus, the only 'legal' argument offered by the Court was the coherence of the EU legal system. This was, it seems, convincing to both domestic judiciaries (even though they were disempowered by the judgment) and legal commentators, allowing them to readily accept the centralisation of review powers over EU law.

D. General Principles of Law

Given that both legal and non-legal actors in society expect the ECJ to justify its decisions by legal arguments, it was necessary for the Court to expand the notion of a legal argument. In the Dworkin-like legal world, in which the Court sees itself, legal arguments are legal rules, but also principles. Thus, unwritten principles, presented as inherent in the EU legal system, such as estoppel or legal certainty, can justify legal decisions. This explains why the theory of unwritten legal principles has become so important in the EU legal order.[111]

However, even if the Court insists that the legal principles it has found are part of the EU system, the very choice of a legal principle which leads to (or justifies) the decision of the Court is influenced by what judges think is right to decide. Thus, the choice of the legal principles to be used as legal arguments in adjudication is in itself influenced by the judges' personal values.

Not surprisingly, therefore, the narrative on general principles of law as necessarily binding in the EU legal order is not readily accepted by all the actors in the system. The recent decision of the Danish Supreme Court in the case *Ajos*[112] is the latest demonstration of such a rebellion. The case was decided after a preliminary reference to the ECJ in Case C-441/14 *Ajos*,[113] in which the ECJ confirmed that the prohibition of discrimination on the ground of age exists in EU law as a general principle of law and has direct effect, including in relations between individuals.[114] The consequence of such a choice is, according to the ECJ,[115]

---

[110] *Foto-Frost* (n 99) para 18.

[111] cf K Lenaerts and JA Gutiérrez-Fons, 'The Constitutional Allocation of Powers and General Principles of EU Law' (2010) 47 *CML Rev* 1629.

[112] Decision 15/2014 of the Danish Supreme Court in the *Ajos* www.supremecourt.dk/supremecourt/nyheder/pressemeddelelser/Documents/Judgment%2015-2014.pdf.

[113] Case C-441/14 *Dansk Industri (DI), acting on behalf of Ajos A/S v Estate of Karsten Eigil Rasmussen* EU:C:2016:278.

[114] This case law was initiated by *Mangold* (n 37), and continued by *Kucukdeveci* (n 37). *Mangold* caused a lot of criticism in scholarly articles and discussions by the Court's Advocates General. For a discussion, see T Ćapeta 'The AG: Bringing Clarity to ECJ Decisions? A Case Study of Age Discrimination Cases' (2011–12) 14 *Cambridge Yearbook of European Legal Studies* 563. There were also political reactions accusing the ECJ of judicial activism. See Herzog and Gerken (n 73).

[115] *Ajos* (n 113) paras 35–37.

the obligation of the Danish Court to set aside domestic law that is in conflict with the general principle, and which the Danish Court claimed not to be able to interpret as being in conformity with EU law requirements. However, the Danish Court refused to follow. Its justification was based on a formalistic legal argument that the Treaty of Accession of Denmark to the EU does not contain a provision which provides for the application of unwritten EU general principles of law in the Danish legal order:

> A situation such as this, in which a principle at treaty level under EU law is to have direct effect (thereby creating obligations) and be allowed to take precedence over conflicting Danish law in a dispute between individuals, without the principle having any basis in a specific treaty provision, is not foreseen in the Law on accession.[116]

The Danish Court decision can be interpreted in many ways: as a reflection of the political trend of renewed nationalism in Europe; as a constitutional issue about final authority on the question of federal delimitation of competences between the EU and Member States; as a result of a change on the bench in the Danish Court; or as a rebellion against perceived ECJ activism.[117] The latter interpretation is of interest for the topic of this contribution. It might be seen as an expected result of the ECJ's continuous reliance on unwritten principles of law, based on exclusively formal legal-systemic arguments, without any substantive explanation of what has motivated the Court to establish principles it 'found' in the EU legal order. Even if motivated by political reasons, the Danish Court responded with another formalistic decision. At the same time, both sides are in bad faith. The ECJ has created a fictitious legal world of general principles which it uses to hide its own value choices by presenting them as inherent in the EU legal system. The Danish Court arguably hides its political preferences behind its formalism. The latter view is backed by the following comments of three Danish scholars:

> Yet by far the most striking issue arising from the SCDK's [Danish Supreme Court] actions concerns the decision to portray itself as legally virtuous against the CJEU political activism. Although *Ajos* is drafted in the spirit of judicial restraint, giving weight to legislative texts and especially to the intention of the legislator (including preparatory works from Parliament), it is likely to be viewed and received in very different terms. Judicial self-restraint simply fails to materialise as the guiding rationale of the decision. The approach of supposedly avoiding politics, the formal *Leitmotiv* of the decision and its formalism (defined as 'playing by the Danish rules'), comes across as political: it effectively changes the dynamics of EU-Danish law and politics.[118]

---

[116] Decision of the Danish Supreme Court in *Ajos* (n 112) 45.

[117] cf comments by MR Madsen, HP Olsen and U Sadl, 'Competing Supremacies and Clashing Institutional Rationalities: The Danish Supreme Court's Decision in the Ajos Case and the National Limits of Judicial Cooperation' (2017) *iCourts Working Paper Series No 85, University of Copenhagen Faculty of Law Research Paper No 2017-32* https://papers.ssrn.com/sol3/papers.cfm?abstract_id=2904012 (forthcoming in *European Law Journal*).

[118] MR Madsen, HP Olsen and U Sadl, 'Legal Disintegration? The Ruling of the Danish Supreme Court in AJOS' http://verfassungsblog.de/legal-disintegration-the-ruling-of-the-danish-supreme-court-in-ajos/.

Had the ECJ not been in bad faith, but had rather more openly connected the general principles of law it 'finds' with the system of values it wants the EU to reflect, one could have expected the dialogue between that Court and the Danish Supreme Court, or any other high national court, to have been more sincere and more meaningful.

VI. Conclusions

In this contribution I have argued that ideology is present in the adjudication process at the ECJ. This is so, notwithstanding the repeated public statements by its judges to the contrary.

The judges' denial of ideology does not mean that they personally do not have political preferences (I certainly hope they do). It is rather a claim that they manage to keep them out of the adjudication process. I then asked why judges try to persuade us that they are successful in being 'objective'. One possible answer is that the current fiction of a pluralist democratic society based on the separation of powers cannot admit to ideology in the courts.

Judges who are aware that ideology has influenced decision-making in the court, but who continue denying it, act in bad faith. In his contribution to this volume, Duncan Kennedy asks whether a judge's bad faith can be justified if a judge hid the truth for a good reason. Explaining the question from the perspective of a left liberal judge, he concludes that it can be justified. He allows the liberal activist judge, who believes that the proportionality method does not always demand deference to a conservative non-egalitarian decision even if such a legislative decision under review is based on rational grounds, to masquerade as a formalist, and not to reveal his thoughts, if this is necessary in order 'to prevent serious bad consequences for the body politic'.[119]

I have argued in my contribution that the bad faith of ECJ judges hiding the presence of ideology in adjudication can be understood if this is done because these judges believe that this is necessary to preserve the political and legal system of the EU. One may compare this with the academic debate about the existence of free will. There are many who claim that free will does not exist. There is even some scientific evidence that it does not exist.[120] However, some scientists argue that even though they are persuaded that there is no free will, the myth of its existence must be maintained, as the organisation of our society depends on it. They claim that 'if the choice is between the true and the good, then for the sake of society, the true must go'.[121] In the same way, in order to preserve the fiction of

---

[119] D Kennedy, 'Proportionality and "Deference" in Contemporary Constitutional Thought' (in this volume).

[120] S Cave, 'There's No Such Thing as Free Will' (June 2016) *Atlantic* 69, 70–72.

[121] ibid, citing Smilansky, 73.

a democratic society based on the separation of powers, it might be necessary to preserve the fiction that judges can step outside their individual cultural heritage and beliefs and solve a case by applying objective legal rules by using the legal method. We believe this story is worth maintaining, as it has proven better than some other fictions that were attempted in the past, or are still being lived by others. Continuing the fiction of the non-existence of ideology in adjudication and of the existence of one correct answer serves a 'good' purpose in the same way that maintaining the fiction of free will serves a 'good' purpose. Judges can thus be justified for their bad faith.

Ultimately, however, I would like to question such a proposal. The serious elaboration of thoughts on the question whether hiding ideology is really necessary for preserving a system of the separation of powers merits another chapter. Thus, I will offer here only a few suggestions why its justifiability can be questioned.

First, any effort to hide the truth in order to preserve the system one believes to be good prevents any change, and thus progress. In this way, accepting bad faith might in itself be conservative.

Second, admitting ideology in adjudication will not necessarily destroy a system of separation of powers. Growing up, children (sooner or later) realise that there is no Santa Claus. This does not prevent them from continuing, once they grow up, to place presents under the Christmas tree and still enjoy the ritual. Admitting that judges introduce ideology in judging would not make legislators disappear. It would, however, allow society to discuss the outcomes of adjudication more clearly, and to reposition the separated branches of government more successfully.

Finally, if the law allows for different solutions, either in its text or after being appropriately construed, but still without denying its existence (thus within the margins of staying faithful to legal materials), is not deciding contrary to one's own ideology precisely the type of bad faith that nobody wants? In such a case, a judge necessarily fails any ideal of justice.

6

Judicial Appointments, Judicial Independence and the European High Courts

MITCHEL DE S-O-L'E LASSER*

I. Introduction

In 2009 and 2010, the European Court of Justice (ECJ) and the European Court of Human Rights (ECtHR) both underwent surprisingly significant and surprisingly similar institutional/procedural reforms: judicial nominations to each were henceforth to be screened in advance by blue ribbon panels of experts. Why did this come to pass? The two great pan-European courts had been in existence for over 50 years. What had happened that suddenly required both courts to become subject to new measures of that type at that time?

There are a great many interesting ways to try to understand and explain these reforms. This chapter focuses on only one of them.[1] To use the classic labels of political science and international relations theory, this chapter seeks to make sense of these judicial appointments reforms by deploying an intergovernmental-ist prism that focuses on the interests of state actors. Such an approach has obvious limitations. It tends to focus attention on governmental actors, potentially at the expense of the great diversity of other actors—such as institutions, NGOs, scholars, activists and so on—who play important roles in the development of domestic and international arrangements. It also tends to treat state interests as given, flow-ing naturally from the state of world affairs. The now classic constructivist litera-ture has described such limitations in detail; and it has done so convincingly.[2] But this should not foreclose the powerful insights that an intergovernmentalist focus on state actors and interests can nonetheless provoke.

* Jack G Clarke Professor of Law, Cornell Law School.
[1] In a forthcoming book, I hope to offer several more.
[2] For classic statements of constructivist theory in the political science and international relations literature, see, eg, Emanuel Adler, 'Seizing the Middle Ground: Constructivism in World Politics' (1997) 3 *European Journal of International Relations* 319; Peter J Katzenstein (ed), *The Culture of*

This chapter expands somewhat the scope of the object of analysis proposed by the book's editors. Rather than limit itself to studying the reforms undertaken with regards to the ECJ, it also includes those directed towards the ECtHR. The experience of each informs the other in productive ways; and while the reforms of each undoubtedly differ from those of the other, they nonetheless share a great deal substantively, conceptually and politically. Furthermore, their differences are also fruitful for examining procedural, intellectual and pragmatic variations between how the different reforms have functioned at the two European judicial institutions.

At the same time as this chapter expands the scope of its analysis to embrace both the ECJ and the ECtHR, it limits its subject matter within the greater field of judicial appointments reform. In particular, it focuses its attention primarily on the issue of judicial independence: to what extent can the judicial appointments reforms undertaken at the ECJ and ECtHR be understood as judicial independence mechanisms?

In order to address this question, this chapter considers, deploys and, to a lesser extent, critiques a set of theoretical texts that approach judicial independence as a tactical response to unsettled judicial and political conditions. These texts range from such classics as Martin Shapiro's analysis of constitutional courts and Landes and Posner's interest group theory of judicial independence, to more contemporary work such as Lee Epstein, Jack Knight and Olga Shvetsova's study on selecting judicial selection mechanisms and Garoupa and Ginsberg's analyses of judicial independence and judicial councils.[3]

As will become apparent, I do not necessarily agree with many of the specific conclusions that these texts might suggest. But I do not see this as a problem. Their tactical approaches to judicial independence nonetheless help to shed light on important facets of the European judicial appointments reforms. These insights will, I hope, prove sufficiently interesting in their own right; but they should prove essential when eventually combined with those generated by more neo-institutionalist and constructivist readings that emphasise a broader array of actors, interests and mutually constitutive interactions.

National Security: Norms and Identity in World Politics (New York, Columbia University Press, 1996); John G Ruggie, 'What Makes the World Hang Together? Neo-utilitarianism and the Social Constructivist Challenge' (1998) 52 *International Organization* 855; Alexander Wendt, 'Anarchy is What States Make of It' (1992) 46 *International Organization* 391.

[3] See Martin Shapiro, 'The European Court of Justice' in Peter H Russell and David M O'Brien (eds), *Judicial Independence in the Age of Democracy: Critical Perspectives from Around the World* (Charlottesville and London, University of Virginia Press, 2001) 273; William Landes and Richard Posner, 'The Independent Judiciary in an Interest-Group Perspective' (1975) 18(3) *Journal of Law and Economics* 875; Lee Epstein, Jack Knight and Olga Shvetsova, 'Selecting Selection Systems' in Stephen B Burbank and Barry Friedman (eds), *Judicial Independence in the Age of Democracy* (Thousand Oaks, Sage Publications, 2002) 191; Nuno Garoupa and Tom Ginsberg, 'The Comparative Law and Economics of Judicial Councils' (2009) 27 *Berkeley Journal of International Law* 53; Nuno Garoupa and Tom Ginsberg, 'Guarding the Guardians: Judicial Councils and Judicial Independence' (2009) 57 *American Journal of Comparative Law* 103.

The chapter is organised as follows. Section II gives a very brief introduction to the European judicial appointments reforms at the ECJ and the ECtHR. These reforms, it turns out, date much farther back than the 2009–10 reforms that instituted expert screening panels for judicial nominees to the high European courts. Section III introduces the scholarly literature that adopts a 'tactical' perspective towards judicial independence. This literature makes important links between judicial independence, judicial accountability, and legal and political uncertainty. Section IV brings the judicial independence literature to bear on the European judicial appointments reforms. It offers conclusions that run counter to the specifics suggested by some of the tactical analyses; but it also confirms and leverages the more fundamental insights offered by that literature. In particular, it stresses the legal and political uncertainty that has so motivated the European judicial appointments reforms. Finally, Section V concludes by suggesting the other layers of analysis that will need to be added to the intergovernmentalist perspective deployed in this chapter in order to yield a more complex and textured understanding of the European reforms.

II. The Reforms

The most dramatic reforms in the ECJ and ECHR judicial appointments processes were instituted only months apart in 2009 and 2010. Article 255 of the Treaty of Lisbon, which entered into force at the end of 2009, established a novel mechanism for vetting candidates put forward by the Member States to serve as judges of the ECJ and the General Court. Article 255 states:

> A panel shall be set up in order to give an opinion on candidates' suitability to perform the duties of Judge and Advocate-General of the Court of Justice and the General Court before the governments of the Member States make the appointments referred to in Articles 253 and 254.

> The panel shall comprise seven persons chosen from among former members of the Court of Justice and the General Court, members of national supreme courts and lawyers of recognised competence, one of whom shall be proposed by the European Parliament. The Council shall adopt a decision establishing the panel's operating rules and a decision appointing its members. It shall act on the initiative of the President of the Court of Justice.[4]

The Treaty of Lisbon had put into being an entirely new institutional mechanism for the specific purpose of screening judicial candidates.

---

[4] Consolidated versions of the Treaty on European Union and the Treaty on the functioning of the European Union (Treaty of Lisbon) http://register.consilium.europa.eu/doc/srv?l=EN&f=ST%20 6655%202008%20INIT.

Less than one year later, the Council of Europe effectively did the same. In a Resolution recalling 'the importance of ensuring the impartiality and quality of the Court', the Committee of Ministers established a Panel 'of seven members, chosen from among members of the highest national courts, former judges of international courts, including the [ECtHR] and other lawyers of recognized competence'.[5] This Panel, which would be 'geographically and gender balanced', would therefore be composed primarily of domestic and international high court judges, who would be appointed to once renewable three-year terms by the Committee of Ministers, 'following consultations' with the President of the ECtHR.[6] After more than 50 years of existence, both European institutions had thus instituted similar judicial screening devices within months of each other.

Indeed, this sudden change is all the more dramatic given the full extent to which the European Member States had controlled judicial appointments to the European courts from their inception. For the ECJ, the 1957 Treaty of Rome declared that appointment was to be made 'by common accord of the Governments of the Member States for a term of six years'. This mechanism, which has been in place ever since, effectively meant that each government could select its judge without serious challenge: the unanimous 'common accord' arrangement empowered each individual government not so much because it could exercise veto powers over the judges proposed by others, but because it could appoint its own judges with impunity, lest it play tit-for-tat with any potential challenging government's own judicial candidate. Appointment to the ECtHR was of course somewhat more complicated, given the nomination of three candidates for election by the Parliamentary Assembly of the Council of Europe (PACE). But even so, matters were rather firmly under governmental control. It took little for the national governments to make their preferences known; and as the PACE is composed of representatives of national parliaments, these representatives were unlikely to override the revealed preferences of national governments in other parliamentary systems.

What, then, had suddenly happened to trigger nearly simultaneous and rather parallel action regarding appointments to the European high courts? In order to begin to work towards an answer to this question, one must first make sure not be misled by the 2009–10 dates. For one thing, the ECJ reforms only came into force in 2009, but they had been negotiated significantly earlier. The Lisbon Treaty had been signed in 2007. Indeed, much of the Treaty of Lisbon merely transposed the substance of the doomed 2004 European Constitutional Treaty; and such was the case with the judicial screening provision: Article 255 of the Lisbon

---

[5] Committee of Ministers, Resolution CM/Res(2010)26 on the Establishment of an Advisory Panel of Experts on Candidates for Election as Judge to the European Court of Human Rights (10 November 2010). According to this Resolution, the Contracting States may submit proposal for appointment to the Panel. ibid para 3.

[6] ibid paras 2–3. Furthermore, 'Proposals for appointment [to the Panel] may be submitted by the High Contracting Parties'.

Treaty reproduces Article III-357 of the Constitutional Treaty essentially verbatim. This provision was in turn negotiated during the Constitutional Convention's 2003 'Discussion Circle on the Court of Justice'.[7] Indeed, the Discussion Circle's proposal itself reproduced the proposal put forward three years earlier by the Report by the Working Party on the Future of the European Communities' Court System, known as the 'Ole Due Report', commissioned in 1999 by the European Commission.[8]

Finally, the Ole Due Report built upon the Report that the ECJ had produced in May 1995 in preparation of the 1996 Intergovernmental Conference that would eventually lead to the Treaty of Amsterdam. This generally tactfully bland and diplomatic document also addressed potential reforms to the appointment process. In a series of telling paragraphs, however, the Court revealed the clear connection that it made between such potential reforms and its judicial independence:

> 17. The Court does not intend to express any opinion with regard to the procedure for the appointment of its members or the term of their appointment, beyond those aspects which concern the preservation of its independence and its functional efficiency.
>
> The Court stresses that the procedure for appointment laid down by the Treaties and the practice generally followed in renewing the terms of office of its members have satisfactorily ensured its independence and the continuity of its case-law.
>
> The Court would not, however, object to a reform which would involve an extension of the term of office with a concomitant condition that the appointment be non-renewable. Such a reform would provide an even firmer basis for the independence of its members and would strengthen the continuity of its case-law.[9]

The Court could hardly have stressed the connection more strongly: it returned to judicial independence in every sentence. Indeed, it was on the basis of such judicial independence that the Court objected to a proposal that must have been under consideration at the time: empowering a committee of the European Parliament to hold hearings with judicial nominees. This, stated the Court,

> would be unacceptable. Prospective appointees would be unable adequately to answer the questions put to them without betraying the discretion incumbent upon persons whose independence must, in the words of the Treaties, be beyond doubt and without prejudging positions they might have to adopt with regard to contentious issues which they would have to decide in the exercise of their judicial function.[10]

The Treaty of Lisbon's 2009 establishment of a panel of experts to screen nominees to the Court was thus the culmination of a sustained series of discussions and

---

[7] See Final Report of the Discussion Circle on the Court of Justice, CONV 636/03 http://european-convention.europa.eu/pdf/reg/en/03/cv00/cv00636.en03.pdf.

[8] See Report by the Working Party on the Future of the European Communities' Court System http://ec.europa.eu/dgs/legal_service/pdf/due_en.pdf.

[9] Report of the Court of Justice on certain aspects of the application of the Treaty on European Union, published in the Court's 1995 Annual Report 19, 28, para 17.

[10] ibid.

proposals dating back to the mid-1990s. And from the beginning, these debates were intimately linked to the issue of judicial independence. In the (seemingly alarmist) words of the ECJ's 1995 Report:

> Any decision affecting the structure of the judicial system must therefore ensure that the [European] courts remain independent and their judgments binding. Were that not to be the case, the very foundations of the Community legal order would be undermined.[11]

The same basic set of associations holds true for the Council of Europe and its court, the ECtHR. They actually launched their debates and reforms regarding judicial appointments and independence a little earlier than did the EU. I do not have the space here to do justice to the debates raging in the early 1990s concerning the need to undertake the reforms that would ultimately take the form of Protocol 11 to the European Convention on Human Rights, which finally established a 'new', permanent, full-time and single Court with compulsory jurisdiction over individual complaints.[12] But these debates over large-scale institutional and procedural reforms were intimately intertwined with increasingly overt and protracted debates over 'judicial independence'. Thus, it was in 1994—the very same year that the Committee of Ministers of the Council of Europe signed onto Protocol 11—that the Committee also passed its Recommendation 'On the Independence, Efficiency and Role of Judges'.[13]

The Committee's Recommendation was but the first of a long series of Strasbourg documents directed towards reinforcing judicial independence at both the domestic and supranational levels. It was followed by the 'European Charter on the Statute for Judges', passed in 1998 and 1999 by a more informal group of European participants, judges and judicial associations organised by the Council of Europe.[14] This document repeated much from the Committee's Recommendation, but began to focus attention on the establishment of independent judicial councils as a means to promote 'the competence, independence and impartiality' of the judiciary.[15] This was followed by the strongly worded Opinion No 1 on 'Standards Concerning the Independence of the Judiciary and the Irremovability of Judges', adopted in 2001 by the newly created Consultative Council of European Judges, which the Committee of Ministers had established the year before. Indeed, the list of such measures goes on and on. Not only have other institutions, such as the Venice Commission, generated their own judicial independence texts,[16] but

---

[11] ibid 21, para 4.

[12] See Council of Europe—Explanatory Report to Protocol No 11 to the Convention for the Protection of Human Rights and Fundamental Freedoms, restructuring the control machinery established thereby ('Explanatory Report to Protocol 11') 3–4 https://rm.coe.int/CoERMPublicCommonSearchServices/DisplayDCTMContent?documentId=09000016800cb5e9.

[13] Committee of Ministers Rec R (94) 12 (13 October 1994).

[14] See Consultative Council of European Judges, Opinion No 1 on Standards Concerning the Independence of the Judiciary and the Irremovability of Judges, CCJE (2001) OP N° 1, para 4.

[15] See European Charter on the Statute for Judges, DAJ/DOC (98) 23 (1998) para 1.1.

[16] See, eg, European Commission for Democracy Through Law (Venice Commission), European Standards on the Independence of the Judiciary: A Systematic Overview, CDL-JD(2008)002

the Committee of Ministers and the Consultative Council of European Judges (CCJE) have returned to the issue several times, generating updated or expanded versions of their earlier pronouncements.[17]

All of these measures took as their starting point the centrality of judges in democratic systems governed by the rule of law. The Explanatory Report to the Committee of Ministers' 1994 Recommendation 'On the Independence, Efficiency and Role of Judges' opens with characteristic language:

1. Within the framework of the activities undertaken to promote and guarantee the efficiency and fairness of civil and criminal justice, it was decided to prepare a recommendation on the independence, efficiency and role of judges.

2. Indeed, the Council of Europe includes among its aims the institution and protection of a democratic and political system characterised by the rule of law and the establishment of a constitutionally governed state, as well as the promotion and protection of human rights and fundamental freedoms.

3. The recommendation on the independence, efficiency and role of judges recognises and emphasises the pre-eminent and significant role played by judges in the implementation of these aims. The independence of judges is one of the central pillars of the rule of law. The need to promote the independence of judges is not confined to individual judges only but may have consequences for the judicial system as a whole.[18]

The Committee of Ministers made no attempt to minimise the critical role that they were expecting an independent judiciary and fundamental rights to play in such a scheme:

The independent allotted task of judges is that of safeguarding the rights and freedoms of all persons within the scope of their duty to administer justice ... Ultimately, the obligation has to do with the defence of democracy and the rule of law, safeguarding against oppression and the totalitarian state as expressed in the Statute of the Council of Europe.[19]

The independence and importance of the judiciary were thus intimately linked from the moment the ECtHR was to become a fulltime court with compulsory jurisdiction over individual human rights complaints.

In order to promote this judicial independence, the organs of the Council of Europe adopted a series of more precise measures. The original 1994 Committee

www.venice.coe.int/webforms/documents/default.aspx?pdffile=CDL-JD(2008)002-e; 'Report on the Independence of the Judiciary—Part I: The Independence of Judges' CDL-AD(2010)004 www.venice.coe.int/webforms/documents/default.aspx?pdffile=CDL-AD(2010)004-e.

[17] See, eg, Committee of Ministers, Establishment of an Advisory Panel of Experts on Candidates for Election as Judge to the European Court of Human Rights—Implementation, CM/Del/Dec(2010)1101/1.7E (2010); CCJE, Magna Carta of Judges (Fundamental Principles) CCJE (2010) 3 final (17 November 2010).

[18] Committee of Ministers, Explanatory Memorandum, Recommendation Rec R (94) 12 on independence, efficiency and role of judges (13 October 1994) 6 www.coe.int/t/dghl/standardsetting/cdcj/CDCJ%20Recommendations/CMRec(2010)12E_%20judges.pdf.

[19] ibid 14.

of Ministers' Recommendation made broad and seemingly categorical statements about domestic practices concerning judicial selection, promotion and discipline:

> All decisions concerning the professional career of judges should be based on objective criteria, and the selection and career of judges should be based on merit, having regard to qualifications, integrity, ability and efficiency. The authority taking the decision on the selection and career of judges should be independent of the government and the administration. In order to safeguard its independence, rules should ensure that, for instance, its members are selected by the judiciary and that the authority decides itself on its procedural rules.[20]

Ensuing measures then took increasingly precise steps designed to impose this vision on national governments making judicial appointment decisions in both the domestic and the supranational (ie, European) contexts.

These more precise measures tended to run in two different, if ultimately related, directions. The first was institutional: the judicial independence and appointments debates increasingly demanded the creation of some kind of independent authority that would be responsible for governing matters relating to judicial selection, promotion and discipline. The European Charter on the Statute for Judges, published in 1998 by a group of European participants, judges and judicial associations organised by the Council of Europe under the auspices of the 'Themis Plan',[21] thus pronounces:

> In respect of every decision affecting the selection, recruitment, appointment, career progress or termination of office of a judge, the statute envisages the intervention of an authority independent of the executive and legislative powers within which at least one half of those who sit are judges elected by their peers following methods guaranteeing the widest representation of the judiciary.[22]

This was followed in 2001 by the CCJE, which had been established the year before by the Committee of Ministers. In its first policy paper (its 'Opinion No 1'), which tellingly addresses 'Standards Concerning the Independence of the Judiciary and the Irremovability of Judges',[23] the CCJE also honed in explicitly on institutional structure. Building upon the European Charter's call for an 'independent authority' (in effect, a judicial council) to govern all aspects of the judicial profession, it also proposed the establishment of formal and public procedures to govern its operation:

> The CCJE recommended that the authorities responsible in member States for making and advising on appointments and promotions should now introduce, publish and give effect to objective criteria, with the aim of ensuring that the selection and career of judges

---

[20] Committee of Ministers Rec R (94) 12 (13 October 1994) 2.

[21] *European Yearbook* vol 46 (The Hague, Boston, London, Martinus Nijhoff, 1998) 64.

[22] ibid para 1.3.

[23] Consultative Council of European Judges, 'Opinion No 1 on Standards Concerning the Independence of the Judiciary and the Irremovability of Judges' CCJE (2001) OP N⁰ 1 ('CCJE Opinion 1').

are 'based on merit, having regard to qualifications, integrity, ability and efficiency'. Once this is done, those bodies or authorities responsible for any appointment or promotion will be obliged to act accordingly, and it will then at least be possible to scrutinize the content of the criteria adopted and their practical effect.

… Therefore, the CCJE considered that every decision relating to a judge's appointment or career should be based on objective criteria and be either taken by an independent authority or subject to guarantees to ensure that it is not taken other than on the basis of such criteria.[24]

The CCJE was calling for the establishment of formal norms, to be applied via 'formal procedures' by a formally established 'independent authority with substantial judicial representation'. This call for the formalised institutions to apply formalised norms has since continued.[25]

The second direction that characterised these measures was their focus on the competence and quality of candidates for judicial office. This trend can already be seen in the 1998 European Charter on the Statute for Judges, whose preamble states:

Being concerned to see the promotion of judicial independence, necessary for the strengthening of the pre-eminence of law and for the protection of individual liberties within democratic states, made more effective;

Conscious of the necessity that provisions calculated to ensure the best guarantees of the competence, independence and impartiality of judges should be specified in a formal document intended for all European States;

Desiring to see the judges' statutes of the different European States take into account these provisions in order to ensure in concrete terms the best level of guarantees;

Have adopted the present European Charter on the statute for judges.[26]

The Charter makes this link between judicial independence and judicial competence particularly apparent. Its first substantive paragraph thus states:

1.1. The statute for judges aims at ensuring the competence, independence and impartiality which every individual legitimately expects from the courts of law and from every judge to whom is entrusted the protection of his or her rights. It excludes every provision and every procedure liable to impair confidence in such competence, such independence

---

[24] ibid paras 25, 37.

[25] The updated 2010 Committee of Ministers' Recommendation makes the point particularly clearly. It states:

'Decisions concerning the selection and career of judges should be based on objective criteria pre-established by law or by the competent authorities. Such decisions should be based on merit, having regard to the qualifications, skills and capacity required to adjudicate cases by applying the law while respecting human dignity … Where judicial authorities establish systems for the assessment of judges, such systems should be based on objective criteria. These should be published by the competent judicial authority' CM/Rec(2010)12 paras 44, 58.

[26] European Charter on the Statute for Judges, DAJ/DOC (98) 23 (1998) 5.

and such impartiality. The present Charter is composed hereafter of the provisions which
are best able to guarantee the achievement of those objectives. Its provisions aim at raising the level of guarantees in the various European States ...[27]

Indeed, the Charter's Explanatory Memorandum only makes the link even more
explicit:

> The Charter endeavours to define the content of the statute for judges on the basis of the
> objectives to be attained: ensuring the competence, independence and impartiality which
> all members of the public are entitled to expect of the courts and judges entrusted with
> protecting their rights ...

> These safeguards on individuals' rights are ensured by judicial competence, in the sense
> of ability, independence and impartiality.[28]

In this final sentence, the link between judicial independence and judicial competence has become so strong that independence is all but folded into—or subsumed
within—the more fundamental category of competence.

Of course, this focus on judicial competence leaves open the question: of what
does such competence actually consist? Unsurprisingly, the question admits of
no easy answer. To its credit, the Charter's Explanatory Memorandum makes an
attempt to address the issue:

> The choice [of judicial candidate] made by the selection body must be based on criteria
> relevant to the nature of the duties to be discharged.

> The main aim must be to evaluate the candidate's ability to assess independently cases
> heard by judges, which implies independent thinking ... The ability to apply the law
> refers both to knowledge of the law and the capacity to put it into practice, which are two
> different things ...

> In order to ensure the ability to carry out the duties involved in judicial office, the rules
> on selection and recruitment must set out requirements as to qualifications and previous
> experience ...

> Candidates selected to discharge judicial duties must therefore be prepared for the task
> by means of appropriate training, which must be financed by the State.[29]

This vague passage, which defines judicial competence largely in terms of judicial
independence and 'independent thinking', as well as in terms of 'qualifications' and
'experience', represents an early salvo in what was to become an increasingly long
set of measures regarding the competence, qualifications and quality of European
judicial candidates.

Before we turn to these measures, it is worth pausing to note the rather smooth
transition in these debates from domestic to supranational judicial appointments.

---

[27] ibid para 1.1.
[28] ibid.
[29] ibid, Explanatory Memo, paras 2.1–2.3.

What held for one, the argument now ran, should hold for the other. The CCJE's Opinion No 1 thus states:

> The CCJE considered that the ever increasing significance for national legal systems of supranational courts and their decisions made it essential to encourage member States to respect the principles concerning independence, irremovability, appointment and term of office in relation to judges of such supranational courts.[30]

Indeed, the CCJE went even further. It extended its analysis not only to the Convention system of which it was, after all, a part (it had been established by the Committee of Ministers), but also to the European Union:

> 56. The CCJE agreed that the importance for national legal systems and judges of the obligations resulting from international treaties such as the European Convention and also the European Union treaties makes it vital that the appointment and re-appointment of judges to the courts interpreting such treaties should command the same confidence and respect the same principles as national legal systems. The CCJE further considered that involvement by the independent authority referred [to above] should be encouraged in relation to appointment and re-appointment to international courts. The Council of Europe and its institutions are in short founded on belief in common values superior to those of any single member State, and that belief has already achieved significant practical effect. It would undermine those values and the progress that has been made to develop and apply them, if their application was not insisted upon at the international level.[31]

If, by the mid-1990s, the judicial independence literature had emerged more or less in tandem with the judicial appointments literature, by the late 1990s those literatures had returned—complete with their institutional and competence components—to the European appointments debates.

The result was a flurry of activity, particularly in Strasbourg. In 1995, the PACE's Committee on Legal Affairs and Human Rights proposed its Draft Resolution and Report 'on the procedure for examining candidatures for the election of judges to the European Court of Human Rights'. Preparing for the entry into force of Protocol 11, the Committee proposed 'to improve [the PACE's] own procedure for examining the candidatures and for the selection of candidates, for more efficiency and professionalism'.[32] This yielded two important procedural developments. First, candidates to fill vacancies on the ECtHR were henceforth 'invited to fill in a model curriculum vitae, so that the Assembly will have comparable information at its disposal' when selecting among the slate of three candidates put forward by the Member States. Furthermore, Member State governments were to transmit these three CVs in alphabetical order, in order to limit the capacity of these governments

---

[30] CCJE's Opinion No 1 para 55.

[31] ibid para 56.

[32] PACE Committee on Legal Affairs and Human Rights (Rapporteur: Lord Kirkhill), Report on the procedure for examining candidatures for the election of judges to the European Court of Human Rights 1, Doc 7439, 1403-15/12/95-1-E (1995).

to influence the PACE's judicial election.[33] Second, the three candidates would 'be interviewed by a sub- committee of the Assembly, for their qualities to be assessed', which would then lead to a recommendation to the Assembly.[34]

To these measures, which were addressed to the European level of the ECtHR appointments process, were added a long and detailed list of measures addressed to the domestic level of the process. These (often redundant) measures—including the 1999, 2004 and 2009 PACE Recommendations on 'National procedures for nominating candidates for election to the [ECtHR]', 'Candidates for the [ECtHR]', and 'Nomination of candidates and election of judges to the [ECtHR]'[35]—oblige the domestic authorities to institute and abide by formal and transparent procedures for the selection and nomination of candidates to fill vacancies on the ECtHR, to issue a formal call for candidates in the appropriate specialised press, to include at least one woman in their slate of three nominated candidates, and so on.[36]

As should now be quite apparent, the establishment in 2009 and 2010 of the EU's Article 255 Panel and the Council of Europe's Advisory Panel of Experts was hardly a sudden or one-off event. It was part and parcel of a long trajectory of developments that had begun in the mid-1990s and has progressed incrementally— but determinedly—ever since. Such Panels had begun to be proposed years earlier; and they were inscribed in a broad set of reforms that explicitly wove together the issues of judicial appointments, judicial independence, judicial self-regulation (via judicial councils), and judicial competence and quality.

III. The Theory: Tactical Approaches to Judicial Independence

The classic literature on judicial independence tends to focus on the values underlying such independence and the key features required to maintain it.[37] These analyses typically distinguish between the independence of the judiciary

---

[33] See PACE Recommendation 1429 (1999), 2004 PACE Recommendation 1649 (2004) and PACE Resolution 1432 (2005).

[34] PACE Committee on Legal Affairs and Human Rights (Rapporteur: Lord Kirkhill), Report on the procedure for examining candidatures for the election of judges to the European Court of Human Rights 1, Doc 7439, 1403-15/12/95-1-E (1995).

[35] PACE Recommendation 1429 (1999), PACE Recommendation 1649 (2004), PACE Resolution 1646 (2009) on the Nomination of Candidates and Election of Judges to the European Court of Human Rights.

[36] See ibid.

[37] See, eg, Peter H Russell, 'Toward a General Theory of Judicial Independence' in Russell and O'Brien (eds) (n 3)1, 3; Peter H Russell, 'Conclusion: A General Theory of Judicial Independence Revisited' in Adam Dodek and Lorne Sossin (eds), *Judicial Independence in Context* (Toronto, Irwin Law, 2010) 599.

as a whole or of the individual judge; and this distinction yields another between external and internal pressures on judicial action. The first triggers concerns regarding the separation of governmental powers; the second raises concerns regarding professional pressures from within the judicial hierarchy. These classic distinctions themselves turn on the fundamental distinction between law and politics: judicial independence distinguishes between judicial decision-making on the basis of unfettered judicial application of law and judicial decision-making on the basis of political factors, be they of an external/political or internal/professional nature.

In contrast to such classic approaches to judicial independence in the legal literature, a number of authors more interested in positive political theory, law and economics and behavioural economics have put forward more tactical accounts of judicial independence. These authors tend to approach the judiciary as merely one more political institution among others (albeit a distinctive one), governed by the same type of self-interested and coldly calculating behaviour that characterises all the other political actors and institutions that surround it. Such an approach prompts us to conceive of judicial independence as a tool and not merely as a distinctive principle operating in its own right or in the furtherance of other rule of law values. By thinking of judicial independence in this more tactical manner, these authors redirect attention towards the ways in which judicial independence interacts with particular political forces and political actors in a particular context.

As will eventually become apparent in Section IV, I do not necessarily agree with the specific conclusions that their accounts might suggest in the European context that is the focus of this volume. But I do not see this as a problem. Their theories prove extremely useful for teasing out and discussing the tensions that characterise the multi-level European judicial/political arena.

Martin Shapiro is likely the best-known proponent of such a tactical understanding of judicial independence, especially in the realms of constitutional and European law. In his view, the judicial independence of constitutional courts (including the ECJ) is but a shorthand description of two core features of all courts (and perhaps especially constitutional courts). The first feature describes the essence of 'triadic conflict resolution': parties to a conflict must be able to turn to mutually acceptable 'third party adjudicators' to resolve their disputes in a manner that losers will tolerate.[38] The second is that in the constitutional context, political institutions understand that the judiciary, when acting as such a third party adjudicator in constitutional disputes of a structural nature, will function as a 'junkyard dog': political institutions establish the judiciary and set it loose specifically to police constitutional bargains and boundaries, despite the risks that the judiciary obviously poses for all other constitutional actors whenever it exercises this authority.[39] Political institutions therefore establish and tolerate judicial

---

[38] See Shapiro (n 3) 273–74.
[39] ibid 275–76.

independence because they believe that it is in their self-interest to do so, even though they are quite conscious of the fact they will periodically regret unexpected and unfavourable judicial interventions.

Shapiro thus fundamentally reorients the way that one might conceive of judicial independence, which now emerges as little more than a pragmatic and calculated mechanism for political institutions to advance their self-interest within a constitutional framework. Lee Epstein, Jack Knight and Olga Shvetsova reinforce this perspective in their important 2001 essay, 'Selecting Selection Systems'. They state:

> To apply this general framework to explain the choice of selection and retention systems for judges, we begin with the basic assumption that designers of constitutional courts prefer institutional rules that will best serve their long-term political goals. But, because attaining this goal requires them to determine the relationship between their present political preferences and the long-term effects of the rules governing constitutional courts, their preferences over judicial selection and retention mechanisms will vary depending on their beliefs about present and future political conditions. So, for example, the more uncertain those conditions—in the fundamental sense that the actors do not know the political circumstances they will face in the future—the less the designers of the court will be able to constrain (with confidence) the court and, thus, the greater the independence the institutional rules will provide the justices.[40]

Although they focus more on particular political actors than on constitutional institutions, Epstein, Knight and Shvetsova thus adopt a diagnosis of judicial independence that stresses the same type of self-interested and calculating behaviour as does Shapiro: political actors adopt a stance on judicial independence in accordance with their assessment of their own political futures. The more those actors believe that they face political uncertainty moving forward, the more they will seek to entrench a system of judicial independence. But the more those actors are certain that they will remain in power, the more hostile they will be towards institutionalising judicial independence, which could only serve to frustrate their political dominance. Under this perspective, judicial independence is but a tool wielded by constitutional designers to serve their political fortunes over time.

In two interesting sister articles published in 2009, Nuno Garoupa and Tom Ginsberg also adopt a similarly dynamic, if more mechanical, understanding of judicial independence.[41] To them, judicial independence is part of a larger dynamic between judges, politicians and public policy. They state:

> It is our view that the periodic reforms of judicial appointments and management that we observe within and across countries reflect a dialectic tension between the need to de-politicize the judiciary and the trend toward judicializing politics. Independence is needed to provide the benefits of judicial decision-making; once given independence,

---

[40] Epstein, Knight and Shvetsova (n 3) 214.
[41] Garoupa and Ginsberg, 'Comparative Law and Economics of Judicial Councils' (n 3); Garoupa and Ginsberg, 'Guarding the Guardians' (n 3).

judges are useful for resolving a wider range of more important disputes. As the judiciary begins to take over functions from democratic processes, however, the pressure for greater accountability mounts.

When judges have little influence over public policy and politics, concerns over independence tend to dominate, and reformers may push for a move from a politically dependent, weak judiciary to a strong, self-regulated judiciary. This shift gives rise to a judiciary that has some control over its own affairs. Frequently, though not inevitably, judges use this independence to increase their influence over public policy, perhaps because of exogenous events. However, once politics is judicialized in a significant way, pressures arise for greater political accountability. The judiciary remains strong but is subject to more oversight and control. Sometimes these pressures for more accountability can lead to assaults on judicial independence, particularly if a small group of principals is able to control the process of supervision. In such circumstances, a politically accountable, strong judiciary may revert back to a politically dependent, weak judiciary, as in a rising authoritarian regime. This dynamic framework provides a tool for understanding the various institutional adjustments observed in different countries.[42]

On this view, judicial independence can be seen as a part of a grand cyclical process, in which the judiciary is subjected to greater independence or accountability in response to governing politico-judicial conditions: judicial independence and accountability rise and fall as those conditions sway back and forth between an excessively politicised judiciary and an excessively judicialised politics.

In each of these models, ranging from Shapiro to Epstein et al to Garoupa/Ginsberg, judicial independence functions as part of a larger dynamic that links the judiciary to political institutions and power. Judicial independence is deployed; it is curtailed; it is promoted; but it does not simply exist in and for itself. And especially for Shapiro and Epstein et al, its primary benefit is as a mechanism for helping to manage political uncertainty over time. In Epstein et al's account, when savvy and powerful actors face future systemic or individual political uncertainty, they can hedge their bets by entrenching an independent judiciary: this helps to protect them against large-scale reversals in their political fortunes. And in Shapiro's account, political institutions may well prefer to set loose an independent judicial 'junkyard dog' than to live with the uncertainty of unenforceable constitutional bargains.

These accounts therefore forge an all-important theoretical link between judicial independence and political uncertainty. In this respect, they are all descendants of the path-breaking 1975 article 'The Independent Judiciary in an Interest-Group Perspective'.[43] In this seminal piece, Bill Landes and Dick Posner offered an elegant analysis of judicial independence. As they explained, the value of legislative bargains depends directly on how long interest groups can expect them to be enforced.

---

[42] Garoupa and Ginsberg, 'Comparative Law and Economics of Judicial Councils', ibid 61; Garoupa and Ginsberg, 'Guarding the Guardians', ibid 117–18.

[43] Bill Landes and Dick Posner, 'The Independent Judiciary in an Interest-Group Perspective' (1975) 18 *Journal of Law and Economics* 875.

The key to creating such legislative stamina is to make it difficult for subsequent legislatures not only to overturn those bargains by legislative means, but also to pressure the judiciary to overturn them by interpretive means. On this view, judicial independence is effectively an entrenchment mechanism for interest groups to guard against political uncertainty over time: it frees the judiciary from having to bow to a sitting legislature, which allows it to seek in good faith to enforce the original legislative deal. If this can be accomplished, interest groups can lock in their desired policy outcomes with much greater confidence.

IV. Connecting the Tactical Theory to the European Practice

A. A Little More History

The key insight of the judicial independence literature of the type we examined in Section III is the relationship between judicial independence and political and/or legal uncertainty. According to such tactical theories, judicial independence helps to settle such uncertainty by providing a mechanism for entrenching policy judgments and enforcing expectations that are valued by currently dominant political forces, albeit at the price of creating a more autonomous judiciary that can be expected to generate unexpected and even unappreciated rulings on a periodic basis.

This insight puts us in a much better position to grasp the dynamics that eventually led in 2009 and 2010 to the creation of the expert panels to vet judicial candidates to the two European courts. The first part of the analysis is to look at the history, as we did in Section II. This exercise pushes the dates back some 15 years, ie, to the mid-1990s. From that point forward, judicial appointments reform proceeded in an unbroken chain of developments that continues to this day. This more extended timeline allows us to take the second important analytic step, which is to draw the appropriate historical and thematic link between the judicial appointment issues/reforms with the judicial independence issues/reforms, which emerged at precisely the same era and have been intimately linked ever since.

Finally, this earlier date not only highlights the link between judicial appointments and independence, but also allows the driving historical impetus for these reform efforts to come clearly into view: the large-scale accession of new Member States from the former Eastern Bloc in the wake of the fall of the Berlin Wall. This sudden and dramatic explosion in the membership of both the EU and the Council of Europe was in fact the major political and legal turning point.

True, both the EU and the Council of Europe had seen their membership gradually increase over time. The Council of Europe had 14 Contracting Parties in

1950 and its membership had risen very modestly to 21 in 1987. But it would add 17 new Member States by 1996 and its membership would explode to 41 by 2000. Similarly, the EU, which had begun as a Community of six in 1952 and 1958, had slowly but surely added Member States over the course of the ensuing four decades: it had added three in 1973, one in 1981, two in 1986 and three in 1995, leaving it with a total of 15. But by 1995, something quite different was on the immediate horizon: accession from the East would almost double the size of the 15-member EU, bringing its membership to 27 by 2004, including 10 new entrants in 2004 alone. And once again, one should not be misled by the eventual dates of accession, such as the great EU accession date of 2004: in 1994, 1995 and 1996—ie, *precisely* when the judicial appointments and independence debates suddenly burst onto the scene—no fewer than 10 former Eastern Bloc countries formally applied for accession to a European Union that was then comprised of only 12 Member States.[44] The speed and size of the transformations were breathtaking. But the political implications were even more so: to admit Spain and Austria into the EU or the Council of Europe was one thing, but to admit Romania and Russia was something else.

This dramatic European enlargement obviously generated enormous uncertainty, as no one could be quite sure what its effects might be. This uncertainty could be managed in assorted ways on the political and institutional fronts. Thus, voting weights in the Council were haggled over quite fiercely; and the application of free movement norms was delayed in a manner that was clearly and unabashedly directed at the labour force of the new Member States. But such adjustments were much more difficult to accomplish in the judicial domain: the one State, one judge principle was almost too straightforward to finesse. The math and its implications were therefore painfully simple: for all intents and purposes, the ECJ and ECtHR were about to double in size. And at least as a brute numerical matter, the one Bulgarian judge would carry as much weight as her one German colleague.

Once we recognise that European enlargement was the key impetus for the sudden rise of the judicial appointments and independence debates in the mid-1990s, a whole series of associated themes comes clearly into focus. The judicial appointments and independence measures, for example, elaborated a set of governing principles regarding the importance of the judiciary for a properly functioning constitutional democracy. This pedantic new theoretical construct—which was hardly universally recognised even within the *Western* European Civilian jurisdictions of the period—placed courts at the very centre of the national and supranational constitutional orders, ideally as a coequal branch of government: judges and courts must be the central institution for defending individual rights and

---

[44] In chronological order, those countries were Hungary, Poland, Slovakia, Romania, Latvia, Estonia, Lithuania, Bulgaria, Czech Republic, Slovenia. See http://europa.eu/legislation_summaries/enlargement/2004_and_2007_enlargement/e50017_en.htm.

freedoms, safeguarding democracy and the rule of law, guaranteeing the separation of powers, and protecting against oppression and the totalitarian state.[45]

This 1990s civics lesson—so typical of the 'rule of law' and law and development' literatures of the period[46]—was clearly directed towards the 'transition democracies' of Central and Eastern Europe. On the judicial appointments front, it posited an overt and recurring distinction between a) well-established democracies with 'long-entrenched and democratically proved systems' and a 'force of tradition and informal self-discipline' that can bring informal mechanisms to bear for curtailing 'undue political influence' over judicial appointments and b) 'newer democracies', 'former communist countries' and 'countries which do not have other long-entrenched and democratically proved systems' and which are therefore in no position to exercise such 'self-discipline'.[47] And this generated a recognisable set of institutional demands, almost all framed in terms of judicial independence. This led to a long series of increasingly specific measures that were designed to guarantee independent judicial decision-making free of party, executive, legislative or other improper influence. At the most general level, judicial independence should be constitutionally entrenched.[48] At the more detailed and practical level, judicial councils should be formally established to govern all aspects of judicial appointment, training, promotion and discipline;[49] and these councils should exercise such powers by applying formally established norms on the basis of formally established procedures.[50]

These reforms were to operate at the European as well as the domestic levels. This meant that judicial appointments to the high European courts were suddenly to be cut free from the control of national governments, which had for over four decades zealously guarded their prerogatives in this domain. This led to the imposition of increasingly detailed and formalised European norms, such as the Council of Europe's requirement that domestic authorities issue a formal call for ECtHR judicial candidates in the specialised press, institute formal and transparent procedures for their selection, put forward a gender-mixed slate of candidates, transmit their CVs in alphabetical order, and so on, as well as the establishment of formal procedures at the European level—such as the requirement that the three

---

[45] See, eg, CCJE Opinion 1 (n 23).

[46] See, eg, Robert Cooter, 'The Rule of State Law and the Rule-of-Law State: Economic Analysis of the Legal Foundations of Development' in *Annual World Bank Conference on Development Economics 1996* (Washington, The World Bank, 1997) 191–217; Martin Golding, 'Transitional Regimes and the Rule of Law' (1996) 9(4) *Ratio Juris* 387–95; Andrzej Rapaczynski, 'The Rule of Law in Theoretical and Comparative Perspective' in Roger Michener (ed), *The Balance of Freedom: Political Economy, Law, and Learning* (St Paul, Paragon House, 1995) 81–106.

[47] See, eg, CCJE Opinion 1 (n 23) paras 32–45, quoting Committee of Ministers Rec R (94) 12 (13 October 1994) 2.

[48] See Venice Commission, 'Report on the Independence of the Judiciary—Part I: The Independence of Judges' CDL-AD(2010)004 para 82.

[49] CCJE, Magna Carta of Judges (Fundamental Principles) CCJE (2010) 3 final (17 November 2010).

[50] See, eg, CM/Rec(2010)12 paras 44–58.

candidates 'be interviewed by a sub-committee of the Assembly, for their qualities to be assessed', which would then lead to a recommendation to the Assembly.[51]

Finally, it was in the context of these large-scale historical and political transitions that issues of judicial competence and quality came increasingly to the fore, leading eventually to the establishment of the two expert panels for vetting judicial candidates and to their ensuing elaboration of relatively detailed substantive criteria for assessing those candidates. Indeed, it is hard to overstate the full extent to which such quality concerns came to dominate the judicial appointments debates. As we have noted, the issue of judicial competence had made its first real appearance in the 1998 European Charter on the Statute for Judges. But the theme of judicial quality became only more strident and even alarmist over time, bursting onto the scene at two specific and quite telling moments.

For the EU, judicial quality roared into the open in 2003, that is, on the eve of the great 2004 accession of 12 new Member States. The Discussion Circle on the Court of Justice, which met in Brussels on 17 February 2003 under the framework of the European Constitutional Convention, simultaneously 'stressed' 'the importance of establishing criteria which would guarantee the professional quality, independence and impartiality of the candidates' and put forward the controversial proposal of establishing 'a panel to assess the candidates'. It offered suggestions regarding such a panel's composition: 'it could include a former President of the Court, Presidents of Constitutional or Supreme Courts of the Member States; it was also suggested that the European Parliament might designate a member of the panel'.[52] It even mooted the idea that the Panel 'interview the candidates'.[53] With the benefit of hindsight, we can of course clearly see that this proposed institutional innovation, which was directly linked to 'the importance of establishing criteria which would guarantee the professional quality, independence and impartiality of the candidates', was the embryo of what would eventually become the Article 255 Panel.

Furthermore, the 255 Panel then took quite seriously its need to establish and expound upon such 'criteria' of quality. In its first Annual Report, it formally published and elaborated upon the six substantive criteria by which it would make its assessment of candidates:

> Although the criteria established by the Treaty on the Functioning of the European Union are exhaustive, the panel nevertheless considers that they could be more clearly and precisely explained. The panel's assessment ... is therefore made on the basis of six considerations: the candidate's legal expertise, professional experience, ability to perform

---

[51] See, eg, PACE Recommendation 1429 (1999), PACE Recommendation 1649 (2004), PACE Resolution 1432 (2005), PACE Ctte Report on the procedure for examining candidatures, PACE Resolution 1646 (2009) on the Nomination of Candidates and Election of Judges to the European Court of Human Rights.

[52] Record of the meeting on 17 February 2003 of the discussion circle on the Court of Justice, CONV 573/03 http://european-convention.europa.eu/pdf/reg/en/03/cv00/cv00573.en03.pdf.

[53] See ibid.

the duties of a Judge, assurance of independence and impartiality, language skills and aptitude for working as part of a team in an international environment in which several legal systems are represented.[54]

The Panel then spent the next two and a half pages working methodically through these six criteria.[55]

For the Council of Europe, these debates over the establishment of an expert panel to vet the quality of judicial candidates, which had first emerged at the same time as the Discussion Circle at the 2003 EU Constitutional Convention,[56] suddenly resurfaced in 2010. In preparation for the 2010 Interlaken Ministerial Conference on the Future of the European Court of Human Rights, Secretary General Thorbjørn Jagland linked 'the idea of a mixed screening panel composed of prominent former high level national or international judges' not only to 'ensur[ing] the highest levels of expertise and relevant experience on the part of the Court's judiciary', but also to 'the standing and credibility of the Court itself' and to the 'authority of the Court's case law'.[57] In response, the Conference approved an 'Action Plan' that wholeheartedly adopted the language of quality:

> 8. Stressing the importance of maintaining the independence of the judges and of preserving the impartiality and quality of the Court, the Conference calls upon States Parties and the Council of Europe to:
>
> a) ensure, if necessary by improving the transparency and quality of the selection procedure at both national and European levels, full satisfaction of the Convention's criteria for office as a judge of the Court, including knowledge of public international law and of the national legal systems as well as proficiency in at least one official language. In addition, the Court's composition should comprise the necessary practical legal experience.[58]

Less than four months later, the sitting President of the ECtHR, Jean-Paul Costa, took the next step. He sent an impassioned letter to the permanent representatives of the Member States of the Council of Europe advocating the establishment of what was soon to become the APE. His letter opens as follows:

> Dear Ambassador,
>
> As you know, point 8 of the Interlaken Action Plan calls upon the states parties and the Council of Europe to 'ensure, if necessary by improving the transparency and quality of the selection procedure at both national and European levels, full satisfaction of the

---

[54] First Activity report of the panel provided for by Art 255 of the Treaty on the Functioning of the European Union, Brussels 17 February 2011, 6509/11 Cour 3 Jur 57 ('First Annual Report') 8–9.

[55] See ibid at 9–11.

[56] See Limbach et al, 'Judicial Independence: Law and Practice of Appointments to the European Court of Human Rights' (2003) www.interights.org/jud-ind-en/index.html. See also Report of the Group of Wise Persons to the Committee of Ministers, CM (2006) 203 paras 117–18.

[57] Contribution of the Secretary General of the Council of Europe to the Preparation of the Interlaken Ministerial Conference, SG/Inf (2009) 20 18 December 2009.

[58] High Level Conference on the Future of the European Court of Human Rights, Interlaken Declaration of 19 February 2010, Action Plan para 8 www.echr.coe.int/Documents/2010_Interlaken_FinalDeclaration_ENG.pdf.

Convention's criteria for office as a judge of the Court, including knowledge of public international law and of the national legal systems as well as proficiency in at least one official language.'

In terms of the future of the Court and therefore the Convention system, one of the decisive factors will be the quality of its Judges. Whatever reforms are undertaken, the system will fail if judges do not have the necessary experience and authority.

The quality of the Judges is important not only to guarantee the high standard of the decisions delivered and the jurisprudence developed. It is also essential because, in a subsidiary system where human rights protection falls primarily to the national courts, the European Court as the ultimate arbiter of human rights issues must be composed of persons of sufficient standing and authority to command the respect of national judges, including senior national judges. If this is not the case, the Court itself will suffer from a deficit of authority and the system will lose credibility and effectiveness.[59]

On 10 November 2010, barely six months after Costa had signed his letter, the Committee of Ministers formally established the APE to help vet judicial candidates to the ECtHR.[60] The issues of judicial independence, judicial quality and judicial appointments were thus linked together to bring into being the expert judicial panels.

B. Aligning the Tactical Judicial Independence Theory to the European Practice

The tactically oriented theory that we summarised in Section III tends, as does most judicial independence theory, to draw a basic distinction between judicial independence and judicial accountability.[61] Thus, Lee Epstein et al posit that the more political actors expect to stay in power, the more they will favour judicial accountability/subservience (in order to have their wishes followed); but the more they face political uncertainty, the more they will favour judicial independence (in order to insulate themselves and their programmes from political reversals). Indeed, Garoupa and Ginsberg treat the relationship between judicial independence and judicial accountability as so fundamental that they depict judicial orders

---

[59] Letter from Jean-Paul Costa, President of the European Court of Human Rights, addressed to member states' Permanent Representatives (Ambassadors) on 9 June 2010 ('Costa Letter'), in Committee on Legal Affairs and Human Rights (Rapporteur: Wohlwend), Report on National procedures for the selection of candidates for the European Court of Human Rights, PACE document 12391 (6 October 2010) Appendix, http://assembly.coe.int/nw/xml/XRef/X2H-Xref-ViewPDF. asp?FileID=12764&lang=en.

[60] See Committee of Ministers, Resolution CM/Res(2010)26 on the Establishment of an Advisory Panel of Experts on Candidates for Election as Judge to the European Court of Human Rights (10 November 2010).

[61] For more classic literature on judicial independence and accountability, see, eg, Stephen Burbank and Barry Friedman, 'Reconsidering Judicial Independence' in Burbank and Friedman (eds) (n 3) 9; Stephen Burbank, 'What Do We Mean by "Judicial Independence"?' Faculty Scholarship. Paper 948 http://scholarship.law.upenn.edu/faculty_scholarship/948.

as swinging back and forth between the two, yielding alternately an excessively judicialised politics and an excessively politicised judiciary. This core theoretical dichotomy prompts us to ask a surprisingly vexing question: should the European judicial appointments reforms be understood as judicial independence measures or, to the contrary, as judicial accountability measures?

On the one hand, the European appointments reforms appear quite clearly to be judicial independence measures. As we demonstrated in Section II, the measures coincided quite clearly with the rise in the mid-1990s of judicial independence as both a discursive theme and as a reform agenda. But this seemingly straightforward answer glosses over some more difficult questions. If Garoupa and Ginsberg are to be believed, calls for judicial independence are the natural backlash to a period of excessive judicial subservience to political authority: 'When judges have little influence over public policy and politics, concerns over independence tend to dominate, and reformers may push for a move from a politically dependent, weak judiciary to a strong, self-regulated judiciary'.[62] But it is very difficult indeed to see how such a description might fit the two great European judicial courts. As has been abundantly clear for decades, the ECJ and the ECtHR have long been major policy and even constitutional players in the European realms; the only debate on the issue has been whether to applaud or critique this state of affairs.[63] If, as per Garoupa and Ginsberg, judicial independence measures are indeed a reaction to judicial weakness, one would therefore be hard-pressed to take the European judicial independence measures at face value. This theoretical problem is only reinforced by the fact that none of the judicial independence measures indicate that they are directed at freeing the ECJ or the ECtHR from the dominance of European political institutions: none of those measures suggest that the European Council, or the Council of Europe, or the European Parliament, or the PACE, or the Commission, or any other European political institution is somehow running roughshod over a dangerously subservient European judiciary.

On the other hand, the European appointments reforms do appear in a certain respect to function as accountability devices: after all, they subject candidates for high European judicial office to the scrutiny of blue ribbon European panels of experts. This interpretation has the advantage of aligning more cleanly with the theoretical framework of Garoupa and Ginsberg, who argue that 'once politics is judicialized in a significant way, pressures arise for greater political accountability'.[64] But such an account immediately faces two problems. First, more or less

---

[62] Garoupa and Ginsberg, 'Comparative Law and Economics of Judicial Councils' (n 3) 61; Garoupa and Ginsberg, 'Guarding the Guardians' (n 3) 117–18.

[63] Hjalte Rasmussen was one of the first legal scholars to bemoan such power openly. See Hjalte Rasmussen, *On Law and Policy in the European Court of Justice. A Comparative Study in Judicial Policymaking* (Dordrecht, Nijhoff, 1986).

[64] Garoupa and Ginsberg, 'Comparative Law and Economics of Judicial Councils' (n 3) 61; Garoupa and Ginsberg, 'Guarding the Guardians' (n 3) 117–18.

none of the endless judicial independence measures that have been passed over the last 20 years say anything at all about judicial accountability. And second, it is hard to see how any of the European reforms has subjected the ECJ, the ECtHR or their respective judges to any greater level of judicial accountability. If anything, the successful push to institute a single non-renewable judicial term at the ECtHR and mounting pressures to do so at the ECJ would appear to militate quite clearly in the opposite direction: a non-renewable term would tend to free judges from— rather than subject judges to—political accountability.[65]

How then are we to make proper use of the tactical literature? The answer is that we need to make two simple but fundamental distinctions of our own. First, we need to distinguish between the domestic and the European levels of the judicial appointments and independence issues. As we have already noted, the ECJ and the ECtHR have hardly been shrinking violets when exercising and expanding their powers. To the contrary: they have consistently made major policy interventions on everything from the supremacy and direct effect of European law, to State liability, to fundamental rights, to labour relations, and on and on.

Note, however, that this only underscores the tremendous power of the ECJ and ECtHR as *courts* when they operate as *institutions* in their *European* legal domain. But the same does not hold true when we consider the very limited power of those courts' *judges* and judicial *candidates* when they operate as *individuals* at the *domestic* level. For here, the European judges and judicial candidates have traditionally been quite vulnerable: as we have seen, both the EU and the Council of Europe had long put the national governments in the driver's seat as to both judicial appointments and judicial reappointments. With minor exceptions, those governments simply exercised 'their rightful role' (*'le rôle qui leur revenait'*) by all but unilaterally appointing 'their' judge on the ECJ and ECtHR.[66] And needless to say, short and renewable terms effectively left the sitting judges at the mercy of the good will of their own governments come reappointment time. Those governments could simply refuse to nominate those judges anew; and if they so refused, the unhappy (ex-)judges faced further difficulty finding worthy positions upon their return home, especially when—as has often been the case—successful reinsertion into the domestic judicial, governmental or professorial ranks also depended on governmental support.

Siniša Rodin is undoubtedly correct to stress that a number of institutional motivations (such as seniority within the Court) have worked to discourage

---

[65] 2010 Protocol 14 to the Convention changed the length of ECtHR judicial office from six-year renewable terms to a single, nine-year term. One might argue that scrutiny of judicial appointments functions as a sort of ex-ante judicial accountability mechanism, but this is not a terribly convincing description, as we shall soon see.

[66] See A Boerger-De Smedt, 'La Cour de justice dans les négociations du traité de Paris instituant la CECA' (2008) 14(2) *Journal of European Integration History* 7, 21 (discussing the dominant French position regarding national governmental control over ECJ appointments during the negotiations for the 1951 Treaty of Paris establishing the European Coal and Steel Community).

national governments from replacing their sitting ECJ judges.[67] But the reality on the ground is that this has by no means stopped numerous governments from refusing to re-nominate their judges through the years. This means that the judges and judicial candidates of the ECJ and ECtHR, for all of the power of their courts as European institutional actors, have traditionally been decidedly personally dependent on the good will of their national governments when they apply for European judicial positions, when they hold those positions and seek to renew them, and even when they willingly face the prospect of returning home at the conclusion of their European judicial service.

This first distinction—between the domestic and the European levels of the judicial appointments issues—therefore suggests that the judicial independence in question is not the independence of the ECJ and ECtHR from European-level political institutions, but of individual ECJ and ECHR judges and candidates from their own national governments. This double distinction (European/institutional versus domestic/individual) regarding judicial independence drives us towards a second, which now manifests on the judicial accountability front: we need to distinguish between accountability *of* judges and accountability *for* judges (and, in particular, for judicial appointments). As we have seen, nothing in the European judicial reforms institutes accountability *of* the ECJ and ECtHR or of their judges. To the contrary, the push for longer and non-renewable judicial terms (proposed at the ECJ and instituted at the ECtHR) militates in the opposite direction. On the other hand, the formal adoption of a long series of formal procedural and substantive requirements, including the establishment of the two European expert panels (the 255 Panel and the APE), has significantly changed the level of national governmental accountability *for* the candidates they propose to fill judicial posts at the ECJ and the ECtHR.

The list of such formal requirements is long and detailed. As we have seen, this is especially evident for appointments to the ECtHR. But the same can be said for the ECJ, especially given the detailed 'assessment criteria' elaborated by the 255 Panel. In its first Annual Report, composed on its own initiative, the 255 Panel laid out its six criteria for assessing judicial candidates; and these criteria included not only bold statements about the need for ECJ judges to have at least 'twenty years' experience of high level duties' and possess 'language skills and aptitude for working in an international environment in which several legal systems are represented', but also the requirement that the nominating governments lay out the procedure by which the candidates were selected, and so on.[68] The net effect of these formal procedural and substantive requirements has undoubtedly been to hold the governments far more accountable for their judicial nominations by putting them in the position of having to justify the mechanics and the results of their judicial selection procedures.

---

[67] See Siniša Rodin, 'A Metacritique of the Court of Justice of the European Union' (2016) 4 *Il Diritto dell'Unione Europea* 193.

[68] First Annual Report (n 54) at 9–11.

These assorted modes of formalisation and quality-control represent a clear change from the previously longstanding regime. Germany, France, England and the Netherlands, for example, even when joined by Spain, Portugal and Greece, had never shown any meaningful interest in vetting each other's judicial nominees. Instead, they had always preferred that European judicial appointments be governed by decidedly informal mechanisms that all but granted national governments the power to appoint their chosen candidates to the ECJ and the ECHR.

The new European judicial measures, which all date from the post-Berlin Wall period, therefore function as a thinly veiled critique directed towards the new accession states, who, it was implied, could not be trusted with similar appointment powers. But they do significantly more. They also function as a rather clever means of *imposing* control *over* judicial appointments at the same time as they function as a means of *freeing* judges *from* control. The latter part is easy to see: hemmed in by formal norms, processes and institutions, as well as by the demands imposed by quality requirements, European judicial appointments (and reappointments) would now be made in a manner less beholden to political power. These reforms thus operated as independence mechanisms.

But that is only part of the story. For the rest, the key is to recognise the fundamental asymmetry between established and the newly acceded European Member States and to analyse that asymmetry in the light of the tactical literature we have been examining. The terrible uncertainty facing the EU and the Council of Europe as they then existed came from the danger of combining a) mass accession of new Member States with b) the tremendous power of the high European courts and c) the personal vulnerability of those courts' judges to their national governments. Components b) and c) were nothing very new. But adding mass accession created a potentially toxic mix that was sufficiently unsettling to induce the existing Member States to be willing to sacrifice some measure of control over their own judicial appointments in order to take away that of their new counterparts. In other words, increasing judicial independence from governmental influence could be achieved by increasing governmental accountability for judicial appointments; and this would in turn help to protect the European status quo from the large-scale disruption that mass accession might potentially produce.

Under this new regime, the established Member States would have done exactly what Epstein, Knight and Shvetsova's theory would have predicted: they would have chosen to manage the large-scale uncertainty generated by mass accession by instituting judicial independence, thereby entrenching, or at least protecting, the European status quo. This protection of existing legislative and other bargains, to use the terminology of Landes and Posner, would have been especially attractive to the established Member States, whose political, economic and institutional interests had for decades co-evolved with the European *acquis communautaire*.[69]

---

[69] One might imagine that they may have also coevolved with what might be termed the European '*acquis humanitaire*' ie, the accretion of European human rights norms developed largely by the ECtHR. But this would be a more difficult argument to make; and I do not have the space

The price that those established Member States had to pay for such protection was a loss of control over their own judicial appointments. That said, this price turned out to be significantly less than might at first be imagined. The reason for this lies in the asymmetry between established and the newly acceded European Member States. The first reason is fundamentally numerical. The imposition of judicial quality standards—including requirements regarding seniority, experience, language skills and so on—operates quite differently in Germany than it does in Slovenia. On one level, this is simply due to the massive difference in size between the two countries. As a simple demographic matter, Germany is some 40 times the size of Slovenia, and would therefore have a pool of potential judicial candidates easily 40 times as large. But this demographic disparity is magnified on a second level: precisely because Germany has been a member of the EU and the Council of Europe since the 1950s, its educational and professional institutions have developed several generations of European jurists, ranging from professors, to EU and human rights specialists, to domestic lawyers whose substantive fields have long intersected meaningfully with European law. The brute demographic disparity is therefore multiplied by longstanding historical factors that have generated important differences in institutional and professional structures.

As a result, the imposition of the long list of judicial quality measures necessarily generates quite different effects in Slovenia than in Germany. These measures impose meaningful constraints on the Slovene government: for the new accession States, there is simply not a very large pool of viable judicial candidates to choose from, especially when one considers, for example, that the ECtHR process requires three such candidates at every appointments cycle and that the sitting judge can no longer be reappointed. And, of course, this demographic and institutional asymmetry recurs throughout contemporary Europe. Thus, if one removes Poland, the seven new Member States that acceded to the EU in 2004 (the Czech Republic, Estonia, Hungary, Latvia, Lithuania, Slovakia and Slovenia) have a combined population of some 33.5 million; meanwhile, Spain has a population of 46 million all by itself! Indeed, whereas the five biggest EU countries have been EU Members for over 30 years,[70] seven of the eight smallest EU Member States (by population) joined the Union in the post-2004 period;[71] and a dozen years is hardly sufficient for such small States to train a large core of European jurists qualified not only to fill key governmental positions (of which the European judicial posts are but one example), but also to train the next generation of such European jurists.

---

to try to make it here. For the use of the term *acquis humanitaire* in the international humanitarian law context, see Dug Cubie, 'Clarifying the *acquis humanitaire*: A Transnational Legal Perspective' in David D Caron, Michael J Kelly and Anastasia Telesetsky (eds), *The International Law of Disaster Relief* (New York, Cambridge University Press, 2014) 338.

[70] Germany, France and Italy are founder members and the UK and Spain joined the EU in 1973 and 1986, respectively.
[71] Those seven are Croatia, Cyprus, Estonia, Latvia, Lithuania, Malta and Slovenia. The eighth small country is Luxembourg, which is a Founder Member State.

The net effect of this paucity of qualified and available applicants is to limit the capacity of the ruling government in the new (and often small) accession States to play favourites on ideological, personal or other grounds and/or to demand fealty from the relatively few judicial candidates legitimately in play. But the same cannot be said for Germany and other established Member States, where the large demographic pool and/or the longstanding institutional/educational/professional structures have long yielded a deep roster of qualified candidates from which the government can pick and choose. The same quality standards, when applied across the board, yield very different practical results.

As if this were not enough, *different* standards have been applied to old and new Member States, this time regarding the judicial selection processes used by the national authorities to nominate their candidates to the ECJ and the ECtHR. Although the PACE, the Committee of Ministers, the APE, the Article 255 Panel, and so on have elaborated a long series of requirements formalising the process by which Member States should go about selecting their judicial candidates for European judicial office (such as the requirement that domestic authorities issue a formal call for candidates in the appropriate specialised press, institute and abide by formal and transparent procedures for the selection of judicial candidates, establish independent judicial selection organisms, and so on), those European institutions have been unwilling or unable to hold established Member States to those standards. Instead, they have created 'tradition'-based exceptions to the European requirements for those established Member States that have refused to abide by them. As early as 1994, for example, the Committee of Ministers instituted the following major exception to the judicial selection rules it was developing:

> Although the recommendation proposes an ideal system for judicial appointments, it was recognised (see sub-paragraph 2) that a number of the member states of the Council of Europe have adopted other systems, often involving the government, parliament or the head of state. The recommendation does not propose to change these systems which have been in operation for decades or centuries and which in practice work well.[72]

With this tradition-based distinction, the Committee of Ministers excused established Member States of the West from having to abide by the independence-based procedures that it was imposing on the new accession States of the former Eastern Bloc.

Although the Article 255 Panel has been far more discreet, it has accomplished similar results. On the one hand, it instituted a procedural demand that Member State governments explain the national procedure by which their ECJ candidates had been selected; but on the other, it held that the failure to institute a proper procedure could not be 'prejudicial' to a given candidate:

> The panel specifies that the method for selecting the candidate chosen at national level *may not be prejudicial to him or her.* In particular, the lack of a procedure enabling candidates' merits to be assessed in an independent and objective manner may not in itself

---

[72] Committee of Ministers Rec R (94) 12 (13 October 1994) at Explanatory Memorandum para 16.

constitute a handicap. It would, after all, be illogical to disadvantage candidates whose merits are to be assessed on the grounds of a selection process over which they have no control.[73]

Once again, the Panel's assessment would simply rest on the quality of the candidate.

Finally, the asymmetry between the old and new Member States emerges in the very composition of the two European expert panels established to vet the candidates proposed to sit on the ECJ and the ECtHR. The membership of these blue ribbon panels, which are composed overwhelmingly of national supreme or constitutional court judges with strong European ties, has been heavily skewed towards established and wealthy Member States from Western Europe. Of the 11 jurists who have served on the 255 Panel in its first and second term, only one—Peter Paczolay of Hungary—has come from Central or Eastern Europe. And although two of the seven current members of the APE hail from Central and Eastern Europe (Nina Vajić of Croatia and Maria Gintowt-Jankowicz of Poland), this doubling of the 255 Panel's geographic diversity hardly represents a major triumph, given that fully half the 48 Member States of the Council of Europe are located somewhere between Germany and Russia.

In short, the asymmetry between the old and new Member States surfaces at the level of the background demographics and professional institutions, at the level of the norms being applied, and at the level of the composition of the institutions applying those norms. For the new Member States, this combination puts significant bite into the judicial independence protections that have been instituted to deal with the uncertainty threatened by mass accession from the former Eastern Bloc. But it also takes a significant amount of sting out of those very protections as they apply to the longstanding Member States from Western Europe. Those established Member States have therefore been able to purchase judicial stability at relatively low cost to their capacity to manage their own judicial appointments.

This is not to say that the established Western Member States have not in fact lost some measure of control over the selection of 'their' ECJ and ECtHR judges. They have. This can be seen most clearly, for example, in such embarrassing rebukes as the 2011 refusal of the APE to accept a political ally of then President Sarkozy, Michel Hunault, as a suitable candidate to be included in the list of three to be sent to the PACE for election to fill the French opening on the ECtHR. This undeniably had consequences, as the PACE's Sub-Committee on Elections refused even to interview the French candidates, leading eventually to the withdrawal of Mr Hunault's candidacy.[74] The established Member States no doubt

---

[73] Art 255 Panel, Third Annual Activity Report 14.

[74] See Le Monde, 'Petite manœuvre pour placer un ami' 14 March 2011 http://libertes.blog. lemonde.fr/2011/03/14/petite-manoeuvre-de-lelysee-pour-placer-un-ami/; Norbert Paul Engel, 'More Transparency and Governmental Loyalty for Maintaining Professional Quality in the Election of Judges to the European Court of Human Rights' (2012) 32 *Human Rights Law Journal* 448.

draw conclusions from such encounters: they are now on notice that there are limits to what they can expect to get away with free of charge.

According to the tactical theories we have been considering, however, such a (minor) limitation and its associated costs represent no more than the (acceptable) price that the established Member States were willing to pay in order to gain what they were really seeking: protection against the (unacceptable) uncertainty that mass accession was threatening in the all-important field of judicial decision-making. For this uncertainty, to speak in the terms of Landes and Posner, threatened to undermine the totality of the legislative and even constitutional bargains that had been elaborated (ie, purchased) over the previous 40 to 50 years. In other words, large-scale accession of the new Member States from the former Eastern Bloc threatened nothing less than the *acquis* itself.

V. Conclusion: A More Complex Picture

The tactical literature offers a very compelling analysis of the judicial appointments reforms that have been instituted at the European level over the last 20 years. By foregrounding the complex if intimate relationship between judicial appointments, judicial independence, judicial accountability and political uncertainty, this literature invites us to adopt a somewhat jaded picture of the European judicial reforms, one that stresses the threatened interests of such major political players as the Member States themselves. This insight points us towards the major historical impetus behind the reforms: the mass accession of former Eastern Bloc countries to the Council of Europe in the mid-1990s and to the EU in the mid-2000s. Viewed through this lens, the creation of the Article 255 Panel and the APE in 2009–10 is but the latest (if particularly noteworthy) mechanism for managing the tremendous uncertainty threatened by the mass accession that followed the fall of the Berlin Wall.

This compelling perspective, which does indeed allow us to grasp a great deal about the European judicial reforms, should not, however, be taken as revealing the totality of the story. Member State governments represent only some of the actors and interests at stake in these ongoing developments, albeit particularly important ones. Thus, for example, a large number of judicial institutions and players—ranging from the ECJ and the ECtHR, to the domestic supreme courts, to the judges on all those courts, to such important European institutions as the Article 255 Panel, the APE and the PACE Committee on the Election of Judges, to various academic players—have played critically important roles in shaping, promoting, resisting and managing assorted aspects of these reforms.

The tactical literature, deployed in the rather State-centred and intergovernmental manner that I have used it here, should therefore be supplemented by a more neofunctionalist and neoinstitutionalist methodology that would bring these other institutional actors and interests into the centre of the picture.[75] This perspective would examine how such institutions and players have developed and advanced their own agendas and interests, sometimes in ways that are manifestly at variance with what the national governments might have predicted or desired. Such an analysis would take such institutional interventions seriously in their own right: rather than reducing them to little more than the acceptable price that the 'real' actors in the drama are willing to pay in order to advance their own agendas, it would treat those institutions as key agents in the reform process, agents who initiate, define, critique, redefine and implement much of what has come to pass.

Finally, these approaches should also be supplemented by a more constructivist prism that would resist the impulse to treat European judicial independence, judicial authority or judicial quality—or even the judicial maintenance of European legal stability—as fixed values and interests that predate their elaboration by all the players involved. Such a constructivist approach would instead examine how the assorted players, interests and alignments have themselves been developed over time through a series of contentious encounters that have gradually elaborated a series of conceptual linkages that have eventually come to appear straightforward and even natural. By layering such intergovernmentalist, neofunctionalist/ neoinstitutionalist and constructivist methodologies, we should be able to better understand the intricate interweaving of interests, issues, concepts, institutions and reforms that has, over the last 15 to 20 years, turned the once sleepy issue of European judicial appointments into an increasingly pressing matter of concern.[76]

[75] For classic statements of neofunctionalist and neoinstitutionalist theory, see, eg, Ernst Haas, *The Uniting of Europe: Political, Social, and Economic Forces, 1950–1957* 3rd edition (Notre Dame, University of Notre Dame Press, 2004); Wayne Sandholtz and Alec Stone Sweet (eds), *European Integration and Supranational Governance* (Oxford, Oxford University Press, 1998); Wayne Sandholtz, Alec Stone Sweet, Alec and Neil Fligstein (eds), *The Institutionalization of Europe* (Oxford, Oxford University Press, 2001).

[76] For the now classic statement regarding 'matters of concern', see Bruno Latour, 'Why Has Critique Run Out of Steam? From Matters of Fact to Matters of Concern' (2004) 30 *Critical Inquiry* 225.

Part IV

Substantive Law of the EU and the Transformation of Europe

7

Transformation or Reconstitution of National Regulatory Policies at the EU Level: Insiders and Outsiders under Free Movement Rules

TAMARA PERIŠIN*

I. Introduction: An Old Paradigm through a New Lens

It is no novelty that EU law grants certain fundamental freedoms to those inside the EU, and not to those outside. The core of EU law is the *internal* market embodying four fundamental freedoms of movement, while *external* trade or movement is not given the same fundamental status. This chapter seeks to examine this well-known paradigm through the lens of critical theory.

It is generally understood that the internal market has transformed Europe, but this chapter discusses whether this internal transformation is in fact only a reconstitution of national protectionist policies at the EU level by giving (now a larger and different group of) insiders substantial rights which are not matched by rights for outsiders (especially outsider people). Full transformation would require also 'better' treatment of the external movement and of the outsiders. The chapter examines the role of the European Court of Justice (ECJ) in this transformation or reconstitution. It argues that the Court has some leeway to step away from the formal differentiation of internal trade/movement rules that are given the status of fundamental freedoms on the one hand, and powerless external

* Jean Monnet Professor, University of Zagreb. Thanks to Nika Bačić Selanec, Martijn van den Brink, Melita Carević, Tamara Ćapeta, Iris Goldner Lang and Pierre Schlag for comments on earlier drafts; to Daniela Caruso, Duncan Kennedy, Roberto Unger and Ilaria Vianello for useful discussions relevant to the chapter; and to Sam Koplewicz for his research assistance and passionate conversations on the world order. Finally, special thanks to Karma Perišin for being a role model in critical thinking, courage and compassion, all being equally essential in personal development as well as in the transformation of Europe.

trade/movement rules on the other. The chapter provides counterarguments to potential conservative critics of the Court by showing that the Court can legitimately take progressive steps.

It should also be said here that during the process of writing this chapter, and even since the Zagreb critical legal studies (CLS) conference in June 2015, Europe has undergone several transformations. The escalation of the migration crisis in the summer of 2015 triggered the best and the worst in EU citizens and their leaders. German Chancellor Angela Merkel famously invited refugees to Germany and said it was her 'damn duty' to help them.[1] Finland's prime minister offered his second home to a refugee family.[2] In many other European countries both the leaders and the people attempted to welcome the refugees. However, as the numbers of migrants were rapidly growing, fears of terrorism, of economic costs and of cultural differences grew as well. These fears led to walls being built or razor-wire fences being installed on the EU's internal borders, even within the Schengen area. Fears have also led to an 'EU–Turkey deal'[3] which was supposed to control irregular migration into the EU. There has also been a rise of nationalism within the EU.

It is well known that free movement, free trade and globalisation lead to economic advantages, but not for everyone. Adam Smith's theory of absolute advantage and David Ricardo's theory of comparative advantage show that individual producers benefit from specialising in an area where they have an advantage, and then trading.[4] This is also to the benefit of consumers who get to enjoy a wider selection of goods and services at lower prices, ultimately benefiting the country as a whole. Of course, the uncompetitive producer loses. Still, instead of protecting the 'losers' through protectionist policies, it is expected that governments will put into place various instruments of social policy that will make change easier.

---

[1] Merkel-Pressekonferenz, 'Wir brauchen jetzt deutsche Flexibilität' Spiegel Online (1 September 2015), www.spiegel.de/video/angela-merkel-mit-flexibilitaet-fluechtlingen-helfen-video-1603986.html; T Paterson, 'Angela Merkel: "It's Our Damned Duty to Help Refugees"' Independent (8 October 2015) www.independent.co.uk/news/world/europe/angela-merkel-its-our-damned-duty-to-help-refugees-a6686631.html.

[2] A Withnal, 'Refugee Crisis: Finland's Prime Minister Pledges to Give Up his Home to Accommodate Refugees' *Independent* (6 September 2015) www.independent.co.uk/news/world/europe/refugee-crisis-finlands-prime-minister-pledges-to-give-up-his-home-to-accommodate-refugees-10488580.html.

[3] EU-Turkey Statement (18 March 2016) www.consilium.europa.eu/en/press/press-releases/2016/03/18-eu-turkey-statement/.

[4] Adam Smith, *An Inquiry into the Nature and Causes of the Wealth of Nations*, Edwin Cannan (ed), (first published 1776, London, Methuen and Co, 1904) www.econlib.org/library/Smith/smWN.html; D Ricardo, *On the Principles of Political Economy and Taxation* (London, John Murray, 1821) www.econlib.org/LIBRARY/Ricardo/ricP1.html.

Brexit clearly confirms that not everyone benefits from European integration or globalisation. 'The benefits of globalization aren't universal, and even if they are positive, they aren't well understood'.[5] There are people in Europe who are de iure insiders as they have EU nationality, but feel as de facto outsiders since they do not feel the benefits of EU integration. They voted to leave the EU, believing that by blocking the inflow of other EU citizens, primarily those from Central and Eastern Europe, and by stopping the immigration of third-country nationals, they could regain some benefits that existed in a closed market.

However, one cannot turn back time. The development of technology, including cheap and fast travel and the internet, has strongly connected the world. And the spread of English has made global communication so easy. Goods, services, capital and people move more easily across the globe than ever before. Brexit, or most types of protectionism, is a bad reaction to the fact that the world is interconnected, and will not address underlying problems,[6] such as job losses for certain categories of workers, and growing inequality.

The EU and national institutions, including the courts, should be aware that limiting the rights of outsiders will not do much to help those who are inside the EU to feel as true insiders of the EU project. While it is certain that EU leaders need to work on popular support for the EU project,[7] this should not be done through simplistic populist measures or in ways which would worsen the treatment of outsiders. I thus argue that the European Court of Justice can legitimately do more to improve the treatment of outsiders in the EU. For example, while the General Court has recently rejected jurisdiction for reviewing the legality of the EU–Turkey deal on controlling irregular migration,[8] on appeal the Court of Justice could legitimately accept jurisdiction, and substantively do more for the rights of outsiders despite any current political pressure.

Following this introduction, the analysis is structured in two main parts. The first main part explains the key concepts and premises—it lays out the traditional narrative of European integration; it defines insiders and outsiders under EU law; it identifies parts of CLS that give a fresh perspective on this segment of EU law, namely the critique of rights and of legal education. The second main part focuses on the role of the ECJ in this field and shows what space the ECJ has for policy decisions on the treatment of insiders and outsiders. This is followed by a conclusion.

---

[5] B Francesca, '"Brexit" Vote Gave Me a Harsh, Belated Wake-Up Call' *New York Times* (2 July 2016) www.nytimes.com/2016/07/03/world/europe/brexit-vote-gave-me-a-harsh-belated-wake-up-call.html?_r=0.

[6] Miguel Poiares Maduro, 'A falsa escolha e uma falsa solução' *Observador* (24 June 2016) http://observador.pt/opiniao/a-falsa-escolha-e-uma-falsa-solucao/.

[7] Manuel Muniz, 'Brexit Exemplifies the Anti-Elite Era' *Social Europe* (27 June 2016) www.socialeurope.eu/2016/06/brexit-exemplifies-the-anti-elite-era/.

[8] Case T-257/16 *NM v European Council* EU:T:2017:130.

II. Key Concepts and Premises

A. The Traditional European Narrative

The narrative of European integration often starts with the story of Robert Schuman and his famous Declaration delivered on 9 May 1950.[9] The narrative explains that Schuman's aim was to ensure peace and wellbeing on the European continent that had been severely harmed by two world wars. This was to be done through the cooperation of European states first in the field of coal and steel, then through wider economic integration and finally through integration in many other fields that would make European states so closely connected that war would be inconceivable. This narrative is supported by the text of the founding treaties which also place market integration at the core of the European project, but with the aim of ensuring progress and closeness in Europe. For example, the original Article 2 of the EEC Treaty signed in 1957 stated that the aim of the European Community

> shall be ... by establishing a Common Market and progressively approximating the economic policies of Member States, to promote throughout the Community a harmonious development of economic activities, a continuous and balanced expansion, an increased stability, an accelerated raising of the standard of living and closer relations between its Member States.[10]

However, this well-known narrative omits to mention an important part of Schuman's idea. Schuman does not speak of 'European peace', but instead he opens with these words: '*World* peace cannot be safeguarded without the making of creative efforts proportionate to the dangers which threaten it.'[11] In his declaration, 'an organized and living Europe' is not an end in itself. That Europe has to make a 'contribution ... to civilization' which is 'indispensable to the maintenance of peaceful relations'.[12] And coal and steel 'production will be offered to the *world* as a whole without distinction or exception, with the aim of contributing to raising living standards and to promoting peaceful achievement'.[13] Schuman specially emphasises that '[w]ith increased resources Europe will be able to pursue the achievement of one of its essential tasks, namely, the development of the African continent'.[14]

---

[9] Declaration by French Foreign Minister Robert Schuman, 9 May 1950.
[10] Art 2 Treaty Establishing the European Economic Community, 1957.
[11] Schuman, Declaration (n 9) (emphasis added).
[12] ibid.
[13] ibid (emphasis added).
[14] Roberto Mangabeira Unger, *Democracy Realized: The Progressive Alternative* (London, Verso, 1998) eg 45, 53, 87.

Schuman's idea does not have to be seen as that of European imperialism in the world.[15] Rather, it can easily be viewed as an idea informed by the global connectedness and mutual dependence that was supposed to be suitable for the post World War II world. What the world wars have shown is that there is no long-term world peace without peace in Europe, and, equally, there is no peace in Europe without world peace.

I am not trying to make an originalist argument in the sense of Scalia originalism. I do not think that the Treaties must be interpreted in the way Europe's founding fathers envisaged them. Instead, this chapter is an attempt to show that the set-up of the EU and its key policies give judges space to seek to secure justice when deciding on precise cases. The Court of Justice has heavily relied on what it has called the teleological interpretation of the Treaties, and it can easily be construed that the *telos* of European integration is global wellbeing and global peace. All this is relevant for assessing the EU's treatment of insiders versus outsiders.

B. Defining Insiders versus Outsiders of European Integration

Much of the current critique of the EU, including that coming from the CLS, is for the difference in treatment of insiders and outsiders. There are two ways in which one can distinguish who is an insider and who an outsider in the European Union: the nationality-based differentiation (de iure) and the benefits-based differentiation (de facto).

i. Nationality-based Differentiation of Insiders and Outsiders

The first and relatively obvious way of differentiating insiders and outsiders is the nationality approach based on the country of origin (de iure). Insiders are those who hold EU nationality, regardless of whether these are persons or goods.[16] Outsiders are all the others. And under EU law, insiders and outsiders defined in this way receive very different treatment.

a. Movement of Goods

In the area of movement of goods, insiders, ie goods produced within the EU, are granted the fundamental freedom of movement. EU law has in many ways transformed the traditional lifestyles in EU Member States by taking a very proactive approach in eliminating (arguably) all obstacles to the movement of goods. In the

---

[15] For the opposite argument, see Peo Hansen and Stefan Johnsson, *Eurafrica: The Untold History of European Integration and Colonialism* (London, Bloomsbury, 2014).

[16] The problem does not in the same way arise in the area of capital movement as the EU has an interest in foreign capital investment.

famous *Dassonville* judgment, the Court held that '[a]ll trading rules enacted by member-States which are capable of hindering, directly or indirectly, actually or potentially, intra-Community trade are to be considered as measures having an effect equivalent to quantitative restrictions' and are thus prima facie prohibited.[17] The principle of mutual recognition introduced in *Cassis de Dijon* additionally requires that a product lawfully produced and marketed in one Member State has to be granted market access in another Member State unless there is a justified reason for preventing this.[18] This elimination of barriers through deregulation (negative integration) is accompanied by the EU's reregulation (positive integration) where the EU legislature actively tries to set rules to eliminate obstacles to movement.

Concerning outsider goods, ie products from third countries, there are a number of EU rules that make their access to the EU market very difficult. First, these can be deliberate obstacles to trade. Prime examples are custom duties (tariffs) and subsidies which remain significant in some sectors, such as agriculture. Second, complicated decision-making processes can also lead to obstacles to trade. For example, in the famous WTO dispute *EC–Biotech*, the problem was that the EU was so divided on the issue of genetically modified organisms (GMOs) that it was unable to adopt a functioning regulatory framework, and this led to a five year moratorium on the approval (or rejection) of GMOs.[19] The Council was unable to reach a qualified majority either to approve or to reject new GMO products.[20] The problem in this case was thus not that GMO products were rejected, but that the EU had unmanageable gridlocked procedures. Third, the EU regulatory process often brings about regulatory peaks which are obstacles to external trade. In a situation where Member States have different rules, it often happens that the strictest of these national rules (the regulatory peak) are adopted at the EU level as the EU standard. For example, after three Member States banned snus, a type of oral, smokeless tobacco, it was banned by the EU; after two Member States banned seal products, they were banned by the EU.[21] There are a number of reasons why the EU regulatory process works in this way, but what is relevant here is that while such EU-wide strict standards (arguably) eliminate obstacles to internal trade,[22]

---

[17] Case 8/74 *Procureur du Roi v Dassonville* EU:C:1974:82.

[18] Case 120/78 *Rewe-Zentrale AG v Bundesmonopolverwaltung fur Branntwein* EU:C:1979:42 (hereinafter: *Cassis de Dijon*).

[19] *European Communities—Measures Affecting the Approval And Marketing of Biotech Products*, Reports of the Panel, WT/DS291/R, WT/DS292/R, WT/DS293/R, 29 September 2006.

[20] See Council of the European Union, Press Release (provisional version) of the 2849th Council Meeting Agriculture and Fisheries, 6199/08, Presse 33, 18 February 2008, 6, www.consilium.europa.eu/ueDocs/cms_Data/docs/pressData/en/agricult/98819.pdf.

[21] T Perišin, 'EU Regulatory Policy and World Trade: Should All EU Institutions Care What the World Thinks?' (2015) 11(1) *European Constitutional Law Review* 99.

[22] For an argument that regulatory peaks also create obstacles to internal trade, see, eg, T Perišin, 'Is the EU Seal Products Regulation a Sealed Deal?—EU and WTO Challenges' (2013) 62(2) *International and Comparative Law Quarterly* 373.

they cause significant obstacles to external trade and often lead to disputes in the WTO. The EU has (arguably) lost all of the WTO cases on EU regulatory standards (*EC–Hormones*,[23] *EC–Sardines*,[24] *EC–Biotech*,[25] *EC–Seals*)[26] as these measures were not in accordance with WTO rules, having been either protectionist or not based on science.[27]

For outsider goods that manage to overcome these various obstacles to market access, the single market then brings some benefits. Benefits are enjoyed by outsider goods after they are placed on the internal market in any of the Member States. For example, the principle of mutual recognition allows a product from a third country to be placed in one EU Member State, and it then has access to the markets of other EU Member States unless there is a justified reason for denying this. Similarly, EU harmonisation can make the position of a third-country producer easier, especially in the case of minimal harmonisation. In this case, a good from a third country can comply with the rules of a Member State with the least stringent regime and then its market access to other EU Member States has to be recognised.

b. Movement of People

In the area of the movement of people, the difference in the movement of insiders and outsiders is even more visible.

EU insiders, ie EU citizens, can avail themselves of the fundamental freedom of movement of workers, service providers/recipients, and of the right of establishment. Alongside these market freedoms, there is a plethora of legal instruments such as the general principles of law, the Charter, the ECHR and the common constitutional traditions of Member States that grant these persons fundamental rights. Finally, they have a number of rights under the umbrella of EU citizenship, eg 'the right to move and reside freely within the territory of the Member States'.[28]

Unsurprisingly, de iure outsiders, ie third-country nationals, do not enjoy such broad rights. This is at the core of Roberto Unger's critique of the World Trade Organization (WTO), as well as of the EU. Such liberalisation creates structures where things and money can move freely while people remain 'imprisoned' in

---

[23] WTO, EC—Measures Concerning Meat and Meat Products (Hormones), Report of the Appellate Body (16 January 1998) WT/DS26/AB/R and WT/DS48/AB/R.

[24] WTO, European Communities: Trade Description of Sardines—Report of the Appellate Body (26 September 2002) WT/DS231/AB/R.

[25] WTO, EC—Measures Affecting the Approval and Marketing of Biotech Products, Panel Reports (29 September 2006) WT/DS291-293/R.

[26] WTO, EC—Measures Prohibiting the Importation and Marketing of Seal Products, Report of the Appellate Body (22 May 2014) WT/DS400&401/AB/R.

[27] T Perišin, 'Transatlantic Trade Disputes on Health, Environmental and Animal Welfare Standards: Background to Regulatory Divergence and Possible Solutions' (2014) 10 *Croatian Yearbook of European Law* 249.

[28] Art 20 TFEU.

their own states.[29] Instead of broad and deep liberalisation in some areas, and no liberalisation in others, according to Unger a fairer regime would have been the parallel gradual liberalisation of all areas, with safeguards tackling the negative sides of liberalisation.[30] However, as the law stands, there is no global right of free movement of humans.

It is somewhat odd that even some rights categorised by the EU Charter as 'fundamental rights' are not recognised for non-nationals. For example, Article 42 on the right of access to documents and Article 43 on access to the Ombudsman are not open to everyone, but create an entitlement only for 'any citizen of the Union and any natural or legal person residing or having its registered office in a Member State'.[31]

Over the years there has been a trend for third-country nationals to be given more rights either due to their connection with EU citizens or companies (derivative rights) or on their own merit (non-derivative rights).[32] There is a plethora of international agreements,[33] EU Treaties,[34] legislation or case law on the rights of third-country nationals. However, these rights differ depending on how the person is categorised (eg highly qualified employee, student, seasonal worker, etc)[35] and for most categories they are not very broad. The system is 'over-complicated, user-unfriendly and ... falls short of elaborating a truly European approach'.[35] There is nothing like a global free movement right or an obligation of States to facilitate global movement.

c. Contrast between the Movement of Outsider Goods and Outsider People

While there are de iure differentiations of insider versus outsider goods as well as between insider and outsider people, there is another contrast worth highlighting. This is the one between outsider goods and outsider persons.

---

[29] On hypermobility of capital versus lack of mobility for humans, see Unger (n 14) 42, 176.

[30] Unger also has ideas on how to introduce additional measures accompanying global movement (eg a receiving country should compensate the poorer country exporting a skilled worker). Unger (n 14) 178.

[31] Charter of Fundamental Rights of the European Union [2012] OJ C 326/02. There is also discussion on the extent to which Art 41 of the Charter on the right to good administration is open to those who are not EU citizens, as the article starts with the words 'every person', but it is placed in the chapter titled 'Citizens' rights'. See on this Ilaria Vianello, 'EU External Relations and EU Administrative Law: A Long Due Encounter', EUI thesis, 2016.

[32] For an overview, see D Kochenov and M van den Brink, 'Pretending There Is No Union: Non-Derivative Quasi-Citizenship Rights of Third-Country Nationals in the EU' (2015) 7 *EUI Working Papers*.

[33] eg United Nations Geneva Convention relating to the Status of Refugees, 1951; 1967 Protocol Relating to the Status of Refugees.

[34] eg the EU Charter of Fundamental Rights even provides that the right of asylum is a fundamental right (Art 18).

[35] I Goldner Lang, 'The European Union and Migration: An Interplay of National, Regional and International Law' (forthcoming) *AJIL Unbound*.

[36] ibid.

For third-country goods, it is relatively easy to get the same rights as domestic goods. Once a product from a third country is placed on the market of one EU Member State, it gains access to the entire single market. Mutual recognition as developed in *Cassis de Dijon* applies equally to goods produced in the EU and those from third countries once they have been lawfully placed in the market of any Member State.

This mutual recognition and free movement rights given to third-country goods are not given to third-country nationals. In stark contrast to the regime applicable to third-country goods, third-country nationals remain tied to one Member State. This is true both for regular and irregular migrants.[37]

Regarding 'regular' legal migrants, there is no EU-wide free movement right for migrants who are legally within the EU. Article 79(5) Treaty on the Functioning of the European Union (TFEU) reserves for Member States the right to 'determine volumes of admission of third-country nationals coming from third countries to their territory in order to seek work, whether employed or self-employed'. The national regime is seen also in the fact that long-term resident status is given only to non-EU nationals who have legally and continuously resided for a period of five years within the territory of one Member State.[38] Those persons then become quasi-citizens, and gain free movement rights within the EU, but States still have the right to limit the total number of admitted third-country nationals. Some EU official documents testify that there is political will to allow more EU-wide movement of migrants who are legally within the EU, but this will was never strong enough to be turned into legislation.[39]

In similar stark contrast to the mutual recognition applied to the movement of goods is the position of irregular migrants. Rules on asylum, largely embodied in the Dublin Regulation, regulate which Member State is responsible for a particular asylum seeker and define his or her movement rights within the EU, and this is typically the country of first entry.[40] Even after the refugee status of a person is established by one Member State, there is no mutual recognition of that status in other States. Section III of the chapter will examine the Court's case law on this.

---

[37] For details about the movement of third-country nationals within the EU, see Nika Bačić Selanec, 'Article 79 TFEU: Common Immigration Policy—Legal and Irregular Migration' in Hermann-Josef Blanke and Stelio Mangiameli (eds), *The Treaty on Functioning of the European Union (TFEU)—A Commentary* (New York, Springer, forthcoming).

[38] Council Dir 2003/109/EC of 25 November 2003 concerning the status of third-country nationals who are long-term residents. Thanks to Martijn Van den Brink for reminding me of this example.

[39] Presidency Conclusions, Tampere European Council 15, 16 October 1999—Part III—Fair treatment of third-country nationals; The Stockholm Programme—An open and secure Europe serving and protecting citizens [2010] OJ C 115/01, 6.1.4, 6.1.5; Bačić Selanec (n 37).

[40] According to the Dublin Reg, there is a hierarchy of criteria so the criterion of first entry is subsidiary to special criteria concerning minors, existing family ties in the EU, a valid visa, etc. Chapter III, Reg (EU) No 604/2013 of the European Parliament and of the Council of 26 June 2013 establishing the criteria and mechanisms for determining the Member State responsible for examining an application for international protection lodged in one of the Member States by a third-country national or a stateless person [2013] OJ L 180/31.

ii. Benefits-based Differentiation of Insiders and Outsiders

Another way of differentiating insiders and outsiders is the benefits approach that looks at who can benefit from certain opportunities (de facto). Insiders get some opportunities, and outsiders do not. This differentiation can be applied both to goods and to persons, but it is more visible in respect of the latter.

Roberto Unger speaks of the EU's 'insiders' as those belonging to groups that can benefit from the current social structure, and of 'outsiders' that cannot do the same. Insiders work in 'the most advanced [and small] sectors of the economy: the sectors that are now the favoured home of innovation-friendly cooperation and that have become responsible for an increasing part of the creation of new wealth'.[41] By contrast, 'outsiders' represent 'the vast majority of people who are lifted above poverty [but] are excluded from [these sectors] as well as from the education which prepares people for them'.[42] To remedy this inequality, according to Unger, the current set-up of the EU would have to be turned upside down. The EU would have to guarantee not market rights, but social rights, and in particular high-quality lifelong education that develops 'skills and habits of perpetual, piecemeal experimentation ... teach[ing] people how to probe and take the next steps'[43] enabling the individual to be flexible on the job market and 'to participate in a form of production that increasingly becomes a practice of collective learning and pertinent innovation'.[44] In contrast, the lower levels should be allowed to experiment with the market.[45]

More recent work on insiders and outsiders in the EU has mostly focused on the adverse distributive effects that EU law can have on Central and Eastern Europe. For example, Daniela Caruso has written how EU market integration and centralisation in certain fields limits the opportunities of some EU citizens and causes adverse distributive effects, particularly on new Member States.[46] Similarly, Damjan Kukovec has argued that the EU periphery, although formally a part of the EU, remains like an outsider when it comes to certain benefits, as EU antitrust and internal market rules give a structural advantage to the EU centre.[47] This work

---

[41]   Roberto Mangabeira Unger, *Left Alternative* (London, Verso, 2005) 89.

[42]   ibid.

[43]   ibid 92–93.

[44]   ibid.

[45]   'The European Union is now developing according to the principle that economic regulation is centralized while social and educational policy remains local. Exactly the inverse of this regime should prevail. There should be expanding scope for economic experimentation on the ground. By contrast, a core responsibility of the Union should be to guarantee the endowment—especially the education endowment—of all its citizens.' ibid 93.

[46]   Caruso has argued that EU-wide uniform contract rules could have regressive effects on certain sellers, particularly from new Member States. Daniela Caruso, 'The "Justice Deficit" Debate in EU Private Law: New Directions' (23 August 2012) *Boston University School of Law, Public Law Research Paper* No 12-42, 7, http://ssrn.com/abstract=2135111 or http://dx.doi.org/10.2139/ssrn.2135111.

[47]   Damjan Kukovec, 'Economic Law, Inequality and Hidden Hierarchies on the EU Internal Market' (2016) 38(1) *Michigan Journal of International Law*; *EUI Department of Law Research Paper No 7* http://ssrn.com/abstract=2748559.

is relevant because it explains how goods from the EU periphery remain marginalised in the EU single market (de facto outsider goods).

In addition to outsiders in the new Member States, Brexit now clearly highlights that even in the old Member States in Western Europe there can be a significant proportion of people who are or feel like outsiders. Marija Bartl's work on the internal market rationality sheds some light on this.[48] She explains how the neo-liberal agenda has 'reified' the aim of establishment and functioning of the internal market.[49] The aim of the internal market has become incontestable, so both deregulation, reregulation and external activities of the EU are done in the name of achieving this aim.[50] Competing aims and ideologies have caved in under the neo-liberal view of the internal market as pushed by the European Commission (and have only slowed down or slightly moderated the economic agenda).[51] Those who were unable to find their place in the internal market (less educated workers, weaker consumers, the digitally inactive, etc) have become outsiders to the process of integration.[52]

While I would argue that the existence of de facto outsiders might only partly be due to the functioning of the EU, and that it is more broadly caused by the functioning of the global market economy, it is certainly true that Brexit and similar expressions of dissatisfaction in other countries require revisiting the basic (arguably 'reified') assumptions of the EU set-up. Unger's and Bartl's outsiders, and Brexit 'leave' voters are (arguably) the ones who believed that they cannot benefit from European integration, and they did not see Europe bringing them benefits which they wanted. The Brexit voters even believed that the internal market would enable nationals of other EU Member States to 'plunder' Britain's social welfare system paid for by generations of British people. Thus, recently Alexander Somek also writes that '[i]t is essential ... that a European Union reverses its perverse federalist make-up. The current combination of free movement conflicting with nationally-conceived social welfare systems is a recipe for political disaster'.[53] It is reasonable to assume that there will be changes in EU law that will attempt to respond to the legitimacy crisis. What is relevant for this chapter is that parts of the problem can be solved without Treaty amendments, but by simply reading the Treaties in a different light.

---

[48] Marija Bartl, 'Internal Market Rationality, Private Law and the Direction of the Union: Resuscitating the Market as the Object of the Political' (2015) 21(5) *European Law Journal* 572; Marija Bartl, 'Internal Market Rationality: In the Way of Re-imagining the Future' unpublished, on file with author.

[49] Bartl, 'Internal Market Rationality: In the Way of Re-imagining the Future', ibid.

[50] ibid.

[51] ibid.

[52] ibid.

[53] Alexander Somek, 'Four Impious Points on Brexit' (2016) 17 *German Law Journal*, Brexit Special Supplement 107.

C. Critique of Rights and Legal Education

Duncan Kennedy's critique of rights sheds new light on the EU's differentiation of insiders and outsiders. Through the lens of this critique one can express phenomena that we observe in the EU—injustice can happen both to those with and without rights based on EU law. De iure outsiders who do not enjoy the rights of free movement are not well off, but also many de iure insiders who formally have rights of free movement are also not well off as they are de facto outsiders.

While Kennedy's critique of rights is something well known to all versed in CLS, it might not be so familiar to European lawyers so, at the risk of oversimplifying a big idea, I will attempt to summarise it.

The critique tells us that rights are a formal concept that can prevent the delivery of justice. In a rights-based society, a formal distinction is made between those for whom the legal system recognises rights and those who do not have such recognised rights. As Pierre Schlag brought to my attention, this point depends on how one defines rights, whether these are individual rights, group rights or something even broader, and whether rights need to be in some way individualised so as to be justiciable, ie that the entity endowed with the right could serve as a claimant before a court.[54] For the purposes of the present chapter, rights will be understood narrowly as belonging only to individuals or identifiable groups, although some are not necessarily justiciable before courts, but impose some other (softer) obligation on decision-makers and inform the courts. So under this view, because rights and justice are different things, law enforcement and society tolerate the possible injustice that occurs as a consequence. In this system, law and justice are different things.

According to Kennedy, the '[r]ights talk was the language of the group—the white male bourgeoisie'[55] and

[s]ince the bourgeois revolutions, one group after another has defined its struggle for inclusion in the social, economic, and political order as a rational demand for enjoyment of the same rights of freedom and equality that belong to a postulated 'normal,' 'abstract' citizen in a bourgeois democracy.[56]

As Kennedy points out:

[a]n important part of the struggle between liberals and conservatives within these societies has been over how far to go in incorporating those not included in the initial Liberal formulation of the Rights of Man into the order the revolutions established for a select few.[57]

---

[54] Pierre Schlag's comments to the draft of this text.

[55] D Kennedy, 'The Critique of Rights in Critical Legal Studies' in W Brown and J Halley (eds), *Left Legalism/Left Critique* (Durham NC, Duke University Press, 2002) 214, http://duncankennedy.net/documents/The%20Critique%20of%20Rights%20in%20cls.pdf.

[56] ibid.

[57] ibid.

Kennedy argues that this 'rights discourse is a trap'[58] because

> [t]his framework is, in itself, a part of the problem rather than of the solution. It makes it difficult even to conceptualize radical proposals ... [b]ecause it is incoherent and manipulable, traditionally individualist, and willfully blind to the realities of substantive inequality.
>
> ...
>
> [T]o speak of rights is precisely not to speak of justice between social classes, races or sexes.[59]

When one uses Kennedy's perspective on EU law, one sees that EU law is also based on a formal difference in rights. De iure insiders who want to move (themselves, or their services, goods, companies) have not only the freedom to do so, but have a freedom that enjoys a fundamental, 'constitutional' status. In contrast, de iure outsiders who want to move do not have any individual right to do so. Lawyers and laymen alike understand that this difference is based on legal documents, primarily on EU Treaties. The EU Treaties are an agreement between EU Member States that was intended to give the rights of internal movement, and not to guarantee movement for those outside the EU. However, as Kennedy suggests, this formal differentiation should not make one feel comfortable with injustices that can occur as a consequence. Legal rules and their application are a consequence of a balance of power at a particular moment. They are 'frozen politics'.[60] Legal rules are a snapshot of political power and political will at the moment of their adoption.

All legal rules leave considerable space for judges where another snapshot is taken capturing the moment when the judgment is rendered. Thus, the courts have a role in creating a balance of power at the moment when they are giving a judgment. This does not mean that the courts can disregard written law, eg the Treaty differentiation of insiders and outsiders. The courts do have to find some reasonable meaning of the existing rules, but in doing so they tilt the balance of power, and their interpretation and application inevitably favour either one side or the other in the dispute. This remains true both when they are interpreting and applying primary sources such as Constitutions or Treaties in the EU context, as well as when they are acting on the basis of legislation, although legislation could be more detailed, leaving less space for judges.

EU law (or any law) must also not be taught as dogma. Students should be educated to see that Treaty texts are not God given. They are man-made and interpreted by men and women (although the latter occurs more seldom, but that is a matter for another text). I agree with Kennedy who points out that

> [m]ost liberal students believe that the liberal program can be reduced to guaranteeing people their rights and to bringing about the triumph of human rights over mere

[58] ibid.
[59] ibid.
[60] Roberto Mangabeira Unger's conversations with the author.

property rights. In this picture, the trouble with the legal system is that it fails to put the state behind the rights of the oppressed, or that the system fails to enforce the rights formally recognized.[61]

EU law students should not accept as dogma the concept of fundamental freedoms, nor accept that there is a given definition on who is an insider and who is an outsider that can benefit from EU law. This does not mean that one should completely abandon the language of rights, and neither is that Duncan Kennedy's argument, but one should be aware that the legal and real world have space for other categories as well. In reality, injustice can happen both to de iure outsiders because they do not have formal rights, but also to de iure insiders despite formally enjoying special rights.

III. Role of the Court in the Treatment of Insiders and Outsiders

It is quite broadly accepted that the Court of Justice has internally transformed Europe. There is abundant academic writing on how and why this was done.[62] The Court of Justice has played a pivotal role in granting rights to the 'oppressed'. Through its case law, it has developed a number of individual rights such as non-discrimination on the grounds of nationality,[63] gender,[64] age,[65] disability[66] (including obesity),[67] etc. Furthermore, the Court's constructs of direct effect,[68] supremacy,[69] interpretative effect[70] and some other characteristics of EU law have contributed to the actual enforcement of rights.

However, has the Court had the same transformative role when it comes to the treatment of the EU's outsiders, or has the Court participated in the reconstitution of national protectionism against outsiders at the EU level? Is there more that the Court could/should do in transforming the EU's treatment of outsiders?

---

[61] Duncan Kennedy, 'Legal Education as Training for Hierarchy' (1982) 32 *Journal of Legal Education* 521, 598.

[62] Most notably, Eric Stein, 'Lawyers, Judges and the Making of a Transnational Constitution' (1981) 75 *American Journal of International Law* 1; JHH Weiler, 'The Transformation of Europe' in JHH Weiler (ed), *The Constitution of Europe* (Cambridge, Cambridge University Press, 1999).

[63] Case C-415/93 *Bosman* EU:C:1995:463.

[64] Case 43/75 *Defrenne* EU:C:1976:56.

[65] Case C-427/06 *Bartsch* EU:C:2008:517.

[66] Case C-303/06 *Coleman* EU:C:2008:415.

[67] Case C-354/13 *Kaltoft* EU:C:2014:2463.

[68] Case 26/62 *Van Gend en Loos* EU:C:1963:1.

[69] Case 6/64 *Costa v ENEL* EU:C:1964:66.

[70] Case 14/83 *Von Colson and Elisabeth Kamann* EU:C:1984:153.

A. The Role of the Court in the Movement of Goods

In the area of *goods*, the Court has made a sharp distinction between insider goods (those originating in one Member State or those from third countries once they have already been placed in the EU market) and outsider goods. It was said above that there is a distinction between the rights granted to those who trade with insider goods, and those who import outsider goods into the EU. What I want to make clear at this point is that, while this differentiation does have a basis in the Treaty text, it was primarily the Court's case law that made this differentiation so huge.

Relevant Treaty provisions on the free movement of goods are textually not very different from the provisions that can be found in other international agreements such as the General Agreement on Tariffs and Trade (GATT). For example, Article 34 TFEU banning quantitative restrictions and measures having equivalent effect on the imports of goods is textually comparable to Article XI GATT[71] and functionally comparable to Article III:4 GATT.[72] However, the Court has, quite understandably, given this provision a much broader meaning than was done by the GATT or WTO Panels or the WTO Appellate Body. As Schlag's contribution systematises it, the Court used a purposivist interpretation, while the WTO 'judicial' bodies tried to appear very restrained in narrow textualist interpretation.[73] The Court has established that this provision has direct effect so it can be directly invoked by individuals before national courts and trump incompatible national laws. It also trumps incompatible EU legislation. The Court has also given this provision a very broad scope, starting from the *Dassonville* case where it found that any obstacle to trade, even one that only indirectly or only potentially hinders trade, is prima facie prohibited.[74] This broad interpretation was further strengthened in *Cassis de Dijon* when it was the Court (not the Treaty text) that introduced the principle of mutual recognition (explained above).[75] While the Court's interpretation of Article 34 TFEU has changed over time and was in some cases narrowed,[76] the fact remains that the provision is still much broader than any functionally comparable provision, including those in national

---

[71] Art XI:1 GATT states that '[no] prohibitions or restrictions other than duties, taxes or other charges, whether made effective through quotas, import or export licences or other measures, shall be instituted or maintained by any contracting party on the importation of any product of the territory of any other contracting party or on the exportation or sale for export of any product destined for the territory of any other contracting party'.

[72] Art III:4 GATT provides that '[t]he products of the territory of any contracting party imported into the territory of any other contracting party shall be accorded treatment no less favourable than that accorded to like products of national origin in respect of all laws, regulations and requirements affecting their internal sale, offering for sale, purchase, transportation, distribution or use …'.

[73] See Pierre Schlag, 'On Textualist and Purposivist Interpretation (Challenges and Problems)' (in this volume).

[74] *Dassonville* (n 17).

[75] *Cassis de Dijon* (n 18).

[76] Joined Cases C-267/91 and C-268/91 *Keck* EU:C:1993:905.

Constitutions, such as the dormant commerce clause in the US Constitution.[77] The provision (arguably) prima facie bans all measures significantly hindering market access to another Member State, even when the measure has no protectionist purpose, discriminatory text or even discriminatory effect. The Court, as well as numerous commentators, has found support for this interpretation in the ambitious aims of the Treaties. For example, Miguel Maduro explained that the ECJ's interpretation of the EU free movement provisions was even broader than the US Supreme Court's interpretation of the dormant commerce clause because the ECJ was engaged in 'market building' while the US Supreme Court was doing 'market maintenance' since the US already had a single market.[78] What is relevant for this paper is that the broad interpretation of the rights of internal movement of goods and the strong enforcement guarantees were developed by the Court itself.

The Court has not given those trading with outsider goods anything comparable. Even when an EU's international agreement such as one of the WTO's agreements on goods has provisions that are comparable to those concerning the free movement of goods found in the TFEU (earlier in the EC Treaty), this is not of much use to individual traders. The Court has consistently narrowly interpreted the rights of traders from or with third countries. For example, in cases where traders wanted to invoke WTO law, the Court has held that WTO law has no direct effect in the EU legal order.[79] With the exception of two narrow situations,[80] WTO law cannot be directly relied upon either before national courts or the ECJ.[31] The Court has only accepted the so-called indirect or interpretative effect of WTO law, meaning that both European and national legislation must be interpreted in its light.[82] However, the Court has been quite restrictive even in using this interpretative effect. As a consequence, nowadays parties often do not even invoke

---

[77] See DH Regan, 'The Supreme Court and State Protectionism: Making Sense of the Dormant Commerce Clause' (1986) 84 *Michigan Law Review* 1091.

[78] Miguel Poiares Maduro, *We, The Court* (Oxford, Hart 1998).

[79] Case C-21-24/72 *International Fruit Company* v *Produktschap voor Groenten and Fruit* EU:C:1972:115; Case 70/87 *Fediol* v *Commission* EU:C:1989:254; Case C-69/89 *Nakajima* v *Council* EU:C:1991:186; Case 280/93 *Germany* v *Council* EU:C:1994:367; Case C-149/96 *Portugal* v *Council* EU:C:1999:574; See also *US—Sections 301–310 of the Trade Act of 1974* WT/DS152/R para 7.72. For academic discussion of this point, see eg P Eeckhout, 'The Domestic Legal Status of the WTO Agreement: Interconnecting Legal Systems' (1997) 34(1) *CML Rev* 11.

[80] WTO law can only be used to assess the validity of an EU measure when that measure is 'intended to implement a particular obligation assumed in the context of the WTO, or where the Community measure refers expressly to precise provisions of the WTO agreements'. *Portugal v Council* (n 79) para 49, citing *Fediol* (n 79) paras 19–22 and *Nakajima* (n 79) para 31.

[81] *Germany v Council* (n 78). See also Case C-120 & 121/06 P *FIAMM & Fedon v Council & Commission* EU:C:2008:98, Opinion of AG Maduro, paras 28, 29.

[82] See ECJ 10 September 1996, Case C-61/94 *Commission v Germany* para 52 on the interpretative effect of international agreements; see ECJ 16 June 1998, Case C-53/96 *Hermès International v FHT Marketing Choice BV* on the interpretative effect of WTO law.

applicable WTO law before the ECJ.[83] Neither do they invoke WTO law even in cases where a WTO complaint might follow shortly after an ECJ decision.[84]

The Court's differentiation between internal and external traders is further highlighted when comparing remedies in cases of a breach of law. It was the Court in *Francovich* that established the rights of individuals to obtain damages in cases of breach of EU law.[85] So an internal market trader whose freedom of movement of goods was violated by the EU or a Member State can obtain compensation for the damage.[86] In contrast, the Court was not so generous in granting damages to trades with third countries. In the *FIAMM* case, FIAMM was an exporter of stationary batteries from the EU to the US and had sustained damage caused by US retaliatory measures.[87] Namely, following the *EC–Bananas*[88] case in the WTO which the EU lost, the US was allowed by the WTO to introduce retaliatory measures against the EU. The US was thus acting in accordance with WTO law when it increased tariffs on stationary batteries that were supposed to compensate the US for the losses sustained in the lack of export of bananas to the EU. So FIAMM was really an innocent bystander that was hurt in the bananas' cross-fire between the EU and the US. However, it was the EU that acted contrary to WTO law and FIAMM wanted to obtain compensation from the EU. The Court rejected this claim. It held that the WTO cannot be used to assess the legality of action of EU institutions and that there was thus no unlawful action that could trigger the right to damages.[89]

Thus, the Court has built a sharp formal differentiation of rights of traders with insider and with outsider goods. It is clear that there is a plethora of policy reasons that pushed the Court to do this (including the fact that other WTO members do not give more rights to third-country traders or more power to WTO law). However, the consequence is that the Court is not transforming the EU's external trade patterns in the way it has transformed the EU's internal trade. The ideology of the Court's decision-making in external trade is reconstitution, and not transformation. I understand that one might argue that it is not the role of the Court to rewrite the differentiations explicitly written in the Treaties, and I am not even arguing for that. The statement is that the Treaty text is

---

[83] T Perišin, 'EU Regulatory Policy and World Trade: Should All EU Institutions Care What the World Thinks?' (2015) 11(1) *European Constitutional Law Review* 99.

[84] For example, WTO law was not even invoked in the *ATA* case despite arguments that the application of the EU emissions trading system (ETS) to civil aviation might be contrary to WTO law. Case C-366/10 *Air Transport Association of America* EU:C:2011:864; L Bartels, 'The Inclusion of Aviation in the EU ETS: WTO Law Considerations' (2012) ICTSD Global Platform on Climate Change, Trade and Sustainable Energy, Issue Paper No 6.

[85] Joined Cases C-6/90 and C-9/90 *Francovich* EU:C:1991:428.

[86] Joined Cases C-46/93 and C-48/93 *Brasserie du Pêcheur and Factortame* EU:C:1996:79.

[87] Case C-120&121/06 P *FIAMM and Fedon* EU:C:2008:476.

[88] *European Communities—Regime for the Importation, Sale and Distribution of Bananas*, WT/DS27/AB/R, Appellate Body Report, 9 September 1997.

[89] *FIAMM* (n 87).

vague, open-ended and indeterminate and that there is more than one reasonable interpretation that could have been followed. As the law now stands, national protectionism towards third countries, to the extent that has been modified by the actions of EU political institutions, is just reconstituted and conserved at the EU level.

B. The Role of the Court in the Movement of People

As regards the movement of people, it is arguable whether the Court has taken steps to transform the crude de iure national differentiations between insiders who enjoy fundamental freedoms, citizenship and other rights, and outsiders.

It is certainly true that the Court has interpreted the Treaties in a way that has given insiders quite broad rights. In a line of cases on free movement, freedoms of movement of workers,[90] establishment[91] and service[92] have been broadly interpreted so as to prevent not only direct and indirect discrimination on grounds of nationality, but also other obstacles to market access. This was complemented by the Court's case law on the recognition of qualification,[93] non-discrimination on grounds other than nationality,[94] citizenship rights,[95] etc. The rules were interpreted so as to cover not only those economically active in the narrow sense of the word, but also tourists,[96] students,[97] patients,[98] various family members, etc. It is true that some de iure EU insiders still do not feel able to overcome obstacles to movement. They factually do not move, and remain de facto outsiders of the integration process (arguably, for example, pro-Brexit voters). The Court could have a role in improving their position in the future.

Concerning the position of de iure outsiders, limited transformation has happened for third-country nationals who are family members of EU citizens.[99] In some cases where they had no right under the national law of an EU Member State to live with their EU family member, the Court has granted them the right

---

[90] *Bosman* (n 63).
[91] Case C-55/94 *Gebhard v Consiglio dell'Ordine degli Avvocati e Procuratori di Milano* EU:C:1995:411.
[92] Case C-76/90 *Säger v Dennemeyer & Co Ltd* EU:C:1991:331.
[93] Case C-19/92 *Kraus v Land Baden-Württemberg* EU:C:1993:125.
[94] Above nn 65–68.
[95] eg Case C-85/96 *Martínez Sala v Freistaat Bayern* EU:C:1998:217.
[96] eg Case C-186/87 *Cowan v Trésor public* EU:C:1989:47.
[97] Case 39/86 *Lair* EU:C:1988:322; Case C-3/90 *Bernini v Minister van Onderwijs en Wetenschappen* EU:C:1992:89; Case C-337/97 *Meeusen* EU:C:1999:284; Case C-209/03 *Bidar* EU:C:2005:169; Case C-147/03 *C v Austria* EU:C:2005:427; Case C-73/08 *Bressol* EU:C:2010:181; Case C-75/11 *C v Austria* EU:C:2012:605. For a discussion of *Bidar* see also Caruso and Nicola's contribution in this volume.
[98] Case C-120/95 *Decker* EU:C:1998:167; Case C-158/96 *Kohll* EU:C:1998:171; Case C-372/04 *Watts* EU:C:2006:325.
[99] I Goldner Lang, 'The Reach of EU Citizenship Rights for "Static" EU Citizens: Time to Move On?' in AP Dourado (ed), *Movement of Persons and Tax Mobility in the European Union: Changing Winds* (Amsterdam, IBFD, 2014).

to family reunification on the basis of EU law. In some cases the Court has gone
a long way in interpreting internal market rules to achieve family reunification.
For example, in *Carpenter*, the Court held that the deportation of Mrs Carpenter
who was a national of the Philippines was contrary to the freedom to provide
services of a UK citizen, Mr Carpenter, as he would be deterred from travelling
to other EU Member States if his wife was deported.[100] In other cases, the Court
used the citizenship provisions to achieve the same ends. For example, in *Ruiz
Zambrano*, the Court found that third-country nationals who are parents of
minors with Belgium nationality enjoy the right of residence and a right to work
in the EU without a work permit.[101] The Court sees these parents' rights as a
necessary corollary of the minors' EU citizenship, as they could not enjoy citizens'
rights if their parents were deported (and they would likely have to leave the EU
as well).[102] The Court has also given third-country nationals who were family
members of EU citizens additional rights concerning the issuance of visas, since a
Member State was not allowed to deny such a third-country national a visa on the
sole ground that he/she was on the list in the Schengen Information System.[103] It
might seem that in all of these cases the Court chose not to reconstitute a national
policy at the EU level, but to take a progressive step which transformed the law.
However, the problem is that these are not really rights that were given to outsiders.
In all of these cases, the Court was actually enhancing the rights of insiders, eg
the right of an EU service provider in *Carpenter* or the right of EU citizens who
wanted to be unified with their family members in *Ruiz Zambrano*. The rights
of third-country nationals were just derivative consequences of broad insiders'
rights. Thus, while this might be a transformation of national policies, it is not a
transformation that concerns outsiders themselves, since they are benefiting only
from rights given to insiders.

Another example where the Court has taken modest steps to enforce the rights
of third-country nationals beyond the practice of national institutions is the
NS case.[104] In this case, asylum seekers challenged the transfer from one EU Member
State to another Member State which was 'responsible' for them under EU
law. It had been regular practice of national authorities within the EU to transfer
asylum seekers who had left the territory of the responsible State back to that State.
The Court held that EU law prevents Member States and their national courts
from applying a conclusive presumption that the 'responsible' Member State
observes fundamental rights as guaranteed by EU law.[105] In particular, a Member

---

[100] Case C-60/00 *Carpenter* EU:C:2002:434. The case builds upon Case C-370/90 *Surinder Singh*
EU:C:1992:296.
[101] Case C-34/09 *Ruiz Zambrano* EU:C:2011:124.
[102] The rule is further refined in Case C-256/11 *Dereci* EU:C:2011:734; Case C-434/09 *McCarthy*
EU:C:2011:277; and Case C-165/14 *Rendón Martín* EU:C:2016:675.
[103] Case C-503/03 *Commission v Spain* EU:C:2006:74.
[104] Case C-411/10 and C-493/10 *N S v Secretary of State for the Home Department* EU:C:2011:865.
[105] ibid para 105.

State and its courts must not transfer an asylum seeker back to the 'responsible' Member State when

> they cannot be unaware that systemic deficiencies in the asylum procedure and in the reception conditions of asylum seekers in that Member State amount to substantial grounds for believing that the asylum seeker would face a real risk of being subjected to inhuman or degrading treatment.[106]

A recent case, *CK*, goes even further, as an asylum seeker has the right not be transferred to another Member State not only when there are 'systemic deficiencies' in that State, but also when, due to the asylum seeker's health problems, there is 'real and proven risk of a significant and permanent deterioration in his state of health ... [so] that transfer would constitute inhuman and degrading treatment'.[107] These judgments gave rights to third-country nationals, asylum seekers, which went beyond the practice of Member States. The States themselves have considered the EU territory as homogeneous and treated all Member States as 'safe' for asylum seekers, but the Court said that this is not so.

These judgments are quite progressive, especially the *NS* case where, unlike in *CK*, not much depends on some specific individual situation, but on significant differences between EU States. The progressive nature of *NS* derives from the fact that outsiders are given a right even at the cost of 'disintegrating' Europe. The Court, having as one of its main ideologies the integration of Europe, has now partitioned Europe into 'safe' and 'unsafe', so as to give more rights to individuals. In other cases, from *Van Gend en Loos* onwards, the Court's recognition of individual rights has typically been beneficial to European integration and the enforcement of EU law. The vigilance of individuals interested in protecting their own individual rights was used for pushing the enforcement of EU law and tightening European integration. In *NS*, this was somewhat different—the granting of rights to individuals contributed to the recognition that Europe is not very homogeneous. However, here as well, the transformative character of the judgment is not very strong, as this decision relied upon a decision of the European Court of Human Rights in the *M&S* case that was delivered shortly beforehand.[108]

New cases arising from the migration crisis are an opportunity for the Court to interpret a number of rules concerning outsiders.[109] However, the Court is quite cautious in recognising the rights of outsiders. For example, in 2016, in *Alo and Osso*,[110] the Court had an opportunity to decide on the legality of the German

---

[106] ibid para 106.
[107] Case C-578/16 PPU *CK, HF, AS v Republika Slovenija* EU:C:2017:127 para 74.
[108] Case *MSS v Belgium and Greece* App no 30696/09 (ECHR 21 January 2011).
[109] On the crisis ability to do the opposite, ie to reduce the rights of outsiders, see I Goldner Lang, 'Do Refugees Have Fewer Rights in the Case of a Mass Influx? A European Perspective' in Silja Vöneky and Gerald L Neuman (eds), *Human Rights, Democracy and Legitimacy in a World of Disorder* (Cambridge, Cambridge University Press, forthcoming).
[110] Case C-443&444/14 *Alo and Osso* EU:C:2016:127.

system imposing residence on third-country nationals who were beneficiaries of international protection.[111] The German system required these persons to have residence within a geographically limited area, such as a municipality.[112] The Court started off boldly by saying that imposing residence on these persons was contrary to their free movement rights guaranteed by the relevant Directive.[113] It went on to say firmly that imposing a residence requirement on these persons is contrary to EU law, even when the aim of that rule is the appropriate distribution of social assistance burdens between different parts of a Member State (as there are presumably other ways of distributing the costs).[114] However, faced with German fears of the possible unsuccessful integration of unprecedented numbers of third-country nationals and the fear of ghettoisation, the Court held that imposing a residence requirement on these persons was in accordance with EU law when its aim is the facilitation of integration.[115] It left it to the national court to decide whether it was objectively justified to require residence for integration purposes in the particular case.[116] The outcome of this case is thus in no way transformative when it comes to the position of outsiders. Those who are outsiders in terms of nationality remain outsiders when it comes to some benefits such as free movement.

The *Alo and Osso* case also highlights that the position of human outsiders remains worse than that of outsider goods. Outsider goods, once they legally arrive in the EU market, start enjoying the same benefits as insider goods and move equally freely. For humans, this is not the case.

Finally, regarding de iure insiders who are de facto outsiders, the Court has had an important inclusive role in European integration. The Court has made many persons de facto insiders of the European project. For example, many persons became insiders thanks to the broad personal scope of free movement rules covering recipients of services, such as students and patients, or equally thanks to broad discrimination grounds covering discrimination on grounds of foreign qualifications or residence. Furthermore, for a while there has been significant case law on the movement rights of economically inactive persons,[117] but in the most recent cases there has been a regression in this field.[118]

While there is always some political pressure in favour of reducing movement (eg of those who might seek social benefits in another country), the Court has the legitimacy to interpret the rules progressively. The European reality is that it is

---

[111] ibid para 21.
[112] ibid.
[113] ibid para 40.
[114] ibid para 56.
[115] ibid paras 60–64.
[116] ibid para 64.
[117] eg *Martínez Sala* (n 95).
[118] Case C-333/13 *Dano* EU:C:2014:2358; Case C-67/14 *Alimanovic* EU:C:2015:597; Case C-308/14 *Commission v UK* EU:C:2016:436.

not that easy to be an active participant of the internal market. It might be easy to become a consumer of goods or services from other EU Member States, but it is certainly not so easy to export your own goods or services or to move to another Member State. Unlike the United States, the EU is not a single country. Instead, the EU is undergoing a complex and lasting process aiming at the establishment of a single market and an ever-closer union. Different languages, cultures and rights make movement difficult. EU law has responded to this by eliminating many regulatory barriers, but there is still a lot to be done. This task partly lies with the Court.

IV. Conclusion

The EU Court of Justice has had a transformative role in European integration. The ideology of (albeit limited) integration that is present in the EU Treaties is also visible in the decisions of the ECJ. The Court has interpreted the Treaties, creating a new legal order and this was matched with benefits for individuals. In synergy with the ideology of European integration, the Court has taken a number of progressive steps and has pioneered the protection of many individual and group rights. Some groups still perceive themselves as outsiders or indeed are outsiders to European integration, so there is still work to be done, and to some extent this work can be done by the Court.

The internally transformative judicial decision-making which has led to the progressive granting of rights for insiders has thus far not been seen in the external sphere. On several occasions, the Court has had the opportunity to create a more just regime of external movement with greater rights for outsiders. So far, it has mostly resisted taking such steps. To put it differently, decision-making in the external sphere has been quite conservative and has mostly reconstituted the existing (national or EU) regulatory policies.

Pierre Schlag's CLS scholarship on legal academics who have a 'desirable X' criticises the dominance of normative legal thought, and suggests that a piece using the CLS perspective might want to restrain itself from making a normative judgement.[119] He also argues that it is not possible to be just descriptive, as ideology is ineluctable in all indeterminate matters such as law and policy.[120] Along those lines, this paper does not seek to be normative, but it does want to show that the Court's hands in granting rights to insiders or outsiders are not completely tied. There is always some room for policy choices, and actually they are inevitable in adjudication. As we have seen over the last 60 years of European integration, the

---

[119] Pierre Schlag, 'Normativity and the Politics of Form' (1991) 139(4) *University of Pennsylvania Law Review* 801; Pierre Schlag, 'Law as Continuation of God by Other Means' (1997) 85 *California Law Review* 427.

[120] Schlag, 'Normativity and the Politics of Form', ibid, particularly 811–14.

Court has used its room for manoeuvre to improve the position of insiders and to create a more just internal system. Similarly, the Court has some space for improving the position of outsiders. Considering that even Schuman's Declaration spoke of Europe's role in securing wellbeing and peace in the world, progressive steps in the external sphere would not endanger the Court's legitimacy.

One might argue that Schuman's post World War II ideas are not applicable in today's world which some have suggested is approaching a World War III.[121] Proxy wars, terrorism and a huge migration crisis all seem to trigger nationalism, protectionism and fear of the foreign. This is true in Europe, in the United States and elsewhere in the world. At such times, the courts must not sink into populism, and can legitimately use the judicial room for manoeuvre they were given.

---

[121] King of Jordan, 'We are Facing a Third World War' *Reuters video* (17 November 2015) www.reuters.com/video/2015/11/17/king-of-jordan-we-are-facing-a-third-wor?videoId=366356889; PW Singer and August Cole, 'Here's How World War Three Could Start Tomorrow' *The Telegraph* (24 November 2015) www.telegraph.co.uk/news/uknews/defence/11920013/Heres-how-World-War-Three-could-start-tomorrow.html.

8

Useful Effect of the Framework Decision on the European Arrest Warrant[*]

SINIŠA RODIN[**]

I. Introduction

This chapter discusses a specific field of European Union law, namely the Framework Decision on the European Arrest Warrant (EAW),[1] an instrument of judicial cooperation in criminal matters within the Area of Freedom, Security and Justice (AFSJ). The question the chapter will address is whether the EAW, as interpreted by the Court of Justice of the European Union (CJEU), performs an integrative function that goes beyond a purely national one, and, if it does, to what extent? Or, to put it differently, is the CJEU interpreting the EAW so as to reconstitute national criminal law at the European level, or is it transforming its function into a genuinely European and integrative one?

The chapter is organised in five main parts. Following this introductory part, in part II, I will explain my general understanding of the interpretative framework within which interpretation of European law in general and of the EAW, in particular, takes place. I will suggest that interpretation of EU law is not pre-determined by Europeanising teleology, but seeks to legitimise the European Union and its law by the perpetuation of assumptions of its basic ontology as defined by the Founding Treaties and the key actors. In part III, I will present the normative context within which the EAW operates and my understanding of the added value of

[*] Paper presented at the Conference 'Transformation or Reconstitution of Europe: The Critical Legal Studies Perspective on the Role of Courts in the European Union', University of Zagreb, 26–27 June 2015. For an early version see S Rodin, 'Useful Effect of the Framework Decision on the European Arrest Warrant' (2016) 1 Il Diritto dell' Unione Europea 1.

[**] Judge, Court of Justice of the European Union. The views expressed in this chapter reflect the author's personal views and by no means the views of the Court of Justice of the European Union.

[1] Council Framework Decision 2002/584/JHA of 13 June 2002 on the European arrest warrant and the surrender procedures between Member States (2002/584/JAI) OJ L 190/1.

judicial cooperation in criminal matters generally and of the EAW in particular. In part IV, I will discuss the implementation of the EAW, particularly concerning the possible tension between the integrative objective of the Framework Decision and pursuance of a national function as envisaged by national legislature. In this part, I will discuss how the added value of the EAW translates into its useful effect. In the final part V, I will present my concluding remarks.

II. The Quest for Legitimacy

In my recent writing,[2] I made a distinction between foreign law, understood as law exogenous to the European Union, as a formal element of adjudication, and foreign law as part of a referential framework of judges. I suggested that the value of foreign legal materials in domestic adjudication is primarily cognitive, while their normative value depends on their compatibility with EU constitutional ontology as understood by the Court of Justice of the EU. Within that framework, I questioned the adequacy of the functional comparative method in adjudication within the EU by contrasting the traditional functions of national law of the Member States against the integrative functions of EU law. I argued that ontology of the EU does not seek to reconstitute traditional functions of national legal rules, principles or concepts at the European level, but to form integrative ones.

I owe my fascination with ontology to Pierre Schlag who, writing in 1997,[3] introduced the term 'key ontological identities' and defined them as fundamental identities around which the US constitutional theory constantly revolves. These are the Constitution as the legal basis, the Act of Founding, the people as the Agent, and Consent as the basis of legitimacy of the social arrangement under which constitutional interpretation operates. Starting from Schlag's analysis, I developed a methodology that does not construct European ontology by replicating the analytical process that would deduce European ontological identities from European constitutional thought, but would imagine them, by analogy, from their US counterparts. In the European Union, I suggest, these identities are: the Founding Treaties as the legal basis, the process of construction of Europe as the Act, the Member States and the peoples of Europe as the Agent, and the consent of the Agent as a basis of legitimacy.[4] Defined in this way, European ontology is, indeed, imagined, but, to my mind, does not lack, as Schlag would have put it, 'a robust or stabilized referent',[5] the lack of which would allow an endless

---

[2] Siniša Rodin, 'Constitutional Relevance of Foreign Court Decisions', Conference on Global Influence, Judicial Diplomacy and Legal Dialogue in the Court of Justice of the European Union, American University Washington College of Law, 30 March 2015; Siniša Rodin, 'Constitutional Relevance of Foreign Court Decisions' (2016) 64(4) *American Journal of Comparative Law* 815–40.

[3] Pierre Schlag, 'Empty Circles of Liberal Justifications' (1997) 96 *Michigan Law Review* 1.

[4] For a more detailed elaboration, see Rodin (n 2).

[5] Pierre Schlag, 'Commentary: Law and Phrenology' (1997) 110 *Harvard Law Review* 877.

re-combination of its constituent elements whose results would lack factual verification and would, therefore, be irrefutable. In other words, while being imagined, European ontological identities are not imaginary but are anchored in concrete social facts and artifacts, notably the Founding Treaties supported by the consent of key agents to ensure their application.

Therefore, reference to European ontology is not merely theoretical but addresses some fundamental objections concerning the question of how EU law is interpreted, and proposals for how it should be interpreted. For example, in a recent conference contribution,[6] Professor Derrick Wyatt suggested that the CJEU is more prone to deliver Europeanising than de-centralising outcomes, while the two should be in balance. Professor Wyatt also argued that the Court should favour literal interpretation of EU rules, in order to give effect to the intention of the draftsman. This is, he explained, to replace the result-driven, teleological approach, in other words, judgments driven by judicial policy rather than legal analysis and reasoning. In the political arena, the Treaty phrase, 'ever closer union'[7] is sometimes understood as a target or, at least, guidance for the development of European integration, not excluding by judicial means that entail purposive, teleological interpretation.

While there is a solid and almost uncontested stream of European scholarship that dwells on the desirable or undesirable merits of teleology in the European integration project,[8] to my mind it is not primarily τέλος but ὄντος—the authentic essence of the EU and its law—that informs interpretation of EU law and constitutes its specific identity as distinguished from the identity of national and international law.[9]

---

[6] Derrick Wyatt, 'Does the European Court of Justice Need a New Judicial Approach for the 21st Century' presented at a conference for the Bingham Centre 'A More Literal and Predictable Approach for the Court of Justice of the EU?' 2 November 2015 www.biicl.org/documents/760_derrick_wyatts_paper.pdf.

[7] TEU Preamble: 'RESOLVED to continue the process of creating an ever closer union among the peoples of Europe, in which decisions are taken as closely as possible to the citizen in accordance with the principle of subsidiarity'; TEU Art 1: 'This Treaty marks a new stage in the process of creating an ever closer union among the peoples of Europe, in which decisions are taken as openly as possible and as closely as possible to the citizen'. For a political overview, see eg www.economist.com/news/britain/21676749-does-european-treaty-commitment-matter-why-david-cameron-wants-exemption-ever-closer.

[8] For an inside view on teleological interpretation, see Nial Fennely, 'Legal Interpretation at the European Court of Justice' (1996) 20(3) *Fordham International Law Journal* 656; CN Kakouris, 'Use of the Comparative Method by the Court of Justice of the European Communities' (1994) 6 *Pace International Law Review* 267.

[9] At first sight, teleology and ontology are but two different argumentative forms that seek to demonstrate the existence of what Schlag calls 'desirable X', be it by ontological proof, be it by argument from design, or by magical thinking. Pierre Schlag, 'Law as the Continuation of God by Other Means' (1997) 85 *California Law Review* 427. Admittedly, as both τέλος and ὄντος are creatures of the interpreting subject, a mere shift from teleology to ontology in legal argumentation does not seem to change much in its own right. Moreover, neither τέλος nor ὄντος of EU law appears to be falsifiable in Karl Popper's sense, but depends on non-empirical assessment, that is, on repetition and belief: 'What I tell you three times is true'. For the merits of the non-empirical assessment of theories, see Richard Dawid, *String Theory and the Scientific Method* (Cambridge, Cambridge University

Both being justificatory rather than determinative elements of adjudication, to my eyes, the difference between the two is that ontology, unlike teleology, does not insist on reaching a certain result, but on perpetuation and justification of assumptions that are essential to the existence of a system within which interpretation operates. In the context of EU law, it would be counterproductive for the CJEU to depart from those basic assumptions, since such departure would undermine the basis of its own being. Saying that a certain legal rule has a certain object and purpose or that a certain interpretation would deprive a legal rule of its useful effect is not a ground for a judicial decision but a justification thereof. In other words, teleology and useful effect are but justifications of EU ontology, that is, of the grounds of the very existence of EU law. The practical consequence is that the CJEU does not interpret EU law in a certain way because there are some external constraints, such as teleology, which command exact outcomes, but because of its own quest for legitimacy of the EU legal order. The same holds, I suggest, throughout the body of EU law. While the entire EU law, as defined by the Founding Treaties, generally depends on repetitive justification of its ontology by the CJEU, the same can be said in respect of more specific areas and segments of EU regulation, such as the Area of Freedom, Security and Justice and, within its context, the European Arrest Warrant.

III. Normative Context and Added Value of the EAW

A. Normative Context

Framework Decisions are a legislative instrument of the former third (intergovernmental) pillar of the EU, and form part of Title VI of the Treaty of Amsterdam of 1997,[10] titled Provisions on Police and Judicial Cooperation in Criminal Matters.[11] Under the original Treaty design, Framework Decisions do not have direct effect, that is, they do not, as such, create individual rights which national courts must protect.[12] Nevertheless, after being transposed into

---

Press, 2014); Lewis Carroll, 'The Hunting of the Snark'. There is emerging debate in theoretical physics on whether theories need to be falsifiable or not. See, eg, Olivia Goldhill, 'Philosophers Want to Know Why Physicists Believe Theories They Can't Prove' (Quartz, 10 January 2016) http://qz.com/590406/philosophers-want-to-know-why-physicists-believe-theories-they-cant-prove/?utm_source=atlfb.

[10] Treaty of Amsterdam amending the Treaty on European Union, the Treaties establishing the European Communities and certain related acts, as signed in Amsterdam on 2 October 1997.

[11] They were for the first time introduced by Art K.6.b of the Treaty of Amsterdam.

[12] Art K.6.b of the Treaty of Amsterdam reads: 'Framework decisions shall be binding upon the Member States as to the result to be achieved but shall leave to the national authorities the choice of form and methods. They shall not entail direct effect'.

the national legislation of a Member State, national courts have an obligation to interpret national law in conformity with them.[13] In other words, the national application of framework decisions entails two obligations for the Member States. First, the obligation to adopt national implementing legislation giving a framework decision effect in national law (transposition) and, second, the obligation of national judicial authorities to interpret national law, implementing legislation included, in light of the law of the European Union.[14]

In 2009 the Treaty of Lisbon dramatically changed the original design of framework decisions by merging the third pillar into the mainstream of EU law as Judicial Cooperation in Criminal Matters.[15] The Treaty did away with future framework decisions, erasing them from the catalogue of sources of EU law, but left the existing ones intact. Under the new Treaty, cooperation in criminal matters will be regulated by directives.

Transition to the new Treaty model was subject to a transitional period of five years that expired on 1 December 2014. Until that date, the CJEU had no jurisdiction to give preliminary references in respect of Framework Decisions, except subject to a specific declaration of a Member State to that effect. Also, the European Commission was not authorised to pursue infraction proceedings[16] and its role was limited to monitoring.[17]

---

[13] Case C-105/03 *Criminal proceedings against Maria Pupino* EU:C:2005:386. Both Framework Decisions and Directives are binding on the Member States as to the result to be achieved but leave them a choice of methods how to do so. It is well established in the case law of the CJEU that Directives can have vertical but not horizontal effect, and that both Directives and Framework Decisions have indirect effect. It is also given that until converted into a Directive, a Framework Decision retains its original form and status, all practical consequences included. Art 288 TFEU: 'A directive shall be binding, as to the result to be achieved, upon each Member State to which it is addressed, but shall leave to the national authorities the choice of form and methods'. Art 34(2) EU (Amsterdam): 'Framework decisions shall be binding upon the Member States as to the result to be achieved but shall leave to the national authorities the choice of form and methods. They shall not entail direct effect'.

[14] This is echoed also in national jurisdictions, most recently by the German Federal Constitutional Court: 'This does not entail a substantial risk for the uniform application of Union law, as the powers of review reserved for the Federal Constitutional Court have to be exercised with restraint and in a manner open to European integration. To the extent required, the Federal Constitutional Court will base its review of the European act in question on the interpretation provided by the European Court of Justice in a preliminary ruling under Art 267 sec 3 of the Treaty on the Functioning of the European Union (TFEU)'. See Protection of Fundamental Rights in Individual Cases is Ensured as Part of Identity Review Press Release No 4/2016 of 26 January 2016, Order of 15 December 2015—2 R 2735/14.

[15] Title V, Area of Freedom, Security of Justice, Ch 4, Judicial Cooperation in Criminal Matters.

[16] See Art 10 of Protocol no 36 to the Treaty of Lisbon: 'As a transitional measure, and with respect to acts of the Union in the field of police cooperation and judicial cooperation in criminal matters which have been adopted before the entry into force of the Treaty of Lisbon, the powers of the institutions shall be the following at the date of entry into force of that Treaty: the powers of the Commission under Article 258 of the Treaty on the Functioning of the European Union shall not be applicable and the powers of the Court of Justice of the European Union under Title VI of the Treaty on European Union, in the version in force before the entry into force of the Treaty of Lisbon, shall remain the same, including where they have been accepted under Article 35(2) of the said Treaty on European Union'.

[17] The Commission was restricted to publishing monitoring reports. See, eg, Report from the Commission to the European Parliament and the Council on the implementation since 2007 of the Council Framework Decision of 13 June 2002 on the European arrest warrant and the surrender

As of 1 December 2014, the CJEU acquired competence over matters in the field of judicial cooperation in criminal matters that were adopted before the entry into force of the Treaty of Lisbon. At the same time, the European Commission reclaimed its police powers within the framework of infraction proceedings under Articles 258 to 260 of the Treaty on the Functioning of the European Union (TFEU). In that respect, the Treaty of Lisbon considerably increased the stakes in the area of judicial cooperation in criminal matters by changing the balance between the national legislative and judicial branch, and by positioning the CJEU as an umpire between the two, in questions that may be raised by national courts. In that way, the Treaty emphasised the function of judicial cooperation in criminal matters as a vehicle for the integrative process.

The newly acquired powers, in a field that has not been subject to interpretation by the CJEU, created tension. Namely, legislative choices made by the Member States in the course of the transposition of the EAW at a time when preliminary references to the CJEU were restricted became subject to judicial scrutiny, both national and European, under EU law. Recourse to the preliminary reference procedure that became universally available to national courts after 1 December 2014 opened the possibility for them to challenge the assumptions of relevant national criminal law legislation before the CJEU by putting it to the test of the entire EU law. If there is any value in the belief in EU ontology, the principles of national criminal law of the Member States began to lend themselves to the test too. *Hic Rhodus, hic salta!*

The full application of the Treaty of Lisbon by the expiry of the five year transitional period and the transition of judicial cooperation in criminal matters from intergovernmental to the fully fledged EU method disturbed the existing balance of powers between the legislative and judicial branches of the Member States, but also between the Member States and the institutions of the EU. This is where the anxiety starts. If the Treaty amendment is to have any useful effect that would justify the basic assumptions of EU law, not only the EAW but also hitherto uncontested principles of national criminal law need to be interpreted in a way that goes beyond the original intergovernmental setting, possibly beyond the meaning that national implementing legislation contemplated at the time of the transposition, and certainly beyond the traditional national understanding of criminal law.

B. Added Value of the EAW

In my understanding, the term 'added value' is similar but not identical to the concept of useful effect (French: *l'effet utile*). For the purposes of this essay, it refers

---

procedures between Member States {SEC(2011) 430 final}. The European Commission was able to identify problems of implementation but did not have the power to institute infraction proceedings against defaulting Member States. See the cited Commission Report and the country reports quoted therein, eg concerning the implementation of optional grounds for non-execution.

to the question about what the EAW adds to the already existing legal regime of sovereignty-based inter-state extradition, for example to the possibility of one Member State surrendering its own nationals, or to the mutual recognition of judgments in criminal matters. In a functional sense, added value has the capacity to contribute to the European integration process; to make a difference. The most general question is how to measure the added value of having the European Union rather than not having it, and, since there are no guarantees that the added value of a legal rule will indeed translate into useful effect, what meaning should one give to the rules of EU law in order to create it?

The concept of useful effect itself deserves some explanation. In its plain meaning, it is an interpretative guidance rule that one applies in order to say that every legal rule is to be interpreted as producing some effect. Conversely, no rule should be interpreted in a way that would frustrate the useful effect of another rule belonging to the same system. A rule without effect hardly has any meaning at all, so an interpretation that preserves certain meaning and effects should prevail over an interpretation that does not.[18] At the same time, reference to the useful effect of a rule can be used to delimit its scope of application. Overstretching the scope of one legal rule risks impinging upon the scope of another, either horizontally or vertically, between EU law and the national law of a Member State. The expression *l'effet utile* is sometimes used by the legislature in the context of the implementation of secondary EU law.[19] Yet, this would be a narrow understanding of the concept, implying that without legislative transposition such an effect would not exist. Another meaning is suggested by Judge Cruz Vilaça who explains it as the flip side of the margin of appreciation, that is, the discretion that Member States have in the implementation of directives.[20] Cruz Vilaça understands the principle primarily as a guarantee of the integrity of the European Union legal order that projects itself to a relationship with national legal orders.[21] Therefore, it overlaps with the principle of loyal cooperation under which Member States are under a duty to recognise the effect of EU law when transposing it into national law. The reading according to which Member States' discretion concerning the 'form and methods' of the implementation of directives and framework decisions is limited by their duty not to pre-empt their useful effect comes close to my understanding

---

[18] In a way, the interpretation of man-made law resembles the instrumentalisation of the forces of nature. One would not say that the production of electricity by the rotation of hydropower turbines is a useful effect of gravity. Gravity is not useful or useless in its own right, it just is. Making natural forces useful requires the creation of artefacts. So does law.

[19] See eg Décret n° 2009-1086 du 2 septembre 2009 tendant à assurer l'effet utile des directives 89/665/CEE et 92/13/CEE et modifiant certaines dispositions applicables aux marchés publics NOR: ECEM0905313D, Version consolidée au 06 juin 2015.

[20] José Luís da Cruz Vilaça, 'Le principe de l'effet utile du droit de l'Union dans la jurisprudence de la Cour' in *The Court of Justice and the Construction of Europe: Analyses and Perspectives on Sixty Years of Case-law—La Cour de Justice et la Construction de l'Europe: Analyses et Perspectives de Soixante Ans de Jurisprudence* (The Hague, TMC Asser Press 2013) 279, 285.

[21] Cruz Vilaça, ibid 280.

of the useful effect of EU law which I hold, in the broadest sense, to be recognition that the added value of some rule to the already existing body of law should also translate into actual legal effects in the process of adjudication.

So, what is the added value of the EAW? To give it a fair reading one has to start from the text of its preamble. The fifth recital states that 'the objective set for the Union to become an area of freedom, security and justice leads to abolishing extradition between Member States and replacing it by a system of surrender between judicial authorities' in order to remove 'complexity and potential delay'.[22] This is to be achieved by replacing the old extradition system with a 'system of free movement of judicial decisions in criminal matters'. Free movement is to be achieved by establishing a system of mutual recognition of judgments in criminal matters, as mentioned in the sixth recital of the preamble.[23] As rightly noted by the president of the CJEU Koen Lenaerts in his recent writing, the EAW 'does not undermine the effectiveness of national criminal laws'.[24] Instead, it creates mechanisms of judicial cooperation that build upon and beyond the existing ones, but at the same time creates additional value for the process of European integration. As can be seen from the already rich practice of the CJEU, this does not always go smoothly and calls for reconciliation between the national and the Europeanising functions of the rules at stake.

In addition to the principle of mutual recognition, the EAW, in the tenth recital of the Preamble, introduces the principle of mutual trust, which allows suspension of the EAW mechanism only in the event of a serious and persistent breach of one of the Member States of the principles set out in Article 6(1) TEU, subject to the application of the mechanism under Article 7(1) thereof.[25] These objectives were echoed by the CJEU in the *Radu* case, where the Court held that the EAW:

> Seeks, by the establishment of a new simplified and more effective system for the surrender of persons convicted or suspected of having infringed criminal law, to facilitate and accelerate judicial cooperation with a view to contributing to the objective set for the European Union to become an area of freedom, security and justice by basing itself on the high degree of confidence which should exist between the Member States.[26]

---

[22] Art 3(2) TEU defines the Area of Freedom, Security and Justice as follows: 'The Union shall offer its citizens an area of freedom, security and justice without internal frontiers, in which the free movement of persons is ensured in conjunction with appropriate measures with respect to external border controls, asylum, immigration and the prevention and combating of crime'.

[23] Recital 6 reads: 'The European arrest warrant provided for in this Framework Decision is the first concrete measure in the field of criminal law implementing the principle of mutual recognition which the European Council referred to as the "cornerstone" of judicial cooperation'.

[24] Koen Lenaerts, 'The Principle of Mutual Recognition in the Area of Freedom, Security and Justice,' (The Fourth Annual Sir Jeremy Lever Lecture, All Souls College, University of Oxford, 30 January 2015).

[25] Recital 10 reads: 'The mechanism of the European arrest warrant is based on a high level of confidence between Member States. Its implementation may be suspended only in the event of a serious and persistent breach by one of the Member States of the principles set out in Article 6(1) of the Treaty on European Union, determined by the Council pursuant to Article 7(1) of the said Treaty with the consequences set out in Article 7(2) thereof'.

[26] Case C-396/11 *Ciprian Vasile Radu* EU:C:2013:39, para 34 and the case law cited therein.

More recently, in Opinion 2/13,[27] the CJEU defined mutual trust as a cornerstone of free movement, ie 'an area without internal borders'.[28]

From this basic layout one can identify the motives that informed the European legislature's design of the EAW. The AFSJ has the purpose of creating and maintaining free movement of people without internal borders, one of the fundamental freedoms of EU citizens. The EAW, as its instrument, introduces *mutual recognition* and *mutual trust* as instruments for achieving this goal. On a more instrumental level, mutual recognition is to be achieved through judicial cooperation between national courts and between national courts and the CJEU, and the latter is ensured by the removal of barriers to preliminary references and Commission supervision, starting on 1 December 2014, as described above. This encapsulates the added value of the EAW as part of the AFSJ:

— Free movement of people;
— Mutual recognition of judgments in criminal matters;
— Mutual trust between the Member States;
— Judicial cooperation between national courts; and
— Judicial cooperation between national courts with the CJEU in the preliminary reference procedure.

The full integrative potential of the EAW was unfolded by the Treaty of Lisbon that set the stage and pushed the process of the construction of Europe by putting judicial cooperation in criminal matters in the mainstream with traditional areas of EU law. Its implementation, however, remains partly in the hands of the peoples of the Member States, that is, national legislatures and judiciaries, requiring popular consent. The tension between integration and consent defines the playing field where the CJEU develops its case law.[29]

---

[27] Opinion 2/13 EU:C:2014:2454.

[28] ibid para 191: 'In the second place, it should be noted that the principle of mutual trust between the Member States is of fundamental importance in EU law, given that it allows an area without internal borders to be created and maintained. That principle requires, particularly with regard to the area of freedom, security and justice, each of those States, save in exceptional circumstances, to consider all the other Member States to be complying with EU law and particularly with the fundamental rights recognised by EU law (see, to that effect, judgments in Joined Cases C-411/10 and C-493/10 *NS and Others* EU:C:2011:865, paras 78 to 80; and Case C-399/11*Melloni* EU:C:2013:107, paras 37 and 63)'.

[29] For a recent expression of this tension, see Order of the German Federal Constitutional Court (n 14): 'As a rule, sovereign acts of the European Union and acts of German public authority— to the extent that they are determined by Union law—are, due to the precedence of Union law (Anwendungsvorrang des Unionsrechts), not to be measured against the standard of the fundamental rights enshrined in the Basic Law. However, precedence only applies insofar as the Basic Law and the Act of Assent permit or provide for the transfer of sovereign rights. Its scope is limited by the Basic Law's constitutional identity that, according to Art 23 sec 1 sentence 3 in conjunction with Art 79 sec 3 GG, is neither open to constitutional amendments nor to European integration (verfassungsänderungs- und integrationsfest)'.

IV. Implementation of the EAW and Its Useful Effect

While Consent of the Member States is based on the Founding Treaties and its value framework of reference, it is neither completely nor permanently secured but has to be re-vowed on each occasion of the adoption of secondary EU law. This is so, for among other reasons, because secondary law harmonising a certain area of EU law and not the Founding Treaties themselves is understood as the controlling authority, unless annulled by the CJEU.[30]

Moreover, even in harmonised areas of law, consent ultimately depends on the national interpretation, implementation and application of previously adopted rules.[31] In an area regulated by the EAW, national interpretation plays a prominent role since the field is permeated with well-established and relatively stable concepts of national law, such as '*ne bis in idem*' or 'final judgment'. Further, the EAW often refers to national law, for example concerning the definition of the 'executing judicial authority'. As we shall see, the meaning of these and other concepts is susceptible to change due to interpretations of the CJEU.

The implementation of framework decisions entails discretion for the Member States that can be exercised at a legislative and judicial level.[32] Certainly, legislative choices made in the implementation of the EAW bear consequences for national judicial authorities. Lack of clarity of the EAW itself does not help. Other

---

[30] Certainly, secondary law has to be interpreted in conformity with the Treaties. As long as this is the case, secondary law represents *lex specialis*. See, eg, Ulrich Stelkens, Wolfgang Weiß, Michael Mirschberger, *The Implementation of the EU Services Directive: Transposition, Problems and Strategies* (The Hague, TMC Asser Press, 2012) 235. See also Case C-341/05 *Laval un Partneri* EU:C:2007:291, Opinion of AG Mengozzi, paras 149 and 150: 'A measure that is incompatible with Directive 96/71 will, a fortiori, be contrary to Article 49 EC, because that directive is intended, within its specific scope, to implement the terms of that article. On the other hand, to hold that a measure conforms with Directive 96/71 does not necessarily mean that it meets the requirements of Article 49 EC, as interpreted by the Court'.

[31] In a recent decision, the German Federal Constitutional Court reaffirmed its standing practice of *identity review* according to which certain principles 'are not open to integration', escape the scrutiny of EU law and, accordingly, of the CJEU, remaining exclusively in national jurisdiction: 'To the extent required, the Federal Constitutional Court will base its review of the European act in question on the interpretation provided by the European Court of Justice in a preliminary ruling under Art 267 sec 3 of the Treaty on the Functioning of the European Union (TFEU). c) The constitutional ... identity ... includes the principles of Art 1 GG. The protected interests that, according to Art 23 sec 1 sentence 3 in conjunction with Art 79 sec 3 GG, are not open to integration must not be touched. Against this backdrop, the Federal Constitutional Court, by way of identity review, guarantees, unconditionally and in any individual case, the protection of fundamental rights that is indispensable according to Art 23 sec 1 sentence 3 in conjunction with Art 79 sec 3 and Art 1 sec 1 GG'. The Federal Constitutional Court continues in 2 (aa): 'In Germany, criminal law is based on the principle of individual guilt, which is enshrined in the guarantee of human dignity and in the rule of law (Art 20 sec 3 GG) and which, due to Art 79 sec 3 GG, is part of the inalienable constitutional identity'. Press Release No 4/2016 of 26 January 2016 Order of 15 December 2015—2 BvR 2735/14.

[32] See Lenaerts (n 24) 12ff.

problems that national legislatures had to face were tension between the absence of the direct effect of Framework Decisions and the self-executing wording of the EAW which appears to be addressed to national judicial authorities. In this part, I will discuss three questions. First, on the grounds of which criteria can we determine who the addressees of the EAW are? Second, are there objective criteria according to which one can decide whether the discretion granted by the EAW belongs to legislative or judicial authorities? Third, what kind of definition of the term 'executing judicial authority' preserves the useful effect of the EAW?

A. Who are the Addressees?

The problem can be illustrated by reference to Article 3 EAW laying down conditions for mandatory non-execution and Article 4 that prescribes the grounds for optional non-execution. Both provisions refer to national executing judicial authorities as their addressees. While Article 3 leaves them no discretion and specifies cases where execution of the EAW 'shall be refused', Article 4 is drafted in non-absolute language and uses the expression 'may refuse'. For example, Article 3(1) specifies that national judicial authority *shall* refuse to execute the EAW 'if the offence on which the arrest warrant is based is covered by amnesty in the executing Member State' and Article 4(4) provides that the executing judicial authority *may* refuse to execute 'where the criminal prosecution or punishment of the requested person is statute-barred according to the law of the executing Member State and the acts fall within the jurisdiction of that Member State under its own criminal law'.

How is the latter provision to be interpreted knowing that the EAW is a framework decision which needs to be implemented into the national legal orders of the Member States and which does not create direct effect? Does it allow, for example, national legislative authorities to exercise discretion under Article 4(4) and prescribe a statute of limitations under national law as a ground for mandatory instead of optional non-execution? Or does the EAW create an obligation for the Member States to leave the decision whether to execute or not to the national judicial authorities? In other words, the question is whether the EAW intended the optional grounds for non-execution to be exercised by the legislative or by the judicial branch. According to the former interpretation, once the national legislative branch has defined one of the optional grounds, the option is consumed and the judicial branch has to follow the legislative choice. According to the latter, such legislative discretion does not exist and national legislature has no other possibility but to maintain the judicial discretion granted to national courts by the EAW. If the EAW intended to grant discretion to national judicial authorities, they should be in a position to take into account other objectives of the Framework Decision and EU law in general and ultimately refuse to surrender the requested person only if no EAW-friendly interpretation of national law that would allow surrender under EU law is possible. This follows also from Article 1(2) EAW which obliges the Member States, 'in principle', to execute the EAW.[33]

The European Commission has suggested two possibilities for the transposition of the EAW. While discretion may be left to a national court, the Commission does not exclude an interpretation according to which the Member States are entitled to define optional grounds for non-execution by legislative means.[34] In this way, the optional nature of the grounds for non-execution defined in Article 4 EAW will be consumed by the legislature, after which they will no longer be optional for the judicial authorities. In other words, the option envisaged by the Framework Decision will be consumed by the national legislature, and the national judicial authorities will have to respect the legislative choice made. In the case where national law creates an obstacle for execution in violation of the Framework Decision, the Commission will have the possibility to institute an infraction procedure against the defaulting Member State. This method of implementation does not allow discretion to national judicial authorities, contrary to what the Commission seems to prefer.[35]

B. Whose Discretion?

In pursuance of the aims of the EAW, national authorities, either legislative or judicial, can exercise discretion. The EAW itself is silent on this point and leaves the choice to the Member States. The case law of the CJEU is also open ended and the wording employed to describe the obligation to extradite usually refers to the Member States without specifying whether it is incumbent on the legislative or the judicial branch.[36] Nevertheless, the choice between the two depends on a number

---

[33] *Radu* (26) para 35: 'Under Article 1(2) of Framework Decision 2002/584, the Member States are in principle obliged to act upon a European arrest warrant'. The obligation to execute the EAW is recognised by the German Federal Constitutional Court, subject to scrutiny of Constitutional Rights: 'As a rule, the Framework Decision on the European arrest warrant is accorded precedence in the German legal system; according to the jurisprudence of the Court of Justice of the European Union, the Framework Decision exhaustively deals with extraditions following sentences rendered in absence of the requested person; this, however, does not relieve the Higher Regional Court from its obligation to ensure that the principles laid down in Art 1 sec 1 GG, in its manifestation as principle of individual guilt, are protected in the context of an extradition based on a European arrest warrant as well'. See Order of 15 December 2015—2 R 2735/14 (n 14).

[34] Commission, Report from the Commission based on Art 34 of the Council Framework Decision of 13 June 2002 on the European arrest warrant and the surrender procedures between Member States COM(2005) 63 final, 4: 'However, transposition of the optional grounds varies considerably from one Member State to the next: some States have only adopted them in part or have left a greater margin of discretion to their judicial authorities, while others have made them all mandatory. Although possible in principle, unless case law develops differently (Article 4(3)), this choice of transposal is open to criticism if it goes so far as to make executing judicial authorities themselves prosecute rather than accept an arrest warrant when proceedings are in progress in the issuing Member State (Article 4(2))'.

[35] See n 34.

[36] See, eg, Case C-123/08 *Dominic Wolzenburg* EU:C:2009:616: 'The principle of mutual recognition, which underpins Framework Decision 2002/584, means that, in accordance with Article 1(2)

of considerations. These include: (IV.B.i) the wording and purpose of the EAW; (IV.B.ii) the useful effect of EU law; (IV.B.iii) the duty of sincere cooperation, and (IV.B.iv) the systemic interpretation of the *acquis* of the AFSJ.

i. Wording and Purpose

It is a commonplace that, according to the plain language of the Treaties, framework decisions do not have direct effect. This said, the European legislature, when adopting framework decisions, could not have intended other than to create an obligation for national authorities 'as to the result to be achieved'. In this context, the self-executing language of the EAW is confusing.[37] Namely, phrases like 'executing judicial authority shall ...' create the impression that the primary addressees of the EAW are national courts. At the same time, since framework decisions, just like directives, generally need legislative transposition into national law,[38] the EAW merely creates an obligation for the Member States to implement the EAW by achieving the desired result.

Faithful application of EU law is an obligation of all branches of national government and all national authorities, in general.[39] While this obligation may vary depending on whether an applicable rule can or cannot have direct effect, this does not affect the general obligation of all national authorities to interpret national law, as far as possible, in light of EU law. Regardless of the fact that the EAW is not

---

thereof, the Member States are in principle obliged to act upon a European arrest warrant. Apart from the cases of mandatory non-execution laid down in Article 3 of the Framework Decision, the Member States may refuse to execute such a warrant only in the cases listed in Article 4 thereof (Case C-388/08 PPU *Leymann and Pustovarov* [2008] ECR I-0000, paragraph 51)'.

[37] See, eg, the language of Art 3 EAW: 'The judicial authority of the Member State of execution (hereinafter "executing judicial authority") shall refuse to execute the European arrest warrant in the following cases ...'

[38] See Case 102/79 *Commission v Belgium* EU:C:1980:120, paras 10–11; see also Case 29/84 *Commission v Germany* EU:C:1985:229, para 23 to the effect that legislative transposition may not be necessary where general principles of constitutional or administrative law render implementation superfluous: 'It follows from that provision that the implementation of a directive does not necessarily require legislative action in each Member State. In particular the existence of general principles of constitutional or administrative law may render implementation by specific legislation superfluous, provided however that those principles guarantee that the national authorities will in fact apply the directive fully and that, where the directive is intended to create rights for individuals, the legal position arising from those principles is sufficiently precise and clear and the persons concerned are made fully aware of their rights and, where appropriate, afforded the possibility of relying on them before the national courts. That last condition is of particular importance where the directive in question is intended to accord rights to nationals of other Member States because those nationals are not normally aware of such principles'. See also Case C-365/93 *Commission v Greece* EU:C:1995:76, para 9.

[39] This can be traced back to early case law as formulated by the CJEU in Case 106/77 *Simmenthal* 2 EU:C:1978:49, para 22: 'Accordingly any provision of a national legal system and any legislative, administrative or judicial practice which might impair the effectiveness of Community law by withholding from the national court having jurisdiction to apply such law the power to do everything necessary at the moment of its application to set aside national legislative provisions which might prevent Community rules from having full force and effect are incompatible with those requirements which are the very essence of Community law'.

specific in this respect, the same holds for the obligation to achieve the objectives it envisages. In other words, the same obligation is incumbent on both national legislative and judicial authorities.

While it is not disputed that the Member States can choose the method of compliance, the question remains whether the result envisaged by the EAW can be achieved if national legislative power, when transposing the EAW, preempts judicial discretion. More specifically, can legislative discretion preempt the exercise of judicial discretion and compel national courts to apply national law, which defines optional grounds for non-execution as mandatory?[40] In *Wolzenburg*, the CJEU clarified that national legislature is allowed to limit the optional grounds for non-execution in the sense that surrender is facilitated.[41] This is possible since it reinforces the system of surrender introduced within the AFSJ. The CJEU did not have an opportunity to say whether the transformation of optional grounds into mandatory grounds would be in accordance with the Framework Directive, but it is difficult to imagine the Court endorsing a result that would lead to an erosion of the system.

It should be repeated that the self-executing language of the EAW does not imply its direct effect. While, at first glance, there is tension between the self-executing language of the EAW and the absence of direct effect, it should be recognised that the two are not interdependent. Actually, the absence of the direct effect of the EAW does not flow only from the Treaty, but from the standard and well-established description of direct effect in the case law of the CJEU. The CJEU has habitually defined direct effect as 'creating individual rights which national courts must protect'. In the case of surrender under the EAW, it is, however, questionable whether there is any grant of rights under EU law that an individual could invoke as against the state.[42] Lenaerts also takes note of this by making the point that in respect of the AFSJ, unlike in respect of fundamental market freedoms, EU law restricts and does not grant individual rights.[43] Instead, there is a grant of power to national judicial authorities to exercise discretion, taking into account EU law and interpreting national law accordingly, as well as a corresponding burden, or liability, that a national court can bring upon an individual. In any case, Article 4 EAW does not seem to be 'clear, unconditional and precise' which is another element

---

[40] For the Commission's view, see n 34.

[41] *Wolzenburg* (n 36) paras 58 and 59: '58. It follows that a national legislature which, by virtue of the options afforded it by Article 4 of the Framework Decision, chooses to limit the situations in which its executing judicial authority may refuse to surrender a requested person merely reinforces the system of surrender introduced by that Framework Decision to the advantage of an area of freedom, security and justice. 59. Indeed, by limiting the situations in which the executing judicial authority may refuse to execute a European arrest warrant, such legislation only facilitates the surrender of requested persons, in accordance with the principle of mutual recognition set out in Article 1(2) of Framework Decision 2002/584, which constitutes the essential rule introduced by that decision'.

[42] See *Pupino* (n 13) para 34.

[43] Lenaerts (n 24) 3. See also M. Möstl, 'Preconditions and Limits of Mutual Recognition' (2010) 47 *CML Rev* 405.

of the standard description of direct effect. Quite the opposite, it is the executing judicial authority that is empowered to exercise the choice, the outcome of which does not unconditionally follow from a rule of EU law.

ii. Useful Effect

This said, recognising that all judicial discretion can be preempted by national regulation would vacate some provisions of the EAW of their useful effect. Apparently, it can be assumed that at least some choices need to be left to national judicial authorities since at least some of those grounds do require judicial assessment. For example, in *Joao Pedro Lopes Da Silva Jorge*, deciding on one of the optional grounds laid down by Article 4(6), the CJEU clarified that decisions concerning certain optional grounds for non-execution require judicial assessment, particularly concerning the degree of social integration of the individual concerned.[44]

Clearly, it is not possible for the legislative authorities to perform the analysis of social integration in abstract and to define the incidence and degree of social integration in advance, since that requires judicial appreciation of the individual circumstances of the person concerned. In such a case, reference of the EAW to the judicial authority would be void of any useful effect.

On the other hand, some other grounds for optional non-execution, such as those mentioned in Article 4(4), can be applied without the exercise of judicial discretion. Determination of a limitation period is a binary exercise and the court can only decide that it has or has not lapsed while, at the same time, the legislature can prescribe which legal consequences attach to that.[45] In any case, the right balance of judicial discretion and legislative ordering may vary from one Member State to another, at least until the CJEU clarifies EU law in that respect.

Not less importantly, the CJEU has recognised in some provisions of the EAW the significance of a 'concept of EU law'.[46] For example, the concept of 'same acts' in the context of the application of the principle '*ne bis in idem*' is one of such concepts. As the CJEU clarified in *Mantello*, the concept of 'same acts' which forms part of the *ne bis in idem* principle, which is a mandatory ground for non-execution, is a concept of EU law which needs to be interpreted uniformly by the CJEU.[47]

---

[44] Case C-42/11 *Joao Pedro Lopes Da Silva Jorge* EU:C:2012:517, para 32; and *Wolzenburg* (n 25) paras 62 and 67: 'that ground for optional non-execution has in particular the objective of enabling the executing judicial authority to give particular weight to the possibility of increasing the requested person's chances of reintegrating into society when the sentence imposed on him expires', and that 'when implementing that provision, the Member States have a certain margin of discretion. The Member State of execution is entitled to pursue such an objective only in respect of persons who have demonstrated a certain degree of integration in the society of that Member State …' See also Case C-66/08 *Kozłowski* EU:C:2008:437, para 45.

[45] However, even in such a case, judicial authorities may have to decide more complex situations, eg whether the time lapse has been suspended or when precisely the deadline expired.

[46] For a discussion of the concepts of EU law, see the text cited in n 2.

[47] Case C-261/09 *Gaetano Mantello* EU:C:2010:683, para 38: '[t]he concept of "same acts" in Article 3(2) of the Framework Decision cannot be left to the discretion of the judicial authorities of

In other words, allowing national legislature to define the meaning of such a concept would remove the EAW of its useful effect in EU law and would restrict national courts in submitting preliminary references to the CJEU.

iii. Duty of Sincere Cooperation

The case for national judicial discretion is also advanced by the duty of sincere cooperation and the corresponding obligation to interpret national law in light of EU law.[48] Since the national court needs to take into account the entire body of EU law, lack of discretion to do so would frustrate its clear obligation under EU law to interpret national law in accordance with EU law.[49]

It is only a national court that can decide whether the circumstances mentioned in Article 4 EAW exist or not. This adds to the plausibility of the proposition that the optional grounds for non-execution are optional for national judicial authorities and do not authorise national legislature to exercise the discretion whether a particular ground is optional or mandatory. To my eyes, correct implementation of Article 4 requires that, when transposing optional grounds for non-execution, national legislative authorities may not define the latter as mandatory but, on the contrary, have to allow judicial discretion to decide whether to execute an EAW or not, depending on the circumstances and interpreting the national law in light of EU law. A separate question is whether the mentioned judicial discretion extends to all optional grounds listed in Article 4 EAW or only some of them. As a minimum, to preserve the useful effect of the EAW, national courts should be able to treat grounds for non-execution as not being absolute, to interpret them in light of EU law and have an opportunity to submit a preliminary reference to the CJEU.

In any case, both national and European authorities are bound by guarantees of fundamental rights under the EU Charter of Rights, and the EAW itself recognises this in the twelfth recital of its Preamble.[50] However, when invoked by a party in

---

each Member State on the basis of their national law. It follows from the need for uniform application of European Union law that, since that provision makes no reference to the law of the Member States with regard to that concept, the latter must be given an autonomous and uniform interpretation throughout the European Union …'.

[48] Following the amendments introduced by the Treaty of Lisbon, the duty of sincere cooperation is provided for by Art 4(3) TEU: ' Pursuant to the principle of sincere cooperation, the Union and the Member States shall, in full mutual respect, assist each other in carrying out tasks which flow from the Treaties'. The duty to interpret national law in the light of EU law, unless such interpretation is *contra legem*, follows from the well-established practice of the CJEU.

[49] See *Joao Pedro Lopes Da Silva Jorge* (n 44) para 60: '[t]he national court is required, taking into consideration the whole body of domestic law and applying the interpretative methods recognised by it, to interpret that law, so far as possible, in the light of the wording and the purpose of Framework Decision 2002/584, with a view to ensuring that that framework decision is fully effective and to achieving an outcome consistent with the objective pursued by it'. See also *Pupino* (n 13) para 34.

[50] Recital 12 reads: 'This Framework Decision respects fundamental rights and observes the principles recognised by Article 6 of the Treaty on European Union and reflected in the Charter of Fundamental Rights of the European Union(7), in particular Chapter VI thereof. Nothing in this Framework Decision may be interpreted as prohibiting refusal to surrender a person for whom a European arrest

order to oppose a decision of a national court to execute an EAW, the national court has to apply standards of fundamental rights as interpreted by the CJEU in order to preserve the primacy, unity and effectiveness of EU law, and may not refuse to execute the EAW by applying allegedly higher national standards.[51] This position was, however, clarified and further developed in *Caldararu and Aranyosi* where the CJEU made execution of the EAW conditional upon the absence of 'evidence of a real risk of inhuman or degrading treatment of individuals detained in the issuing Member State'.[52]

In other words, the discretion of national courts is restrained by national implementing legislation on one hand, and by the duty of EU-friendly interpretation on the other.

iv. Acquis of the AFSJ

Another limit to national legislative discretion flows from the need for the systematic interpretation of EU law in the AFSJ. There are two separate problems.

First, the exercise of judicial discretion is necessary to put in balance different obligations under national and EU law. For example, in *Spasić*,[53] the CJEU ruled, in the somewhat different legal context of the Convention Implementing the Schengen Agreement, that the principle of *ne bis in idem* is not absolute and has to be interpreted in light of European rules applicable to the AFSJ, including its objective to avoid impunity. It should be noted that the *ne bis in idem* principle is also laid down as a reason for non-execution of the EAW and that the concept of 'same act' may have a different meaning in the context of internal situations and in the context of EU law.

---

warrant has been issued when there are reasons to believe, on the basis of objective elements, that the said arrest warrant has been issued for the purpose of prosecuting or punishing a person on the grounds of his or her sex, race, religion, ethnic origin, nationality, language, political opinions or sexual orientation, or that that person's position may be prejudiced for any of these reasons'.

[51] Case C-399/11 *Stefano Melloni* EU:C:2013:107, para 60: 'It is true that Article 53 of the Charter confirms that, where an EU legal act calls for national implementing measures, national authorities and courts remain free to apply national standards of protection of fundamental rights, provided that the level of protection provided for by the Charter, as interpreted by the Court, and the primacy, unity and effectiveness of EU law are not thereby compromised'.

[52] Joined Cases C-404/15 and C-659/15 PPU *Pál Aranyosi and Robert Căldăraru* EU:C:2016:198, para 88: 'It follows that, where the judicial authority of the executing Member State is in possession of evidence of a real risk of inhuman or degrading treatment of individuals detained in the issuing Member State, having regard to the standard of protection of fundamental rights guaranteed by EU law and, in particular, by Article 4 of the Charter (see, to that effect, judgment in Melloni, C-399/11 EU:C:2013:107, paragraphs 59 and 63, and Opinion 2/13, EU:C:2014:2454, paragraph 192), that judicial authority is bound to assess the existence of that risk when it is called upon to decide on the surrender to the authorities of the issuing Member State of the individual sought by a European arrest warrant. The consequence of the execution of such a warrant must not be that that individual suffers inhuman or degrading treatment'.

[53] Case C-129/14 PPU *Spasić* EU:C:2014:586, para 63:'The execution condition laid down in Article 54 CISA is to be seen in that context since it is intended, as noted in paragraph 58 of the present judgment, to prevent, in the area of freedom, security and justice, the impunity of persons definitively convicted and sentenced in an EU Member State'.

The second problem appears where a certain field is regulated partly by framework decisions and partly by directives. The picture is complicated by the fact that under Article 9 of Protocol number 36 to the Treaty of Lisbon, framework decisions can no longer be adopted, but 'shall be preserved until [they] are repealed, annulled or amended in implementation of the Treaties'.[54] Among the three mentioned events, I would like to discuss the last mentioned by asking in what measure the direct or indirect application of a directive may affect the interpretation and application of a framework decision. More precisely, in a vertical situation, and assuming a late transposition of a directive, can its clear unconditional and precise rule preclude a rule of national law transposing a framework decision? Imagine a situation where a national prosecutor of an executing Member State decides not to prosecute and, as a consequence, not to execute an EAW. In such a situation, the court of the executing Member State seized with the case would not have an opportunity to perform a judicial review of that decision because the requested person would have no interest to challenge the decision of the prosecution and the prosecution would not submit its own decision to judicial review. At the same time, a victim of the crime could invoke Article 11 of the Directive 2012/29/EU[55] which grants victims of crimes the right to review a decision not to prosecute.

When examining the request of the victim contesting the prosecutorial decision not to prosecute, a national court of the Member State of execution decides, in fact, about the execution of the EAW. Assuming that prosecution in that Member State is prevented by one or more of the mandatory or optional grounds for non-execution, as transposed in the national law of the executing Member State, interpretation of the directive will have effect on the interpretation of the framework decision. In order to ensure the useful effect of the Victims Directive, the national court will need to interpret national law in the light of both the Victims Directive and the Framework Decision on the EAW. In the case of a late transposition of the Directive, the victim of the crime can invoke it against the Member State, since, according to the well-settled case law of the CJEU, it produces direct effects. Arguably, the EAW must not be interpreted in a way that frustrates the useful effect of other rules of EU law and, conversely, EU law restricts the discretion of national authorities in the implementation and interpretation of the EAW.

---

[54] Art 9 of Protocol 36 reads: 'The legal effects of the acts of the institutions, bodies, offices and agencies of the Union adopted on the basis of the Treaty on European Union prior to the entry into force of the Treaty of Lisbon shall be preserved until those acts are repealed, annulled or amended in implementation of the Treaties. The same shall apply to agreements concluded between Member States on the basis of the Treaty on European Union'.

[55] Dir 2012/29/EU of the European Parliament and of the Council of 25 October 2012 establishing minimum standards on the rights, support and protection of victims of crime, and replacing Council Framework Decision 2001/220/JHA. Art 11 reads: 'Member States shall ensure that victims, in accordance with their role in the relevant criminal justice system, have the right to a review of a decision not to prosecute. The procedural rules for such a review shall be determined by national law'.

C. What Executing Judicial Authority?

As provided by Article 1(1) EAW, '[t]he European arrest warrant is a judicial decision issued by a Member State ...'. Obviously, judicial decisions can be adopted only by judicial authorities and, this time, reference to the Member States clearly does not refer to the national legislature. However, since the expression 'judicial decision' may include either national courts or national prosecuting authorities, the definition begs the question what the judicial authorities and what the judicial decisions are?

The Explanatory Memorandum produced by the European Commission and attached to the EAW leaves the choice of the executing judicial authority to the Member States, leaving them the possibility to designate a court or a public prosecutor.[56] While it makes little difference for the issuing Member State, the choice of a prosecutor as the executing judicial authority on the side of the requested Member State is not without problems.

To start with, the concept of 'executing judicial authority', unlike the concept of 'court or tribunal',[57] is not a concept of EU law, meaning that Member States remain competent to determine its meaning.[58] One could imagine three different situations. First, the situation where a requested person consents to surrender does not pose any particular problems related to execution, whether performed by a judge or a public prosecutor. Second is the situation where the requested person opposes the surrender, and the procedure is conducted by a court or tribunal. That jurisdiction will hear the case and decide to execute or not to execute the warrant. This situation also does not seem to be problematic. The third situation is one where the requested person opposes the surrender, and the procedure is conducted by a public prosecutor. If the prosecution decides not to proceed, and, accordingly, not to execute the warrant (for example, on one of the grounds of optional non-execution), a national judge of the Member State of execution will not be seized with the case since the requested person will typically not have a legal interest to contest the prosecutor's decision.[59] More generally, such would be the

---

[56] Commission, Proposal for a Council framework decision on the European arrest warrant and the surrender procedures between the Member States COM(2001) 522 final/2, 7–8: 'With regard to the executing judicial authority, several procedural mechanisms are possible depending whether the simplified procedure applies or not (Article 16). It will be the prosecution service or a judge, depending on the procedure applicable in the Member State. The term "executing judicial authority" will cover one or the other, as the case requires. But it must always be the authority that takes the decision to execute the warrant. Even if Article 5 enables the Member States to confer powers on a central authority in a series of circumstances, that authority will not be covered by this definition'.

[57] See most recently Case C-377/13 *Ascendi Beiras Litoral e Alta, Auto Estradas das Beiras Litoral e Alta SA v Autoridade Tributária e Aduaneira* EU:C:2014:1754, para 23.

[58] According to Art 6(2) of the EAW: 'The executing judicial authority shall be the judicial authority of the executing Member State which is competent to execute the European arrest warrant by virtue of the law of that State'.

[59] With the exception of cases where a victim or other person with recognised legal interest under national law can continue the prosecution.

situation in all cases where a public prosecutor in the Member State of execution of the EAW adopts a decision not to prosecute.[60]

It is a commonplace that only a national court can submit a preliminary reference to the CJEU concerning the interpretation or validity of the EAW, while a public prosecutor, not being a court or tribunal within the meaning of EU law, cannot. Therefore, leaving the execution in the hands of a public prosecutor, without the possibility of judicial review and without the possibility for a national court to address a preliminary reference to the CJEU, which is the situation in cases where the prosecution decides not to prosecute, weakens the useful effect of the EAW and of judicial cooperation with the CJEU. Among a variety of situations under the EAW that keep steadily coming to the docket of the CJEU, it should be mentioned that recently AG Bot opined in *Kossowski*, a case concerning interpretation of the Schengen Convention, that a prosecutor's decision not to pursue criminal proceedings should not be considered a 'final judgment' for the purposes of the *ne bis in idem* rule as guaranteed by Article 50 of the EU Charter of Rights, as long as the substance of the allegations has not been considered by the competent court.[61] The CJEU adopted essentially the same view and defined the concept of 'final judgment' as to require a profound investigation. Failure to have the victim of a crime heard in the capacity of a witness may be an indication of the absence of such an investigation.[62] In other words, a shallow investigation without a genuine assessment of the merits of a case deprives the decision of a national prosecutor that puts an end to prosecution of its character as final decision within the meaning of the Schengen Convention.

V. Final Remarks

The Treaty of Lisbon and the Charter of Fundamental Rights of the EU significantly changed the legal environment in which the EAW operates. Following the

---

[60] The latter was the case in *Piotr Kossowski*. See Case C-486/14 *Criminal Proceedings against Piotr Kossowski* EU:C:2015:812, Opinion of AG Bot, para 17. Admittedly, preliminary reference can be sent to the CJEU by the court of the issuing Member State. However, it is still possible that the executing judicial authority of the issuing Member State was not a court but the prosecutor.

[61] ibid para 85: 'The *ne bis in idem* principle expressed in Article 54 of that convention and in Article 50 of that charter must be interpreted as meaning that an order of discontinuance made by the public prosecutor's office, terminating investigative proceedings, cannot be characterized as a final disposal for the purposes of those articles, where it is clear from the reasons stated in that order that the matters making up the very substance of the legal situation, such as hearing the victim and the witness, have not been examined by the judicial authorities concerned'. This is to be distinguished from the judgment in Cases C-187/01 and C-385/01, where the CJEU held that the *ne bis in idem* principle, laid down in Art 54 of the Convention implementing the Schengen Agreement, applies to a situation where the public prosecutor adopted a decision after having examined the case on the merits. See Joined Cases C-187/01 and C-385/01 *Criminal proceedings against Hüseyin Gözütok and Klaus Brügge* EU:C:2003:87.

[62] Case C-486/14 *Kossowski* EU:C:2016:483, para 54.

expiry of the five-year transitional period on 1 December 2014, the system of inter-EU rendition has grown teeth in the form of European Commission enforcement powers and in the form of preliminary references to the CJEU.

Application of the EAW by national courts and its interpretation by the CJEU are stretched between two normative claims: the claim for the uniform interpretation and application of EU law and the claim for the preservation of what I will call 'traditional national ways of doing things in criminal law'. The origin of this tension seems to lie in the fact that the subject matter of regulation of the EAW is not genuinely European but heavily relies on concepts and traditions of national law. More precisely, the European functional quest of becoming an area of freedom, security and justice by abolishing extradition between Member States and replacing it by a system of surrender between judicial authorities is confronted with mundane and static national concepts such as double criminality, *ne bis in idem*, statutory limitations or amnesty.

Within this tension between the functional and static, the European and national, two kinds of impediments to the useful effect of the EAW arise. On the one hand, there are overt, typically procedural obstacles caused by the almost usual rift between national law and novel European regulation. For example, Article 6(2) EAW defines executing judicial authority as 'the judicial authority of the executing Member State which is competent to execute the European arrest warrant by virtue of the law of that State'. While this provision clearly refers back to the national law of the Member States, it is more or less clear that, for example, a national authority for rescue at sea can hardly fulfil the task, while national courts seem to be far more appropriate. In other words, while leaving discretion to the Member States, EU law still provides for a general framework that is meant to ensure the useful effect of EU law.

On the other hand there are inherent hurdles, such as loyalty to national criminal concepts and practices of extradition. Both kinds of obstacles are amplified by the fact that the EAW is deeply embedded in national criminal law and procedure and that the initial wave of its transposition took place in a much less supranationalised legal environment.

Not less importantly, the EAW regulates an extremely sensitive area of law that is considered to belong to a hard core of national sovereignty. As a result, there is constant tension between the requirements of EU law and national measures that may restrict the possibility for the CJEU to pronounce itself on preliminary references on interpretation of the EAW. Such national measures have the potential of voiding Article 10 paragraph 3 of protocol number 36 annexed to the Treaty of Lisbon, as well as of Article 267 TFEU, of their useful effect.[63] In other words,

---

[63] Para 3 envisages that transitional measures cease to apply five years after the entry into force of the Treaty of Lisbon. Accordingly, after 1 December 2014, the CJEU assumed competence to decide on preliminary references concerning the interpretation or validity of framework decisions, and the European Commission assumed its police powers in infraction proceedings.

since 1 December 2014, EU law requires that national courts have the possibility to address preliminary references on the interpretation and validity of the EAW to the CJEU, and jurisdiction of the Court should not be frustrated by provisions of national law such as those making it possible for a public prosecutor to disallow surrender without the possibility of judicial review by a national court and, consequently, by the CJEU.

EU law encroachments on what is considered national sovereignty is nothing new in the history of European integration. In that sense, it may be useful to recall formative developments in the area of free movement of goods. Once customs duties were abolished in trade between Member States, a number of measures of equivalent effect to quantitative restrictions (MEEs), liable to restrict intra-Community trade, began to emerge. This prompted the CJEU to develop tests and criteria for their legality under EU law. The rationale was the suspicion that the MEEs would render the abolition of customs duties and the free movement of goods void of their useful effect.

There is certain functional resemblance between the MEEs and national measures adopted in the implementation of the EAW. National measures, such as the definition of the optional grounds for non-execution as mandatory and the designation of the prosecution as the executing judicial authority, apparently transpose the EAW but at the same time pose questions of its useful effect. More precisely, once interstate surrender has been liberalised, preservation of the useful effect of the EAW would require the removal of possible alternative barriers.

This time, however, the situation is different. The Treaty of Lisbon amended earlier Treaty provisions laying down the national identity clause and the duty of sincere cooperation. The former allowed for more regulatory discretion of national authorities[64] and the latter converted the duty of loyal cooperation that was incumbent on the Member States into the symmetrical duty binding both the Member States and the European Union. Not surprisingly, this has been echoed by national courts.[65] In the German interpretation, national identity review, as interpreted and performed by the GFCC, is possible in exceptional circumstances subject to interpretation friendly to EU law but, nevertheless, may override EU law in particular cases. In this way, the real question seems to be not which legal system

---

[64] See, eg, A von Bogdandy and S Schill, 'Overcoming Absolute Primacy: Respect for National Identity under the Lisbon Treaty' (2011) 48 *CML Rev* 1417; S Rodin, 'National Identity and Market Freedoms After the Treaty of Lisbon' (2011) 7 *Croatian Yearbook of European Law & Policy* 11.

[65] For the German Federal Constitutional Court, see n 31: 'The identity review conducted by the Federal Constitutional Court safeguards the constitutional identity. As with ultra vires reviews, [identity] reviews may ultimately result in Union law having to be declared inapplicable in exceptional cases. To prevent German authorities and courts from simply disregarding the Union law's claim to validity, applying Art 23 sec 1 sentence 3 in conjunction with Art 79 sec 3 GG in a manner that is open to European integration and the legal concept expressed in Art 100 sec 1 GG both require that declaring a violation of the constitutional identity is reserved for the Federal Constitutional Court. In substance, identity review is a concept inherent in Art 4 sec 2 sentence 1 of the Treaty on European Union (TEU) and does not violate the principle of sincere cooperation within the meaning of Art 4 sec 3 TEU'.

prevails, but which court gets to interpret EU law, and how. Recent judgments of the CJEU in *Caldararu and Aranyosi* on one hand and in *Kossowski* on the other provide recent examples, in criminal law cases, of how the CJEU has responded to national concerns by reconstituting national legal concepts within EU law. This, in my view, is possible not because of certain postulated or inherent teleology of EU law, but because of the CJEU's belief in and perpetuation of European ontology,[66] this time in the context of the Area of Freedom, Security and Justice.

---

[66] ie European ontological identities, notably the Founding Treaties as the Legal Basis, the Process of European Integration as the Act, and the Consent of the Peoples of Europe and the Member States as the Agents.

Part V

Academic Discourse and the Transformation of Europe

9

Reflections on European Legal Formalism

PIETER-AUGUSTIJN VAN MALLEGHEM[*]

There exists a legal-cultural abyss between the United States and Europe, an abyss often summarily referred to under the name 'American Legal Realism'. The anti-formalism of the American Legal Realists transformed American understanding of the role of the judiciary in society, even of law *tout court*. The phenomenon often manifests itself in interactions between American and European lawyers. Many a European lawyer has been confronted, in their exchanges with American colleagues, with the challenge that their views are 'formalist'. This damning epithet alludes to the fact that American legal thought devalues the importance of abstract legal reasoning by contrast with extra-legal factors influencing legal and judicial decision-making, among which politics takes a prominent place. The American prejudice that Europeans are hopelessly formalist has deep roots in American legal theory and education. It is commonly thought that the emergence of American Legal Realism in the first half of the twentieth century solidly implanted anti-formalist legal thought in American legal consciousness, contrasting boldly with the formalism of European legal culture.

With his *Judicial Deliberations*, Mitchel Lasser has made a vital contribution to this European-American debate. Through a close examination of the argumentative practices of the American Supreme Court and two European courts, the French Cour de Cassation and the Court of Justice of the European Union (ECJ), Lasser was able to put forward a persuasive argument that Europeans are far less formalist than is commonly thought in America. Indeed, alongside a visibly deeply formalist primary discourse of these two courts, Lasser discovers a less visible, dramatically less formalist accompanying discourse. Europeans are not the formalists Americans understand them to be, but their anti-formalism is expressed in different sites.

This contribution seeks to shed a complementary, albeit fundamentally different, light on the question of formalism and anti-formalism within the European

---

[*] Pieter-Augustijn Van Malleghem is an SJD candidate at Harvard Law School.

context. While I ultimately concur with Lasser, I develop an alternative account of what the concepts of formalism and anti-formalism delineate. Formalism and anti-formalism refer to the power of legal reasoning to yield interpretive closure in the form of correct legal answers. The anti-formalist attitude can be understood as the attitude of distantiation: the refusal to take legal arguments at face value, to doubt their capacity to ultimately decide the legal question at hand. Distantiation is an individual attitude, though it has deeper roots in legal culture, primarily in legal education and legal theory.

I take the question of the (non-)existence of anti-formalism in European legal thought to be central to the emergence of a Critical Legal Studies movement in Europe. American anti-formalist thought indeed formed the fertile soil from which Critical Legal Studies would later emerge. Anti-formalism has been, and remains, a cornerstone of critical legal thought around the globe. If Critical Legal Studies is to be a powerful movement in legal practice and thought in Europe, as it has been in the United States, its success will depend on its ability to build upon and strengthen the legacy of European anti-formalist legal thought.

I. An Account of European Legal Culture

In *Judicial Deliberations*, Lasser proposes a fundamental shift in traditional American conceptions of European legal culture. As Lasser puts it,

> [t]he gist of ... traditional American accounts is that the French Civil judicial system— the poster child of Continental European, civilian legality—represents the misguided and formalist alternative to the American system's judicial pragmatism. France, accord- ing to this American comparative tradition, is in some respect pre-realist or, at best, realist-ignorant.[1]

In this traditional narrative, the Europeans are formalist, whereas the American legal culture is described as realist, the American home-grown variation of anti-formalism.

A prominent example of such a traditional account can be found in the work of Duncan Kennedy. Kennedy describes the dominant European conception of judicial decision-making in the following way:

> On the Continent, the official story is that the role of the judge is to apply the relevant Code to the facts of the case using a presumption of gaplessness. If the case cannot be resolved by semantic or deductive analysis of the meanings of the terms in a validly enacted rule, the judge deploys interpretive techniques based on the presumption that the Code is the coherent working out of a particular conceptual structure. He does the

---

[1] M Lasser, *Judicial Deliberations. A Comparative Analysis of Judicial Transparency and Legitimacy* (Oxford, Oxford University Press, 2004) 27–28.

best he can but does not entertain the possibility that 'there is no right answer.' In the official version, the judge can always do his job, though some cases are harder than others. In this respect, Dworkin is a Continental.[2]

In another passage, Kennedy identifies one specific feature of American anti-formalism and contrasts it with the prevailing European legal culture.

> I mentioned a moment ago that the realists taught 'distrust of abstraction'. By this I mean that they had a general notion that the more abstract the concepts that went into the definition of a legal norm, the more unlikely that it could be elaborated by deduction to produce a subrule that would resolve a particular case.[3]

This specific feature of American anti-formalism is thought to be absent in the European tradition, leading to the understanding that European legal thought is formalist.

> As I've indicated several times already, your ordinary American lawyer is likely to find European solutions to classic legal problems blatantly formalist, in the sense of overestimating the power of deduction, and to find European legal culture in general formalist in the same sense. When Europeans protest that none of them think, or ever did think, that deduction could solve every legal problem, the American lawyer is likely to think they have missed the point, which has to do with an attitude toward abstraction rather than with a theory of law in the jurisprudential sense.[4]

Lasser offers an alternative account of European legal culture, which differs considerably from Kennedy's picture. He argues that 'it has been a recurring mistake for the American discipline of comparative law to organize its understanding of Franco-American judicial difference around the formalism/realism divide'.[5] Lasser argues that European legal discourse can be understood as bifurcated (ie simultaneously incorporating features of formalism and anti-formalism), complexifying the identification of European legal discourse with formalism and American legal discourse with anti-formalism. Lasser recognises the decisions of the French Cour de Cassation to be formalist, whereas the decisions of the American Supreme Court are considerably influenced by the anti-formalist American Legal Realist tradition. The bifurcation can be exemplified in EU legal discourse: ECJ decisions are considered more formalist than American Supreme Court decisions (albeit not as formalist as decisions of the French Cour de Cassation) whereas Opinions of ECJ Advocates General are less formalist even than the opinions of the Supreme Court.[6] It is this bifurcation of EU legal discourse between the decisions of the ECJ and the Opinions of its Advocate General which makes it particularly difficult to identify European legal discourse as either formalist or anti-formalist.

---

[2] D Kennedy, *A Critique of Adjudication. Fin de siècle* (Cambridge, Harvard University Press, 1997) 36.
[3] ibid 107.
[4] ibid.
[5] Lasser (n 1) 299.
[6] ibid 251, 258.

Lasser's picture of formalism relies upon textual analysis examining the interpretive openness of the language used in legal argument. The decisions of the French Cour de Cassation are considered formalist because of the 'terse, unsigned, univocal, and single-sentence textual syllogism' of its judgments.[7] Conversely, American Supreme Court decisions reflect 'American judicial pragmatism or realism' thanks to the 'open-ended quality' of their arguments which 'undoubtedly brings far more to the table than a textual syllogism'[8] and 'often offers more than one take on the controversy at hand'.[9] ECJ decisions fall somewhere in between, as they remain 'univocal and unsigned', 'highly magisterial and deductive' yet 'offer[] distinctly visible marks of interpretive openness'.[10] An Opinion of an Advocate General, however, is even more open-ended than American Supreme Court decisions because it 'presents, considers, and responds to the arguments and perspectives of a veritable litany of players' resulting in a 'staggering' 'cacophony of interpretive voices'.[11] Furthermore, opinions use subjective language and are expressed 'in an eminently personalized, perspective-laden, and even insecure fashion that only stresses the plurality of views and the range of interpretive options presented in ECJ controversies'.[12]

II. Formalism and Anti-formalism

I propose an alternative account of the tension between formalism and anti-formalism in order to challenge both Kennedy's and Lasser's understanding of American and European legal culture. This account defends the view that the concepts of formalism and anti-formalism refer to interpretive closure and undecidability, respectively. Both are reflected in the distantiation of legal arguers with respect to the legal arguments they advance. Distantiation is a phenomenon attributable to an individual who advances a legal argument, yet it has deeper roots within legal culture, traceable to legal education and legal theoretical debate.

A. A Different Approach

The tension between formalism and anti-formalism must be distinguished from an unreflexive, immediate approach to legal reasoning. One way of engaging in the practice of legal argument is to focus on the legal question at hand, and attempt to

---

[7] ibid 244.
[8] ibid.
[9] ibid 245.
[10] ibid.
[11] ibid 249.
[12] ibid 250.

resolve it. Legal argument as a practice is simply accepted as is, no questions asked. Legal argument is the fuel of a complex machinery composed by, among others, the judiciary, bar associations and legal academy. The machine can run without us. What matters is how we operate it.

The reason why the unreflexive, immediate approach to legal reasoning is unsatisfying is that the practice of legal reasoning is recurrently experienced as problematic. The machine sputters. Call it the epistemic problem: our knowledge of the law falls short of what legal practice requires.[13] The process of legal reasoning, for one, repeatedly stumbles upon (perceived?) gaps in the legal materials. Similarly, legal argument relentlessly reveals series of potentially contradictory legal arguments responding to identical legal questions. Gaps and contradictions may depend on particular interpretations of legal rules: under one interpretation, a gap or conflict exists, under another, it does not (or they do not). Despite gaps, conflicts and interpretive ambiguities, answers need to be given to legal problems, and they need to be justified by the legal materials.

One can also observe that legal arguers often operate with an implicit sense of what is 'just', a sense which can be distinguished from the meaning of the legal materials themselves. This sense of justice adds an additional layer of complexity. The practice of legal argument ought to reconcile the legal materials with this view of justice. The possibility of an outright conflict between what the law requires and what justice requires cannot be excluded a priori.[14]

Formalism and anti-formalism can both be understood as mediated, reflexive understandings of legal argument. On the one hand, they take into account the necessities of legal practice. It is understood that legal argument serves a purpose in the real world, ie the determination of certain outcomes as either complying with legal requirements or not. On the other hand, they are aware of the deficiencies of legal argument. They confront the challenge of gaps, conflicts, inconsistencies and injustices in legal argument. It is the combination of both elements that yields a formalist or anti-formalist understanding of legal argument.

Formalism is a mediate, reflexive understanding of legal argument which emphasises the ability of legal argument to yield interpretive closure. It aims to respond to the challenge by offering a theory of legal reasoning. Traditionally, the concept of formalism refers to the idea that interpretive closure can be reached by relying upon legal arguments and traditional logic alone, paradigmatically on deductive legal reasoning. The definition proposed here goes further in that it understands as equally formalist those theories which aim to achieve interpretive closure by relying upon non-deductive arguments, such as teleological arguments, or even non-legal arguments, such as moral, economic or political considerations. What matters is our ability to point towards a 'correct answer'.

---

[13] One might think, for instance, of the interpretive challenges and problems identified by P Schlag in this volume.

[14] Canonically, G Radbruch, 'Gesetzliches Unrecht und übergesetzliches Recht' (1946) 1 *Süddeutsche Juristen-Zeitung* 105.

A paramount example of formalism is what Duncan Kennedy has called 'conceptual interpretive formalism' which '"constructs" general principles thought necessary if the legal system is to be understood as coherent. It uses the principles to resolve uncertainty about the meaning of extant valid norms, and applies the principles according to their meaning to fill apparent gaps ...'.[15] Alongside conceptual interpretive formalism, Kennedy recognises an array of existing conceptions of formalism, among which are textual interpretive and precedential interpretive formalism. Unger offers a more expansive definition, arguing that formalism can be understood as 'a commitment to, and therefore also a belief in the possibility of, a method of legal justification that contrasts with open-ended disputes about the basic terms of social life-disputes variously dubbed ideological, philosophical, or visionary'.[16]

Formalism offers a metaphysics of legal reasoning. Legal argument is the palpable evidence of law in the 'real world'. Formalism goes beyond the realm of these appearances by constructing a theory which overcomes the shortcomings of these appearances: the gaps, conflicts, ambiguities and injustices of law which we encounter in concrete instances of legal argument. Whether in the guise of the legal concepts, principles or purposes, or of moral, political or economic concepts driving legal argument, formalist theories interpret the practice of legal argument in light of a world of ideas that transcends it.

Anti-formalism is a mediate, reflexive understanding of legal argument which emphasises the moments of undecidability within legal argument: moments where legal argument does not yield a compelling answer, despite the requirement that a decision be taken. It therefore downplays the ability of legal argument to yield interpretive closure. The anti-formalist is committed to a practice of internal critique: emphasising the inability of legal argument to produce, on its own terms, definitive responses to the question of what is legally required. This form of internal critique operates in a realm beyond the correct and the incorrect.

Notice that the anti-formalist must understand the practice of legal argument as deeply troubling. In the anti-formalist view, legal practice is ridden with moments of undecidability—yet legal practice depends upon the existence of a final determination of the correct legal outcome. The anti-formalist conception of legal argument therefore suggests the possibility of an existential crisis for the practice of legal argument. The collective practice of legal argument seems absurd: it is clearly oriented at the resolution of legal questions, yet, for the rigorous anti-formalist, that very practice will be unable to yield such a resolution in a problematically high number of cases.

The anti-formalist tends to be ambivalent towards the formalist metaphysics of legal argument. Anti-formalists will all doubt the capacity of formalist theories

---

[15] D Kennedy, 'Legal Formalism' in *International Encyclopedia of the Social & Behavioral Sciences*, vol 13 (Amsterdam, Elsevier, 2001) 8634, 8635 with reference to F Gény, *Méthode d'interprétation et sources en droit privé positif: Essai critique* (Paris, Chevalier-Marescq, 1899).

[16] R Unger, *The Critical Legal Studies Movement* (London, Verso Books, 2015) 83.

of law to yield correct answers. Some will prefer exploring the surface of legal argument with all of its uncertainties, to the depths of metaphysical truth advanced by the formalist. Others will transform the formalist metaphysics into its opposite: a straightforward denial of the possibility of 'right answers' in legal argument.

B. Of Case Law and Legal Method

Notice the potential differences with Lasser's argument. One component of Lasser's understanding of formalism is its identification with deductive or syllogistic legal argument (both are understood here as synonymous). Anti-formalism is then associated with the rejection of deduction as a paradigm of legal reasoning. But under the conception proposed here, non-deductive legal argument may well be considered formalist, if and when such non-deductive legal argument is thought capable of producing interpretive closure. And, vice versa, deductive or syllogistic legal argument can be identified with anti-formalism, to the extent one refuses the idea that deductive or syllogistic argument can yield correct answers.

The difference is not just theoretical. On the account of formalism and anti-formalism I have proposed above, one can wonder whether America is anti-formalist at all, and, conversely, whether Europe is formalist. Lasser contrasts the 'terse, unsigned, univocal, and single-sentence textual syllogism'[17] of the French Cour de Cassation with the 'judicial pragmatism or realism' of American Supreme Court decisions, characterised by the 'open-ended quality' of their arguments which 'undoubtedly brings far more to the table than a textual syllogism'[18] and 'often offers more than one take on the controversy at hand'.[19]

The clearest way to elucidate the difference is by alluding to the principle of proportionality (for the Europeans) or the doctrine of balancing (for the Americans). In Lasser's terms, it seems fair to associate the doctrine of proportionality with anti-formalism: against syllogistic or deductive legal reasoning, proportionality and balancing appear to be characterised by a high degree of 'interpretive openness'.[20] Yet, in terms of the account of formalism and anti-formalism which I offered above, proportionality appears far more ambiguous. In both legal cultures, this method of legal reasoning has been attacked for its indeterminacy yet defended for its power in guiding legal reasoning.

Take the European debate. Proportionality has been attacked for being capable merely of 'subjective'[21] evaluation, for being a 'formula for disguising judicial

---

[17] Lasser (n 1) 244.
[18] ibid.
[19] ibid 245.
[20] ibid.
[21] B Schlink, 'Der Grundsatz der Verhältnismäßigkeit' in P Badura and H Dreier (eds), *Festschrift—50 Jahre Bundesverfassungsgericht* vol 1 (Tübingen, Mohr Siebeck, 2001) 460.

or interpretive decisionism'.[22] Because of proportionality, the 'danger of irrational rulings increases'.[23] In response, Alexy has rejected accusations of subjectivism and decisionism[24] and has defended the rationality of proportionality reasoning.[25]

The American debate about balancing is strikingly similar. A critic argues that 'balancing is such a weak form of rationality, so inherently indeterminate, that there is no assurance against it functioning as the vehicle for the subjective, arbitrary extra-juristic preferences of the proponent'.[26] Yet contemporary voices plead for the introduction of European-style proportionality in American constitutional law, arguing, for example, that it might 'enhance judicial reasoning', 'improve the outcomes of adjudication' or even be 'democracy-enhancing'.[27]

It is clear that proportionality and balancing differ considerably from the deductive or syllogistic mode of legal reasoning. Yet, as the controversies above show, methods of legal reasoning can be understood as either capable or incapable of yielding a 'correct answer' to a given legal problem. There can be formalist and anti-formalist conceptions of the same method of legal reasoning, in the sense I describe above.

In other words, it is unclear whether the syllogistic nature of the reasoning of the French Court of Cassation is formalist at all, in the sense I defined above. Perhaps the French simply reject the notion that deductive argument is capable of yielding a correct answer to a given legal question. Conversely, American Supreme Court Opinions might not be anti-formalist at all, in the sense defined here. Indeed, the plurality of views on the same legal question is not incompatible with the view that legal arguers are capable of determining the correct legal answer to the question at hand amidst a plurality of divergent arguments.

C. At the Roots of Anti-formalism

If formalism and anti-formalism are not intrinsically related to the type of legal argument used, how are they expressed? Formalism and anti-formalism are reflected in the somewhat sublime and intangible characteristic of distantiation of a lawyer with respect to the practice of legal argument. An anti-formalist

---

[22] E-W Böckenförde, 'Grundrechtstheorie und Grundrechtsinterpretation' (1974) 27 *Neue Juristische Wochenschrift* 1534.

[23] J Habermas, *Between Facts and Norms. Contributions to a Discourse Theory of Law and Democracy* (Cambridge, MIT Press, 1996) 259.

[24] R Alexy, *A Theory of Constitutional Rights* (Oxford, Oxford University Press, 2002) 100.

[25] R Alexy, 'Constitutional Rights, Balancing and Rationality' 16 *Ratio Juris* (2003) 131, 134 ff.

[26] D Kennedy, 'The Hermeneutic of Suspicion in Contemporary American Legal Thought' (2014) 25 *Law and Critique* 91, 101.

[27] V Jackson, 'Constitutional Law in an Age of Proportionality' (2015) 124 *Yale Law Journal* 3094, 3194. See also S Breyer, *The Court and the World. American Law and the New Global Realities* (New York, Knopf, 2015).

places significant distance between the legal argument (s)he puts forward, ie (s)he takes it with a significant pinch of salt. A formalist places significantly less distance between the legal argument and her- or himself, ie (s)he identifies with it more closely. This symbolic distance is unobservable in principle, although it is not uncommon to perceive hints as to what an individual legal arguer's position might be.

To refer to the phenomenon of symbolic distance is to allude to the phenomenon of distance in the physical realm. An individual can be at a greater or lesser distance from an object or another individual. An individual can likewise actively reposition her- or himself in order to be at a greater distance from someone or something, ie distance her- or himself. The verb 'to distantiate' generally refers metaphorically to that very activity of positioning oneself at a distance within the symbolic realm. A politician might desire to distantiate her- or himself from an unpopular argument advanced by a party member. A judge might want to distantiate her- or himself from party politics.

Similarly, we can distantiate ourselves from the activity of legal argument. An individual can be at a greater or lesser symbolic distance from the arguments he makes. At one extreme, an individual can totally identify with his legal argument, experiencing it as completely true and evident. The image is one of passivity, where the individual cannot escape the truth of the matter—legal truth imposes itself on the individual. At another extreme, an individual can adopt an ironic attitude with respect to an argument, ie not take an argument seriously at all. The image is one of resistance, of refusal to accept the truth value of an argument. The ironist stubbornly persists in her or his suspicion that, for a given legal claim, there is probably a plausible counter-claim. One reason to do so might be the recognition that, in some circumstances at least, a plurality of legal arguments can persuasively be defended as truthful.

Imagine a legal arguer advocating the right to same-sex marriage. (S)he argues that the right to same-sex marriage is embodied in some constitutional rights provision. (Note that such an argument could be advanced under US law,[28] as well as under European Convention on Human Rights (ECHR)[29] or partially under EU law.)[30] What does the distantiation argument imply? One can imagine, on the one hand, an individual who completely identifies with the argument put forward. (S)he would defend to the bitter end the truth of the proposition that the constitutional rights provision really does embody a right to same-sex marriage, irrespective of the setting or of the counter-argument. At the other extreme, one can imagine the ironic attitude of an individual who asserts an identical argument within the framework of judicial argument. When questioned on the truth value of her/his legal argument outside the setting of judicial proceedings, (s)he would

[28] *Obergefell v Hodges*, 576 US ___ (2015).
[29] eg *Schalk and Kopf v Austria*, App No 30141/04; *Hamalainen v Finland* [GC] App No 37359/09.
[30] Case C-267/12 *Hay* EU:C:2013:823.

strike a very different tone: the essence of the debate is not about the question whether there 'is' or 'is not' a right to same-sex marriage embodied in the Constitution. The ironist would suggest that the question is not one regarding the truth of the matter, but (for instance) of the choice of the legal arguer. Lawyers and judges alike could choose to develop credible arguments for multiple views.

The ironic attitude indeed plausibly leads to the introduction of another dimension of legal argument. If multiple legal arguments are plausibly legally true, one might understand legal argument as being driven by something other than the question of the 'correct' legal argument in a given legal setting. When the ironist takes these motives to be the effective driver of legal argument, the ironist becomes a cynic.[31] Plausible candidates are the legal arguer's moral, social, economic or political preferences. The cynic conceptualises legal argument as the hybrid product of a visible and an invisible realm. The visible and evanescent realm is that of legal argument. But it is merely superficial. The deeper realm is that of the invisible, of the words neither written nor spoken, but which ultimately do drive legal argument. The cynic perceives the legal arguer to speak with a double tongue: he hears a legal argument, but perceives a deeper, imperceptible but certain, motive underneath it. The cynic suggests that the 'real' grounds on which a legal arguer defends his/her legal position are, for instance, his/her political, ideological or moral beliefs.[32] For the cynic, the legal language of *Obergefell* or *Schalk and Kopf* is not unimportant, but it is mostly valuable because these decisions reveal the political and ideological position of these Courts.

The ironist can avoid the cynic's recognition of a supplementary dimension by remaining at the surface level of legal argument. The ironist might find malicious pleasure in laying bare the logical errors in a given legal argument. This activity is common in legal practice, for instance when it comes to the analysis of the arguments of an opponent. Yet this critical practice diverges significantly from the ironist's attitude, whose activity is not the necessary prelude to discovering the correct answer to the given legal question. Rather, the ironist rejects any implicit claim to the correctness of a legal argument, even if it is one he himself advances.

One caveat immediately imposes itself here. Within certain settings, lawyers cannot credibly adopt an ironic or cynical attitude with respect to legal argument. In a court setting, for instance, legal arguers by definition have to 'play the game' in the sense that they have to at least appear to accept the purpose of the exchange

---

[31] Note that this typology of legal attitudes towards legal argument is far from exhaustive. For more elaborate attempts, see Kennedy (n 2) 180 ff; M Xifaras, 'Figures de la doctrine, essai d'une phénoménologie des "personnages juridiques" dans la doctrine administrative française' in *La doctrine en droit administratif, actes du colloque de l'Association Française de Droit Administratif* (Paris, Editions Litec, 2010) 175 ff.

[32] It seems to me the contribution of T Ćapeta in this volume comes close to this position, by recognising the necessary presence of ideology in adjudication. A more general example in EU legal discourse would be the alleged bias of the Court towards greater European integration.

of legal arguments in the judicial setting. The ironist could hardly credibly spend his time, in a court setting, deconstructing the logical flaws of previous case law or of his own arguments. One might think the ironist has much to gain from showing the logical flaws of his opponent's argument—but he would only stand to gain if the *telos* of that endeavour were the strengthening of his own argument. And that attitude would be antithetical to the ironist's deeper motivation. Similarly, it would be counterproductive for the cynic to claim, within a court setting, that his motive or that of his opponent, or that of the judge is not to do what is legally correct, but rather to pursue some ulterior motive. Because the ironist and cynic refuse to play by the book, they stand to lose a lot in the process.

One might recognise that an openly cynical or ironic legal arguer who made clear as much in a court setting would find himself in a performative contradiction. What he says would contradict what he does: he would argue that the legal arguments he advances do not really matter in resolving the case at bar, yet his presence in the courtroom would indicate that he hopes to obtain a favourable judicial decision by means of the legal arguments he advances.

Notice that the assertion that formalism and anti-formalism are related to distantiation is to frame the issue as related to a mental attitude,[33] rather than merely focusing on the relative degree of interpretive openness of a written legal argument or the integration of pragmatic policy considerations in judicial reasoning. Of course, such mental attitudes are likely to be reflected in oral or written arguments, becoming somewhat perceptible. But the limiting case might well be one where, on the basis of an analysis of oral and/or written arguments, it is impossible to state with absolute certainty whether a given argument reflects a formalist or anti-formalist attitude, for lack of indication of the underlying mental attitude of the arguer.

Also notice that a legal arguer who engages with a legal question as allowing for an overwhelming variety of plausible interpretive options might still credibly postulate that there is a correct legal answer to the question raised. Perhaps the legal arguer merely was not able to determine what that answer is because of lack of sufficient time, or lack of relevant documentation on the subject. Similarly, the fact that a legal arguer openly engages with policy arguments in the course of legal argument does not necessarily have to imply an anti-formalist attitude as it is understood here. A legal arguer might postulate the existence of correct answers to such policy questions. In each of these scenarios, one can experience legal argument as tending towards a solution which imposes itself on the legal arguer, which the legal arguer cannot escape.

---

[33] Notice the proximity to Kennedy's argument here: in response to the European's objection that his legal culture is not really formalist, 'the American lawyer is likely to think they have missed the point, which has to do with an *attitude* toward abstraction rather than with a theory of law in the jurisprudential sense' (Kennedy (n 2) 107 (emphasis added).

D. Of Advocates-General

The theme of distantiation draws the attention to another aspect of the formalist/ anti-formalist distinction in Lasser's work. For Lasser, anti-formalism is also characterised by the irruption of subjectivity in legal discourse. The Opinion of the Advocate General at the ECJ is associated with anti-formalism because it 'presents, considers, and responds to the arguments and perspectives of a veritable litany of players' resulting in a 'staggering' 'cacophony of interpretive voices'[34] written 'in an eminently personalized, perspective-laden, and even insecure fashion that only stresses the plurality of views and the range of interpretive options presented in ECJ controversies'.[35]

Lasser is right, of course, to underline the important role of the Advocate General in deciphering the nuances, ambiguities and contradictions in the state of the law. It is equally important to point towards this role for an understanding of the evolution of EU law—and, therefore, to the importance of the European judiciary. But is this observation sufficient to take the Opinions of Advocates General as evidence of a deeper anti-formalist legal culture?

It seems not: the Opinions of the Advocate General do not emphasise the moment of undecidability so much as they transcend it in a legal solution put forward for the Court's consideration. In that sense, their Opinions cannot be understood as anti-formalist in the conception I propose here. For institutional reasons, it is obvious why. Indeed, it is the job of the Advocate General to 'make, in open court, reasoned submissions on cases which … require his involvement'.[36] I am not aware of any interpretation of the term 'reasoned submissions' which would include the submission that 'to every argument, there's a plausible counter-argument'. The Advocate General must give, and consistently gives, a reasoned submission as to what the correct answer is to the legal question(s) raised in the case at hand. The plurality of views and interpretive options put forward by the Advocate General is therefore conditioned by the horizon of the 'correct legal outcome' which the Advocate General ultimately submits to the Court. The Advocate General does not undermine the notion of a 'correct legal answer' in and of itself—rather, it opposes one 'correct legal answer' to another (or multiple others).

In other words, the Opinion of the Advocate General is merely another site for the appearance of the problem of ambiguities and inconsistencies in legal argument. It calls for a mediated, reflexive understanding of legal argument—but by no means requires the rejection of a formalist conception of legal argument in favour of anti-formalism.

---

[34] ibid 249.
[35] ibid 250.
[36] Art 252 TFEU.

E. Legal Culture

While distantiation certainly is an individual phenomenon, it can be understood more broadly as a cultural phenomenon. Distantiation can be reinforced or weakened by social institutions which make legal argument second nature to the lawyer. Formalist and anti-formalist attitudes can be understood as *habitus*,[37] ie as reflecting predispositions which structure legal practice and the representation of legal knowledge. These predispositions can make the world of legal practice appear structured and regular, although it is not subject to objective laws governing that realm. These predispositions can also be associated with attitudes typical of one group, although they are not the product of a conscious decision of one individual leading that group.

Formalist and anti-formalist attitudes can be reinforced through legal education, for instance. Kennedy describes 'the intense preoccupation of American legal culture with the techniques of critique of substantive legal regimes and of the judicial opinions that rationalize them' as produced in part by the fact that 'critique is taught as the foundation of legal education through the case method and institutionalized in legal academia as an element in any conventionally acceptable scholarly performance'.[38] It is 'the particular practices and techniques' which are the basis of 'internal critique and hopeful reconstruction of judicial opinions' and which are 'transmitted from generation to generation through the case method and the Socratic classroom' that 'define American legal culture'.[39]

One ought, nevertheless, to underline the ambiguity of the case law method and that of the Socratic method for the anti-formalist *habitus*. Neither is necessarily related to the development of the anti-formalist attitude—both can be deployed with an emphasis on the ultimate existence of a correct answer to legal questions. Indeed, '[t]eachers convince students that legal reasoning exists, and is different from policy analysis, by bullying them into accepting as valid in particular cases arguments about legal correctness that are circular, question-begging, incoherent, or so vague as to be meaningless'.[40] Nevertheless, the Socratic and case law method remain interesting because they can be thought of as particularly fertile breeding ground for the development of these practices and techniques of internal critique and reconstruction.

---

[37] P Bourdieu, *Le Sens Pratique* (Paris, Minuit, 1980) 88 ff.

[38] Kennedy (n 2) 75.

[39] ibid 94–95. See also J Boyle (ed), *Critical Legal Studies* (New York, New York University Press, 1994) xix ('To a greater extent even than the rest of the American legal profession, the professoriate tends to see legal doctrine as manipulable and indeterminate—principles as always being balanced by counter-principles, policy arguments as meeting counter-policy arguments, and so on. They hold this realist view of law because it is deeply coded into their professional lives. Under the relentless and sometimes painful probing of the Socratic method, the first-year student learns how to make exceptions devour rules and rules devour exceptions.').

[40] D Kennedy, 'Legal Education as Training for Hierarchy' in D Kairys (ed), *The Politics of Law. A Progressive Critique* (New York, Basic Books, 1998) 60.

One might observe that, conversely, European legal education is marked by the relative absence of development of these techniques of internal critique. European legal education is typically oriented towards the coherent exposition of applicable rules and norms. Judicial opinions can be reconstructed coherently all the more hopefully in the context of the relative absence of a practice of internal critique. The presentation of the legal materials in *ex cathedra* format, allowing for relatively little interaction, suggests the absence of a plurality of possibly conflicting interpretations concerning the same legal questions. The emphasis on abstract exposition of legal rules which explicate a variety of cases as against an emphasis on the variety of cases from which abstract rules could be induced similarly downplays the possibility of conflicting interpretations.

F. Legal Theory

A second important component of the infrastructure of individual attitudes towards legal argument is the state of debate in legal theory.[41] First, legal theoretical debate offers a forum where these themes, which otherwise always remain implicit, can be explicitly discussed and called into question. Second, legal theoretical debate offers deeper justifications for conceptions of legal argument, which elsewhere often remain undertheorised. The legal theoretical debate can be understood as a theoretical prerequisite for formalist and anti-formalist legal education and individual engagement with legal practice. Because the discourse of legal theory explicitly engages with these questions, little room for ambiguity remains: one either emphasises interpretive closure or undecidability. Formalism simply is a central question of contemporary legal theory which legal theorists traditionally engage with (which does not mean that a particular legal theorist might not try to dodge the question.)

In the United States, there is an established anti-formalist tradition in legal theory. It was born at the turn of the twentieth century, when liberals controlled the legislature but conservatives controlled the judiciary.

> Most liberals simply continued arguing that each specific conservative judicial decision was judicial legislation because there was a right legal answer that the court disregarded in favour of its own subjective ideological preference. But some liberals 'couldn't take it anymore' and began to argue that the problem was that there were no correct legal answers to these questions.[42]

The authors associated with this strand of legal thought had a deep influence on American lawyers during the first half of the twentieth century, and are often

---

[41] It is interesting to note that Critical Legal Studies as a movement in the United States seems to have contributed as much to the legal theoretical debate (as well as the broader social theoretical debate) as to the doctrinal debate in different areas of law.

[42] Kennedy (n 2) 81.

associated with American Legal Realism. It was intensified after the Second World War by scholars associated with the Critical Legal Studies movement. In American legal thought, the critique of formalism is an established position in legal theory today.

The same cannot be said about European legal theory. The anti-formalist position is not as clearly entrenched in European legal theory as it is in the United States. That is not to say that it is not there, on the fringes.[43] The anti-formalist position has similarly been defended throughout the history of European legal theory.[44] But out of this constellation an established contemporary anti-formalist legal theoretical position has not emerged in the way in which it currently exists in the United States.

None of this should be taken as evidence that Americans are straightforwardly 'anti-formalists' and Europeans straightforwardly 'formalists'. Rather, formalism and anti-formalism are contested positions in both the United States and Europe. As Duncan Kennedy put it, 'the body fights the virus'.[45] In the United States, prominent defences of formalism, in the sense to which we refer to it here, exist.[46] In Europe, the anti-formalist position is also defended.[47] What matters is the existence of a sufficient methodological consensus to sustain legal practice as it exists. What characterises the American constellation of positions, as opposed to the European situation, is a relative lack of methodological agreement which makes the practice of legal argument deeply problematic.

III. Legitimacy

The lack of methodological consensus surrounding the nature of legal argument in the United States creates a legitimacy problem for the American legal elite and, in particular, its judiciary. Because of the recognition and exposure of the fragile epistemic foundation of legal arguments, a cornerstone of anti-formalist argument, it may be plausible to suspect the existence of political motivations behind legal arguments. When a legal question has recognisable political stakes, and the legal debate can be resolved either way because of the presence of strong

---

[43] The existence of this very book attests to that. See also the German Law Journal's special issue dedicated to this question, 'Critical Legal Thought: An American-German Debate Twenty-Five Years Later' (2011) 12(1) *German Law Journal.*

[44] One can think, for example, of the critical positions adopted by the *Ecole de la Libre Recherche Scientifique* in France, the Freirechtsschule in Germany (both of which had a major influence on American Legal Realism).

[45] Kennedy, *Critique of Adjudication* (n 2) 91.

[46] Canonically, R Dworkin, 'Is There Really No Right Answer in Hard Cases?' in R Dworkin, *A Matter of Principle* (Cambridge, Harvard University Press, 1985) 119 ff.

[47] eg A Somek, *Der Gegenstand der Rechtserkenntnis. Epitaph eines juristischen Problems* (Baden-Baden, Nomos, 1996).

arguments and counter-arguments, whatever argument is preferred is likely to be chosen on the basis of extra-legal motives. Political motives are prominent candidates. Yet that creates problems for a judiciary supposedly legitimate as the guardian of the rule of law (as opposed to the rule of men). The converse would then appear to be true about European legal culture.

But are the Europeans really unaware of the political dimension of legal reasoning? The hypothesis seems unlikely—probably many Europeans are consciously or unconsciously aware that legal reasoning is politicised.

For instance, one might suggest that Europeans are better cynics than the supposedly cynical anti-formalist. The cynic, as we have argued so far, recognises the political nature of legal argument—perhaps European legal elites have been successful in instrumentalising this understanding of the law to their own advantage. The allusion to Plato's Noble Lie[48] seems relevant here. Just as Plato advocated lying to the population of his ideal city in order to increase the legitimacy of his virtuous political order, European lawyers would attempt to persuade the population of the Noble Lie of the rule of law and the separation of powers.

But this objection is problematic. Is it really likely that Europeans are so deeply aware of the political nature of legal argument if, in comparison with American legal culture, written proof of it remains so scarce in European legal culture, where the opposite position is *nota bene* recurrently argued and accepted in legal theory and, implicitly, in legal doctrine? The objection seems to postulate that Europeans are schizophrenic, or at least speak with a double tongue: talking the language of the rule of law, but thinking in the vocabulary of Machiavellian *Realpolitik*.

For a third reason, the objection must ultimately remain unpersuasive. Just like American societies, contemporary European societies are politically and ideologically divided. It is therefore plausible to assume that legal elites, too, are similarly politically divided (as in the United States). Under those circumstances, it seems highly unlikely that Europeans, despite their awareness of the political stakes of certain legal questions, and despite their anti-formalist conviction that legal argument does not ultimately determine the outcome of a given legal question, would refuse to engage in the practice of denouncing the political motivations behind legal arguments and, in particular, judicial decisions. Given the political stakes of some legal questions, the incentive is simply too important to resist the temptation to engage in political critique of legal argument.

An alternative hypothesis about the European state of affairs seems more likely. European lawyers are well aware of the politics of legal argument. Yet, for contingent reasons, anti-formalism has not gained mainstream recognition. Driven by self-interested motives, European lawyers have been reluctant to glance into the abyss of anti-formalist legal thought. For practitioners, it seems natural to presuppose that legal argument is a meaningful practice in the sense that it allows us to conclude what the correct legal answer to our legal questions is, as the practice

---

[48] *Republic*, 414b–c.

seems to do in everyday legal life. Focused on legal practice, legal academia has been preoccupied with rendering the chaotic and confused mass of legal materials more digestible and comprehensible for legal practitioners (while the professional American Law Schools, paradoxically, had more room to engage with theoretical questions at greater distance of legal practice). Despite the existence of the anti-formalist position in European and global legal theory, European legal theorists have been too preoccupied with theorising and justifying the existing practices of legal argument to perceive and engage with the deeper questions it raises, and to question and challenge it from within. For contingent reasons, the theoretical debate failed to heat up in the way it did in the United States, and to have a cor-relative effect on legal doctrine and practice.

Individuals and legal cultures alike are therefore caught in the tension between formalism and anti-formalism. In other words, the legal mind necessarily suffers from a greater or lesser degree of schizophrenia. It is for this reason that anti-formalism is vital to any critical legal project. When pushed, individuals are likely to recognise the limits of legal argument. The question is rather: how much push-ing is needed, and where does one draw the dividing line? The ideal typical formal-ist and anti-formalist are merely the extremes of this phenomenon. Something similar can be said about legal cultures. Legal theory, as its epiphenomenon, can attest to this. Formalism and anti-formalism merely exist as contested positions within a given context. Pushing the envelope on anti-formalist legal thought opens the door to an internal critique of legal argument, and thereby to a critical recon-struction of law and society.

IV. Conclusion

Lasser contests the common American diagnosis that European legal culture is formalist. Instead, he recognises European legal culture, in particular the legal dis-course of the European Union, to be bifurcated between an open and prominent formalist legal discourse and a somewhat more concealed and subordinate anti-formalist legal discourse. The argument rests, on the one hand, on the mode of argument of European legal actors and, on the other hand, on their recognition of the degree of subjectivity implicated in legal reasoning.

This contribution has attempted to complement Lasser's understanding of for-malism and anti-formalism by proposing to understand, more broadly, formalism as an emphasis on the capacity of legal reasoning to yield interpretive closure in the form of correct legal answers, and anti-formalism, vice versa, as an emphasis on the moments of undecidability in legal argument, its inability to yield interpre-tive closure. On this view, Lasser's argument may well overstate its conclusiveness: the open-ended nature of legal argument in the Opinions of the Advocates Gen-eral at the Court of Justice, their rejection of deductive legal reasoning, even their references, in passing, to the subjective nature of legal argument, are insufficient to show that the discourse of European Union law is genuinely anti-formalist, emphasising the moments of undecidability of legal reasoning. Open-ended, non-deductive legal argument can be understood as yielding interpretive closure. It seems plausible to understand the Opinions of Advocates General as institutionally conditioned by the horizon of a correct legal answer, to be suggested to the Court of Justice when it takes its final decision.

Rather, European legal culture could be understood as anti-formalist in virtue of the distantiation of legal actors with respect to the arguments they advance—the refusal to take legal arguments at face value as determining ultimately the outcome of legal disputes. The phenomenon of distantiation is individual, but also a mark of legal culture, primarily through legal education and legal theoretical debate, which can reinforce the formalist and anti-formalist attitude. The abyss between European and American legal culture becomes visible in the divergent institutional practice of legal education and a very different constellation of positions within the legal theoretical debate—pointing, ultimately, to the recognition that European legal culture displays significant characteristics of legal formalism.

Yet the European position is thoroughly unstable. The European legal theoretical debate is conspicuously vulnerable to the accusation of maintaining an untenable commitment to the ability of legal argument to yield interpretive closure. This recognition may have a transformative effect on legal education in Europe. European critical legal scholars should seize this opportunity to strengthen the anti-formalist position in the European legal debate.

10

Legal Scholarship and External Critique in EU Law

DANIELA CARUSO* AND FERNANDA NICOLA**

I. Introduction: Nostalgia and Engagement

Why, readers might wonder, would a group of Croatian legal scholars spearhead this volume? Why would they care, at this specific juncture in the history of EU law, to reflect on a movement—Critical Legal Studies (CLS)—born in the peculiar and utterly American socio-legal context of the 1970s?

Two explanations come to mind. First, nostalgia. Nostalgia explains many types of human behaviour and may have something to do with the genesis of this volume. Contributors Judge Rodin and President Lenaerts, honourable members of the EU Court of Justice (CJEU), were both exposed at a younger age to CLS teachings in the United States.[1] They remember their encounter with critical legal theory, which freed them from the dogmatic cage of their coursework at home and allowed, for once, exploration of the law's outer boundaries—its implication in power-building, its open-endedness, and its ambivalent relation with the quest for distributive justice. No one ever forgets the travels of one's youth and, in the cleverest minds, intellectual tourism leaves the sweetest of memories.

To be sure, CLS's critique of adjudication—with its insistence on the inextricable link between judicial function and ideology, on the indeterminate nature of

---

* Professor of Law and Jean Monnet Chair, Boston University School of Law.
** Professor of Law, Washington College of Law, American University, Director of the Program on International Organizations, Law and Diplomacy.
[1] Koen Lenaerts received his LLM at Harvard Law School in 1978. His LLM paper, written under the supervision of Duncan Kennedy in 1978, was titled 'The "Negative Implications" of the Commerce Clause and "Preemption" Doctrines as Federalism-related Limitations on State Power: A Historical Review'. The paper provided an internal critique of the US jurisprudence on the dormant commerce clause. Siniša Rodin received his LLM at Michigan Law School in 1992. In 2002 he visited Cornell Law School and his acquaintance with Mitchel Lasser influenced his choice of readings (most notably the works of Pierre Schlag).

legal arguments, and on politics in the court[2]—could make these judges deeply uncomfortable today. However, their contributions to this volume give that critique a nod and then quickly move on to safer ground.[3] Their superior expertise, classical training and explicit identification of firm methodological boundaries in judicial reasoning can reassure the European reader that they have certainly *not* caught the indeterminacy virus.[4] With due caution, nostalgia can be both pleasurable and harmless. Gratitude to one's former teachers for their unforgettable lessons is obviously compatible with parting ways, whether geographically or intellectually.

The other explanation for the birth of this volume is more complex, and has to do with a scholarly project that involves not only notable (male) jurists but also prominent (female) academics professionally anchored in the youngest Member State of the European Union.[5] In one word, we define this ulterior prompt for this volume as 'engagement', legal and political. There are times in history when jurists become particularly aware of their responsibility in shaping the structure of government, in informing the discourse of and about law, and in resisting dangerous political trends.[6] The Croatian scholars at the helm of this project clearly perceive themselves to be at such a juncture, and are acting accordingly.

Our own contribution to this volume stems, on the one hand, from a deep empathy with the editors' project of engagement and, on the other, from familiarity with the CLS movement in the US. We proceed as follows: section II articulates several ways in which the engaged intellectuals who spearheaded this volume may derive both inspiration and tools from American CLS literature. Section III spotlights one particular CLS tool, known as 'external critique', and outlines its targets—namely the distributive effects of CJEU cases, their uneven impact on different groups, and their implications for justice across class, gender, race, nationality or socio-economic status. Section IV discusses the role of progressive scholars in bringing distributive stakes to the fore and vigorously engaging in the external critique of judgment in Luxembourg. Section V illustrates two CLS points that complicate the work of the legal scholar—distributive ambivalence and legal indeterminacy—and concludes by reasserting the value of critical scholarship in spite of its unavoidable limitations.

---

[2] Duncan Kennedy, *A Critique of Adjudication: Fin de Siècle* (Cambridge, Harvard University Press, 1997).

[3] See Siniša Rodin, 'Useful Effect of the Framework Decision on the European Arrest Warrant' (in this volume); Koen Lenaerts, 'Discovering the Law of the EU: The European Court of Justice and the Comparative Law Method' (in this volume).

[4] See Lenaerts, ibid (positing that adopting the comparative method enables the court 'to resolve particular gaps, conflicts and ambiguity without embarking on judicial legislation').

[5] Croatia joined the EU in 2013. Two of the contributors to this volume are established members of the law faculty of the University of Zagreb: Tamara Ćapeta and Tamara Perišin. Judge Siniša Rodin, co-editor of this volume, was a member of the same law faculty until he joined the CJEU in 2013.

[6] Piero Calamandrei, in spite—or perhaps because of—the internal contradictions of his opus, famously exemplifies the 'engaged jurist' in the Italian legal tradition. See Piero Calamandrei, *Lo Stato Siamo Noi* (Milan, Chiarelettere, 2011).

II. EU Law Scholarship as Engagement

There are at least three ways in which working on EU law in a place like Zagreb is a form of social and political engagement. First, as a scholarly discipline, EU law is naturally poised to challenge established layers of authority in the law faculties of the new(er) Member States. This is because, by definition, no bulwark of academic power could until recently be built around this subject. In EU law, expertise is a prerogative of the young—a fact that allows for novel and inverted hierarchies. A testament to the engagement of Croatian scholars in the EU–national law debate is found in the Dubrovnik Jean Monnet Seminars, which have served as a regular forum for East–West dialogue since 2003. These seminars are known for raising anti-formalist issues and for introducing doctoral students to the role of policy and power in the creation and administration of law.[7] The proceedings of the Dubrovnik meetings may be published in the prestigious Croatian Yearbook of European Law and Policy—a peer reviewed journal of regional scope and broad ambition.[8]

A second dimension of engagement appears in the operational dynamics of substantive EU law. Teaching and writing about EU law can be a disruptive, critical project not only in relation to the institutional layers of local academia, but also vis-à-vis the substance of Member States' law. Because the EU demands the approximation of domestic laws around the time of accession and at each new stage of integration, the process of harmonisation forces scholars, judges and legislators to rethink and question the rationale of national rules.[9] The resulting pressure for legal reform brings existing privileges and unspoken judicial policies to the surface.[10] Legal formalism is no excuse for resisting reform, and legal change must be fought for or resisted on the basis of clear distributive arguments. In other words, in the aftermath of accession, EU law often *is* critique. It unveils false necessities in Member States' legal discourse and may identify winners and losers in consolidated domestic legal practices.[11] A loose analogy with CLS is easy

---

[7] See eg Adam Łazowski, 'Who's Got the Power? Division of Competence in EU Membership Acquis', paper presented at the Dubrovnik seminar, www.pravo.unizg.hr/_download/repository/ Dubrovnik_2016_-_Programme.pdf.

[8] *Croatian Yearbook of European Law and Policy*, 'Home' (2016) www.cyelp.com/index.php/cyelp.

[9] Christian Joerges, 'The Europeanisation of Private Law as a Rationalisation Process and as a Contest of Disciplines—An Analysis of the Directive on Unfair Terms in Consumer Contracts' (1995) 3 *European Review of Private Law* 3.

[10] To name just one example, the Product Liability Directive proved hard to transpose in the Member States, because it mobilised corporate lobbying and threatened to undo the quiet pro-consumer revolution conducted by judges since the 1960s. Daniela Caruso, 'The Missing View of the Cathedral' (1997) 3 *European Law Journal* 3.

[11] Gunther Teubner, 'Legal Irritants: Good Faith in British Law or How Unifying Law Ends Up in New Differences' (1998) 61 *Modern Law Review* 11. See also Pierre Legrand, 'On the Singularity of Law' (2006) 47 *Harvard International Law Journal* 517, 520 (discussing, by way of example, the distributive impact of EU-wide sanitary standards on small enterprises and farmers in Poland who are excluded from the new production chains of the internal market).

to establish here. Two defining features of the CLS movement are the denunciation of false necessity in legal deduction and the focus on the distributive and redistributive consequences of legal rules. These very features happen also to be natural by-products of early-stage Europeanisation. CLS was a militant project in the American legal academy of the 1970s and continues to display defiant and utopian features[12] in the many corners of the world where it has seeped under various guises.[13] It is therefore an inspiration for those scholars who, like the editors of this volume, perceive their engagement with EU law as part of a larger project of justice.[14]

Third, and most importantly, this volume reflects a desire to subject EU law itself to a critical rethinking. It is clear by now that the Europeanisation of law has brought about its own set of questionable dogmas: the centrality of the individual,[15] a structural blindness to intra-EU distribution,[16] a strong market paradigm that often crowds out alternate visions,[17] and a practical indifference to the geopolitical externalities of the project.[18] From the standpoint of Croatian scholars in particular, the EU's own role in such post-accession catastrophes as the Euro-zone crisis and the deaths of thousands of migrants in the Mediterranean waters requires closer scrutiny at the very least.[19] When the dust of accession settles and the promises of peace and prosperity fail to materialise, scholarly engagement necessarily takes a sceptical turn and begins to contemplate whether foundational concepts of EU law might themselves be vehicles of distributive and ideological regression. Here, EU law is not the critique. EU law is its object.

The propensity to engage in a sustained critique of EU law marbles several contributions in this volume and certainly animates this chapter. This generally critical stance takes the present stage of legal Europeanisation as a fact and aims

---

[12] Roberto Unger, *The Critical Legal Studies Movement* 2nd edn (Cambridge, Harvard University Press, 1983) (emphasising the often unspoken utopian strand in CLS).

[13] See eg Sylvia Wairimu Kang'ara, 'Beyond Bed and Bread: Making the African State through Marriage Law Reform—Constitutive and Transformative Influences of Anglo-American Legal Thought' (2012) 9 *Hastings Race & Poverty Law Journal* 353.

[14] The Croatian Yearbook self-identifies as a critical project and explicitly aims to embed legal questions 'in a wider political, economic and social context', *Yearbook* (n 8).

[15] See Joseph HH Weiler, 'Van Gend en Loos: The Individual as Subject and Object and the Dilemma of European Legitimacy' (2014) 12 *International Journal of Constitutional Law* 94; Daniela Caruso, 'Limits of the Classic Method: Positive Action in the European Union after the New Equality Directives' (2003) 44 *Harvard International Law Journal* 331.

[16] Damjan Kukovec, 'Law and the Periphery' (2015) 21 *European Law Journal* 406; Marija Bartl, 'The Way We Do Europe: Subsidiarity and the Substantive Democratic Deficit' (2015) 21 *European Law Journal* 23; Fernanda Nicola, 'Invisible Cities in Europe' (2012) 35 *Fordham International Law Journal* 1282.

[17] Marija Bartl, 'Internal Market Rationality, Private Law and the Direction of the Union: Resuscitating the Market as the Object of the Political' (2015) 21 *European Law Journal* 572.

[18] See, eg, Daniela Caruso and Joanna Geneve, 'Trade and History: The Case of EU-Algeria Relations' (2015) 33(1) *Boston University International Law Journal*.

[19] Iris Goldner Lang, 'Is There Solidarity on Asylum and Migration in the EU?' (2013) 9 *Croatian Yearbook of European Law and Policy* 1.

to make full use of the possibilities for political and social justice it can currently support, but at the same time it decries its many structural and dynamic drawbacks. In doing so, this critical project borrows liberally from CLS without fear of misreading or misappropriation. Irreverence in this context is a feature, not a bug.[20] The CLS toolkit is clearly useful to European scholars, but there is no pretence here of fidelity to the original CLS conception.[21] Transformations can be productive on EU soil, and there is no reason not to utilise, albeit in a different epistemic environment, the motivational force of lessons drawn from far-away places or times.[22]

The CLS toolkit can be embraced selectively; its tenets disassembled and recomposed at leisure. For instance, the methodology of internal critique works best when EU legal deduction is simply flawed or when interpretive results presented as necessary are no more plausible than the road not taken.[23] External critique is useful when decisions made at any node of the EU system lead to distributively questionable outcomes. The critique of rights—another staple of CLS scholarship[24]—easily takes apart such constructs as EU citizenship[25] and market access,[26] which may lead to a deficit of substantive justice.[27]

What CLS stands for, when translated onto the operational level of EU legal scholarship, is a thorough rethinking of the project of integration through law in any of its formants,[28] not just the judicial one.[29] With no pledge of adherence to the CLS archetype and no obvious political direction, this loosely critical posture may come across to CLS founders as inchoate and even spineless—in other words, as a non-movement. In the current landscape of EU legal scholarship, critique is indeed piecemeal and disaggregated. If it is a project at all, it is one of scattered resistance with no flag or army. Yet, as the following sections illustrate,

---

[20] Umberto Eco, *Misreadings* (San Diego, Harcourt Brace, 1993).

[21] See, eg, Máximo Langer, 'From Legal Transplants to Legal Translations: The Globalization of Plea Bargaining and the Americanization Thesis in Criminal Procedure' (2004) 45 *Harvard International Law Journal* 1.

[22] See Diego López Medina, 'Por Qué Hablar de Una "Teoría Impura del Derecho" Para América Latina?' in Daniel Bonilla Maldonado (ed), *Teoría del Derecho y Trasplantes Jurídicos* (Bogotá, Siglo del Hombre, 2009) (explaining why misreadings need not be corrected).

[23] Gráinne De Búrca, 'The Road Not Taken: The EU as a Global Human Rights Actor' (2011) 105 *American Journal of International Law* 649.

[24] See Duncan Kennedy, 'The Critique of Rights in Critical Legal Studies' in Wendy Brown and Janet Halley (eds), *Left Legalism/Left Critique* (Durham NC, Duke University Press, 2002).

[25] Joseph Weiler, 'Editorial: Individuals and Rights—The Sour Grapes' (2010) 21(2) *European Journal of International Law* 277.

[26] Damjan Kukovec, 'Economic Law, Inequality and Hidden Hierarchies on the EU Internal Market' (2017) 38(1) *Michigan Journal of International Law*.

[27] Dimitry Kochenov, Gráinne de Búrca and Andrew Williams (eds), *Europe's Justice Deficit?* (Oxford, Hart Publishing, 2015).

[28] Rodolfo Sacco, 'Legal Formants: A Dynamic Approach to Comparative Law' (1991) 39 *American Journal of Comparative Law* 1.

[29] Bryant Garth, 'The Florence Access-to-Justice Project in Law and in Context: Mauro Cappelletti as Importer, Exporter, and Academic Entrepreneur' (2016) *Annuario di Diritto Comparato* 13.

EU law can be better analysed, understood and perhaps transformed when observed through CLS-tinted glasses.

We prioritise here external critique over the many other tools in the CLS kit. By external critique, we mean the scholarly activity of highlighting the distributive stakes—and therefore the political and ideological dimensions—of legal disputes adjudicated by the CJEU.[30] The importance of external critique lies in the fact that adjudication plays a role in eliminating or maintaining privilege, or class and race inequalities.[31] In comparison to the tool of internal critique, which focuses on logical inconsistencies in judicial reasoning and reveals the often ambivalent results of deduction, external critique is a harder sell in Europe,[32] given the still widespread belief in the importance of isolating the judicial function from concern with the political impact of each case's outcome.[33] We nonetheless hope to show first, that distributive arguments are *as a matter of fact* not foreign to judicial reasoning in Luxembourg[34] and, second, that scholarly commentary on the correctness of such arguments, whether expressed or silently woven into the fabric of judgments, is a necessary and important part of the life of engaged jurists.[35]

III. Distributive Arguments in Adjudicatory Practice

Whether judges in Luxembourg, or elsewhere, should take into account the larger distributive consequences of their decisions remains an unsettled question.[36] Prominent scholars object to distributive justice as a goal of adjudication because of the conviction that (re)distribution is more efficiently achieved through taxation

---

[30] The distinction between internal and external perspectives in law predates the CLS movement. See Brian Z Tamanaha, 'The Internal/External Distinction and the Notion of a "Practice" in Legal Theory and Sociolegal Studies' (1996) 30 *Law and Society Review* 163; Charles L Barzun, 'Inside-Out: Beyond the Internal/External Distinction in Legal Scholarship' (2015) 101 *Virginia Law Review* 1203.

[31] Marc Galanter, 'Why the "Haves" Come Out Ahead: Speculations on the Limits of Legal Change' (1974) 9 *Law and Society Review* 95; Duncan Kennedy, *Legal Reasoning: Collected Essays* (Aurora CO, Davies Group Publishers, 2008).

[32] See Siniša Rodin, 'A Metacritique of the Court of Justice of the EU' (2016) 4 *Il Diritto dell'Unione Europea* 193.

[33] This belief is firmly held or at least clearly deployed also in progressive circles. See eg Michelle Everson, 'An Exercise in Legal Honesty: Rewriting the Court of Justice and the Bundesverfassungsgericht' (2015) 21 *European Law Journal* 21.

[34] Below s III (discussing distributive principles in the *E Fritz* case).

[35] Below ss IV and V.

[36] The points summarily articulated in this section are further explored in Daniela Caruso, 'Fairness at a Time of Perplexity: The Civil Law Principle of Fairness in the Court of Justice of the European Union' in Stefan Vogenauer and Stephen Weatherill (eds), *General Principles of Law: European and Comparative Perspectives* (Oxford, Hart Publishing, 2017) 329.

and other forms of transfers, as opposed to judgment in discrete disputes.[37] But in equally reputable milieus, courts are expected to redress, within the boundaries of judicial discretion, the predicaments of situationally disadvantaged parties.[38] This is because—among other reasons—a distribution-insensitive mode of adjudication would not be *neutral*, but rather bound to produce *regressive* results that defy common notions of justice.[39]

In European circles, there is a pervasive assumption that distributive arguments do not belong in judicial reasoning.[40] Most courts, aiming to preserve legitimacy and authority, generally cling to the language of internal coherence; to this goal, they stay within the boundaries of doctrinal abstraction and formalism, or at most put forth an even-handed balancing of distributively neutral policies (efficiency, judicial economy, protection of expectations, etc).[41] CLS notoriously challenges this judicial posture on both normative[42] and descriptive grounds.[43]

In an American CLS perspective, a paradigmatic example of judicial responsiveness to distributive considerations is found in Justice Brennan's opinion in *Penn Central v New York*.[44] The facts are well known and are only summarily recalled here. Appellants, owners of Penn Central Station, had sought a permit to build above the existing station's structure, but because of a zoning regulation aimed at preserving historic landmarks, their request was denied. The appellants then sought monetary compensation. In their view, the denial of the permit resulted in the taking of their *jus aedificandi* and in a significant depreciation of real estate

---

[37] Louis Kaplow and Steven Shavell, 'Why the Legal System is Less Efficient than the Income Tax in Redistributing Income' (1994) 23 *Journal of Legal Studies* 667.

[38] Lee Anne Fennell and Richard McAdams, 'The Distributive Deficit in Law and Economics' (2016) 100 *Minnesota Law Review* 1051 (providing a thorough critique of the assumption that taxation is always a preferable strategy for wealth redistribution).

[39] See Robert Hale, 'Coercion and Distribution in a Supposedly Non-Coercive State' (1923) *Political Science Quarterly* 470.

[40] See Fernanda Nicola, 'Transatlanticisms: Constitutional Asymmetry and Selective Reception of US Law and Economics in the Formation of European Private Law' (2008) 16 *Cardozo Journal of International and Comparative Law* 101 (arguing in favour of an open analysis of distributive consequences in the CJEU's private law judgments).

[41] It is often the case that with judicial balancing, by now a feature of adjudication around the globe, mere lip service is paid to conflicting considerations, but no real solace can be found against regressive outcomes of law and policy choices. Duncan Kennedy, 'Three Globalizations of Law and Legal Thought' in David Trubek and Alvaro Santos (eds), *The New Law and Development: A Critical Appraisal* (Cambridge, Cambridge University Press, 2006). See also Mitchel Lasser, 'Fundamentally Flawed: The CJEU's Jurisprudence on Fundamental Rights and Fundamental Freedoms' (2014) 15 *Theoretical Inquiries in Law* 229.

[42] Kennedy (n 2).

[43] For the argument that, as a matter of positive law, redistributive motives are already pervasive in all corners of adjudication, including private law, see Duncan Kennedy, 'Distributive and Paternalist Motives in Contract and Tort Law, with Special Reference to Compulsory Terms and Unequal Bargaining Power' (1982) *Maryland Law Review* 563. See also Aditi Bagchi, 'Distributive Justice and Contract' in Gregory Klass, George Letsas and Prince Saprai (eds), *Philosophical Foundations of Contract Law* (Oxford, Oxford University Press, 2013).

[44] *Penn Cent Transp Co v City of New York*, 438 US 104 (1978).

value. Famously, Brennan saw things otherwise. In his view, the appellants should only be thankful for the City's time-honoured practice of preserving historic landmarks from disorderly urban development. In fact, strict zoning in the area around the station was precisely the reason for the enormous value of Penn Central's property. In the balancing of property rights against public interest, it therefore became clear that the appellants derived great advantage from the very regulatory practice they now deemed harmful and deserved, as a consequence, no compensation.[45]

The mode of judicial reasoning adopted in *Penn Central* may strike some European observers as excessively open-ended, but it is hard to see how the dispute could be seriously resolved without resorting to Brennan's distributive logic. The case shows that a lucid consideration of benefits and harms is not beyond the realm of judicial functions, but is rather essential to an intelligent adjudication of specific cases. Is this type of reasoning off limits in Luxembourg? Interestingly, it is not.[46]

Take, for instance, *E Friz*, a ground-breaking case decided at the dawn of this decade by the CJEU.[47] In brief, in 1991 Mr von der Heyden received an unsolicited visit by a tax consultant who convinced him to invest, together with other partners, in the modernisation of decrepit real estate in Berlin. For contracts concluded in this haphazard fashion, the EU door-step selling directive grants consumers a right to repent, ie to cancel the deal in a period of no less than seven days from due notice of this right.[48] If the consumer receives no such notice—as was the case in *E Friz*—the possibility to cancel lasts much longer.[49] Accordingly, Mr von der Heyden withdrew from the partnership in 2002, after a period of over 10 years, hoping to recoup the full value of his investment on restitutionary grounds. The partnership, however, refused to refund Mr von der Heyden in full and asked

---

[45] ibid 147.

[46] It is often in the AG's opinion that one finds a more explicit engagement with the distributive consequences of the Court's choices. Take for instance the opinion of Advocate General Eleanor Sharpston, aimed at striking down a reverse discriminatory scheme in Belgium. Case C-212/06 *Govt of the French Cmty v Flemish Govt* [2008] ECR I-1683. Here, Sharpston openly explains that an uneven allocation of resources might be simply discriminatory, and therefore illegal, or it might be aimed to promote growth in underdeveloped territories. In either case, Sharpston makes the point that European judges are well situated to understand the progressive or regressive impact of a domestic regulatory scheme on different local and transnational communities. See ibid para 155. For reasons investigated in depth especially by Mitchel Lasser, *Judicial Deliberations* (Oxford, Oxford University Press, 2009), this position is seldom taken by the Court so openly.

[47] Case C-215/08 *E Friz GmbH v Carsten von der Heyden* [2010] ECR I-2947. The facts and the law of the *E Friz* case have been thoroughly analysed by other scholars, making a full summary here redundant. See Martijn Hesselink, 'The General Principles of Civil Law: Their Nature, Roles and Legitimacy' in Dorota Leczykiewicz and Stephen Weatherill (eds), *The Involvement of EU Law in Private Law Relationships* (Oxford, Hart Publishing, 2013) 131.

[48] Dir 85/577/EEC.

[49] Case C-481/99 *Heininger v Bayerische Hypo- und Vereinsbank AG* [2001] ECR I-09945; Case-412/06 *Annelore Hamilton v Volksbank Filder eG* [2008] ECR I-02383 (discussing the issue of limitation on the time for repentance).

instead that he pay his share of the steep losses suffered over the years. This result would comply with German law and in particular with the judicial principle of 'defective partnership', duly highlighted for the CJEU by AG Trstenjak in her opinion.[50]

The language used by the Court to endorse the latter result was unmistakably sensitive to distributive concerns.[51] In 2010, two full years into the financial crisis, consumers all over Europe and beyond shared Mr von der Heyden's desire to walk back from improvident investments.[52] The *E Friz* judges were surrounded by news of pervasive financial disasters, and were constantly reminded that the consequences of poor financial market regulation would hit some pockets of the EU population much more heavily than others. Apportioning losses fairly, ie protecting those who were hopelessly stuck with the partnership from the sudden flight of those who could withdraw their membership, seemed to be what justice required. Interestingly, the Court went beyond mere judicial necessity, and openly appealed to solidarity between those who could flee and those left behind in the quagmire of financial disaster. It is at least plausible that the judges could see the analogy between the uneven distribution of losses inside the *E Friz* partnership on one hand, and Europe's larger inequities on the other: the widening of the spreads, the plight of the unemployed and the predicament of the PIIGS (Portugal, Ireland, Italy, Greece and Spain), at that time haunted by serious debt restructuring problems. In the midst of sobering reflections on law's complicity in perpetuating Europe's inequalities, it may be important to take stock of narrow, but clear, progress through law.[53]

E Friz confirms that in Luxembourg, whenever an interpretive gap leaves the judge room to manoeuvre, a lucid assessment of circumstances and distributive considerations *may* precede and guide the decision-making process. The case says nothing, however, on the normative *desirability* of such arguments inside the court—a point dear to CLS founders.[54] Some contributions in this volume directly tackle the argument that judges should engage systematically and openly in distribution-sensitive argumentation.[55] We take no stance on such a point in these pages. History is replete with situations in which mere judicial adherence to formalism or to distribution-opaque legal arguments produces results which are

---

[50] *E Friz* (n 47).

[51] ibid.

[52] AG Trstenjak pointed out that 'Investment in [junk] property, which Germans opted for primarily on account of the resultant tax benefits, has often failed to deliver the expected results, and investors have therefore looked for ways of terminating those investments by relying inter alia on the Community directives concerning consumer protection'. *E Friz* (n 47) para 3.

[53] See Ugo Mattei and Fernanda Nicola, 'A "Social Dimension" in European Private Law?: The Call for Setting a Progressive Agenda' (2006) 41 *New England Law Review* 1.

[54] Duncan Kennedy, 'Proportionality and 'Deference' in Contemporary Constitutional Thought' (in this volume).

[55] For a nuanced and profound discussion of this point in this volume, see Tamara Ćapeta, 'Ideology and Legal Reasoning at the European Court of Justice', s V, 'Conclusions', in this volume. cf Kennedy, 'Role of Courts' (n 54); and Lenaerts (n 3) (espousing radically different visions of the role of ideology in the subjective experience of judging).

highly desirable from the perspective of substantive justice. It is not our purpose to challenge this type of judicial work on ethical grounds—at least not here.

Our argument here is rather aimed at informing European legal scholarship only (*la doctrine*), in the hope that a feedback loop between judicial and academic milieus may ultimately lead to substantively progressive outcomes in Luxembourg as well as in the EU's legislative and administrative fora.

IV. External Critique: The Role of European Scholars

As noted by Pierre Schlag, judges are often excessively narrow in their definition of a dispute's context.[56] Academic scholarship, on the other hand, is not bound by the built-in constraints of judicial activity nor by the time pressure under which European judges are compelled to decide. Scholars have the necessary institutional freedom and research capabilities to weave together the different narratives surrounding each case, to identify the perspectives of possible winners and losers, and to focus on the broader distributive consequences of a judgment in Luxembourg.[57]

An external critique of EU adjudication is essential to ensure that judicial decision-making and its often obscure distributive consequences are known and understood, not only in lawyers' circles but also in civil society, where choices of broader political salience should be made.[58] This type of scholarly activity is continually needed not only to decipher the reasoning behind technical judicial language,[59] but also to make explicit the law-making by-products of judicial dispute resolution.[60] In addition, European scholarship is an important site of transnational legal theory—a field now undergoing intense critical scrutiny and major transformations, including greater historical self-awareness and global reach.[61]

---

[56] See Pierre Schlag, 'On Textualist and Purposivist Interpretation (Challenges and Problems)' (in this volume) (portraying judges and lawyers as engaged in 'a fairly localised and discrete juridical mission').

[57] See Bill Davies and Fernanda Nicola (eds), *EU Law Stories: Contextual and Critical Histories of European Jurisprudence* (Cambridge, Cambridge University Press, 2017) (aiming to offer careful accounts of the effects of the CJEU decisions for particular litigants in each case).

[58] See Bartl (n 16).

[59] Phillipe Jestaz and Christophe Jamin, *La Doctrine* (Paris, Dalloz, 2004).

[60] See Daniel R Kelemen, *Eurolegalism: The Transformation of Law and Regulation in the European Union* (Cambridge, Harvard University Press, 2011).

[61] See Fernanda Nicola, 'Critical Legal Histories in EU Law' (2013) 28(5) *American University International Law Review* 1173; William Twining, 'Globalisation and Legal Scholarship' (Nijmegen/Tilburg, Wolf Legal Publishers, 2009).

The external critique of adjudication does not figure predominantly in the corpus of EU law scholarship.[62] Its relative scarcity may be due to a habit of respect for judicial function, or to the widespread belief that legislation, rather than adjudication, is the proper forum for redressing material inequities.[63] It is also the case that external critique of judicial reasoning is less in tune with the civil law tradition, in which judges are not perceived as 'culture heroes [or] parental figures', but rather as civil servants, ie riders 'of a machine built and operated by legislators'.[64] The paucity of scholarly critique grounded in distributive concerns prevents the emergence of a robust, sustained exchange between scholars and the bench that is common in other judicial cultures.[65] The landscape is changing, however, and the Court has experienced deep transformations over its 60 years of existence.[66] The fact that the Court is now staffed by a transnational legal elite and its bureaucracy[67]—immersed in comparative methodologies and moulded by a plurality of legal influences[68]—should facilitate a more fruitful conversation between scholars and the judicial branch.[69]

To be sure, powerful critiques have been deployed against the Court of Justice on grounds other than distribution.[70] Scholars have often demanded increased argumentation and express weighing of competing policies.[71] They have also engaged in internal critiques aimed at denouncing the Court's formalism,

---

[62] There are, of course, prominent exceptions. See eg Hans-W Micklitz 'Mohamad Aziz—Sympathetic and Activist, But Did the Court Get it Wrong?' in Anna Södersten and Joseph Weiler (eds), *Where the Court Gets it Wrong* (Florence, European Constitutional Law Network, 2013) http://www.ecln.net/tl_files/ECLN/Florence%202013/Micklitz%20-%20The%20ECJ%20gets%20it%20wrong%20Aziz-30-11-14.pdf.

[63] Helena Alviar García, 'Distribution of Resources Led by Courts: A Few Words of Caution' in Helena Alviar García, Karl Klare, and Lucy Williams (eds), *Social and Economic Rights in Theory and Practice: Critical Inquiries* (London and New York NY, Routledge, 2014).

[64] See John Henry Merryman, *The Civil Law Tradition: An Introduction to the Legal Systems of Europe and Latin America* 3rd edn (Redwood City CA, Stanford University Press, 2007) 37.

[65] See Alexandra Braun, *Giudici e Accademia nell' Esperienza Inglese: Storia di un Dialogo* (Bologna, il Mulino, 2006).

[66] See Allan Rosas and others (eds), *The Court of Justice and the Construction of Europe: Analyses and Perspectives on Sixty Years of Case-Law* (The Hague, Asser Press, 2013).

[67] See Mathilde Cohen, 'Judges or Bureaucrats' in Davies and Nicola (n 57) 58.

[68] See Fernanda Nicola, 'National Legal Traditions at Work in the Jurisprudence of the European Court of Justice' (2016) 64 *American Journal of Comparative Law* 865.

[69] See Koen Lenaerts and Kathleen Gutman, 'The Comparative Law Method and the European Court of Justice: Echoes across The Atlantic (2016) 64 *American Journal of Comparative Law* 841; Nicola (n 68); and Mitchel Lasser, 'Decoding the European Judicial Appointments Debates' (in this volume).

[70] See, by way of example only, Hjalte Rasmussen, *On Law and Policy in the European Court of Justice: A Comparative Study in Judicial Policymaking* (Dordrecht, Martinus Nijhoff, 1986); Damian Chalmers, 'The European Court of Justice Has Taken on Huge New Powers as "Enforcer" of the Treaty on Stability, Coordination and Governance. Yet its Record as a Judicial Institution Has Been Little Scrutinised' http://blogs.lse.ac.uk/europpblog/2012/03/07/european-court-of-justice-enforcer/.

[71] Joseph Weiler, 'Epilogue: The Judicial Après Nice' in Gráinne De Búrca and Joseph Weiler (eds), *The European Court of Justice* (Oxford, Oxford University Press, 2001) 215. Vlad Perju, 'Reason and Authority in the European Court of Justice' (2009) 49 *Virginia Journal of International Law* 307.

identifying its incoherent use of legal ontologies, and deconstructing its reasoning from within.[72] Yet, no matter how thoroughly argued and internally coherent, a judicial opinion may produce regressive distributive effects that need to be clarified in order to be redressed in a timely manner. By the same token, a judicial opinion may have inconspicuous progressive outcomes, which may remain sporadic in application if not sufficiently highlighted in commentary and then generalised through law and policy. It is the task of scholars across a range of social sciences to engage in this type of analysis.

In our view, legal scholarship should embrace the task of external critique through three different moves. The first consists in emphasising the distributive stakes of each judgment (a).[73] The second is to take a position in support of the marginalised groups that may be saddled with the regressive distributive consequences of a judicial decision (b). A third move engages with deeper political and economic choices, and aims to achieve a more egalitarian, democratic and utopian society (c).

A. Foregrounding the Distributive Stakes

Through the lens of positive sociology functionalism,[74] scholars can highlight which groups or constituencies are impacted by the new allocation of rights and privileges that result from each judgment. This can be done through interdisciplinary, empirical or archival work. Jurists may have to borrow from other social sciences or engage directly in detective work in order to gain a broader sense of the consequences of judicial decisions, which extend beyond the perspective of the parties of any given case.[75] A lesson dear to the CLS movement,[76] but grounded in the earlier tradition of legal realism,[77] is that distributive effects are intrinsic

---

[72] Sacco (n 28); Siniša Rodin, 'Les effets horizontaux du droit de l'Union européenne' in Antonio Tizzano et al (eds) *La Cour de justice de l'Union européenne sous la présidence de Vassilios Skouris (2003–2015)* 491.

[73] See Duncan Kennedy, 'The Stakes of Law, or Hale and Foucault!' (1991) 14 *Legal Studies Forum* 327.

[74] See Fernanda Nicola, 'Family Law Exceptionalism in Comparative Law' (2011) 58 *American Journal of Comparative Law* 777 (explaining the distinction between social purpose and positive sociology functionalism).

[75] See Karl Llewellyn, 'A Realistic Jurisprudence—The Next Step' (1930) 30 *Columbia Law Review* 431.

[76] See especially Kennedy (n 73).

[77] According to David Kennedy, *A World of Struggle: How Power Law, and Expertise Shape Global Political Economy* (Princeton NJ, Princeton University Press, 2016), the link between law and distribution was made particularly explicit in US legal thought by the following writings: Oliver Wendell Holmes, 'The Path of the Law' (1897) 10 *Harvard Law Review* 457; Wesley Hohfeld, 'Some Fundamental Legal Conception as Applied in Judicial Reasoning' (1913) 23 *Yale Law Journal* 16; Robert Hale, 'Coercion and Distribution in a Supposedly Non-coercive State' (1923) 38 *Political Science Quarterly* 470.

to legal rules and that '[l]aw is present whenever gains are distributed, facilitating their aggregation or ensuring their dispersion'.[78]

Take the liberalisation of education in the EU for instance—a timely topic in light of the potentially steep costs of Brexit.[79] Since the 1990s, England experienced a significant influx of EU students entitled by EU law to UK national treatment with respect to both tuition fees and maintenance grants. It was in this context that the CJEU, with its decision in *Bidar*,[80] precipitated a political backlash. Denis Bidar, a French national, entered the UK to complete his secondary education and never had recourse to social assistance. In 2001, when he began to study economics at University College London, he received assistance for his tuition fees, but his application for financial aid to cover his housing costs in London was refused on the ground that he was not sufficiently settled in the UK. Seized with a preliminary question, in 2005 the CJEU held that, given Mr Bidar's 'genuine link' with the UK, he could not be treated as a 'grant-tourist' and as such discriminated against. He would therefore be able to receive the housing subsidy. The court was well aware of the consequences this decision would have for the UK education system. Not surprisingly, in the aftermath of *Bidar*, the UK ramped up its residency requirements to three years for assistance seekers in similar situations.[81] Some scholars applauded *Bidar* as a progressive decision, enabling internal free movement and affirming the principle of nondiscrimination, and praised the Court for putting a premium on 'residence, integration and solidarity: the longer the migrants are resident in the host State, the more integrated they are in the society of the host State in terms of benefits'.[82] Others, however, condemned the regressive distributive consequences of this judgment in particular, and of the EU education saga in general. For instance, Gisella Gori noted that certain states, namely the UK and Belgium, were 'net importers of students' in the context of European education mobility. According to Gori this was, in such states, a matter of public finance: broadening the class of housing assistance recipients would shift the funding of education from the private sector (via loans) to tax payers' contributions (via grants).[83]

The policy implications of *Bidar* appear equally regressive if examined through the lens of local government. Bidar's housing subsidy, allocated to

---

[78] David Kennedy, ibid 204.

[79] See Sir Stephen Wall, 'Leaving the EU?' (2016) 22 *European Public Law* 57. See also Steve Peers, 'The Final UK/EU Renegotiation Deal: Legal Status and Legal Effect' (2016) *EU Law Analysis* http://eulawanalysis.blogspot.com/2016/02/the-final-ukeu-renegotiation-deal-legal.html.

[80] Case C-209/03 *Bidar v London Borough of Ealing* [2005] ECR I-2119.

[81] Michael Dougan, 'Fees, Grants, Loans and Dole Cheques: Who Covers the Cost of Migrant Education within the EU?' (2005) 42 *Common Market Law Review* 943, 972; Gareth Davies, '"Any Place I Hang My Hat?" or: Residence is the New Nationality' (2005) 11 *European Law Journal* 43.

[82] See Catherine Barnard, 'Of Students and Babies' (2005) 64 *Cambridge Law Journal* 560, 563. See also Catherine Barnard, 'Note on *Bidar*' (2005) 42 *Common Market Law Review* 1465.

[83] See Gisella Gori, 'Mademoiselle Gravier and Equal Access to Education: Success and Boundaries of European Integration' in Davies and Nicola (n 57) 446 (at least in the UK).

students residing in the Ealing Borough, had a precise redistributive aim. Ealing is located in West London and is populated in large part by non-affluent and immigrant people.[84] The resident subsidy for students in that particular borough was probably aimed at helping certain vulnerable groups such as the children of Polish, Caribbean and African immigrants rather than foreigners. But in the aftermath of *Bidar*, housing allowances to residents going to London universities became substantially lower with likely negative consequences for the intended beneficiaries of the subsidy.

B. Taking a Stance

The second step in our external critique should enable scholars to explore the politics of judicial decision-making. Jurists know well that the doctrinal and social effects of each case are deeply intertwined. Even though law remains relatively autonomous, scholars can show how a particular interpretation of standing requirements,[85] free movement rights, or of a liability regime can have politically salient implications and favour certain groups at the expense of others. Take for instance *Gonzalez Sanchez*,[86] a hotly contested and arguably conservative decision of the ECJ: in this judgment the Court, through an activist interpretation of relevant rules, denied consumers who had contracted Hepatitis C through blood transfusions the possibility of suing their healthcare providers, and thus let them bear their own costs. Compare this case with *Océano Grupo*,[87] a decision widely acclaimed by pro-consumer advocates. Here, two Spanish sellers sued five buyers for unpaid sums, due under a contract of adhesion, for the sale of encyclopaedias. The ECJ famously allowed a Spanish court to declare the term void of its own motion, setting aside the sellers' argument that this procedural matter should be determined by internal law only. It is important to note, in this regard, that while in cases like *Gonzalez Sanchez* or *Océano Grupo* the progressive or regressive distributive consequences of the Court's holding are obvious, in others they remain rather indeterminate and that, given the nature of EU law, the Court's adjudication on legal questions may not have a clear distributive impact.[88] In such cases it is all the more imperative that scholars point out the distributive ambivalence of the Court's pronouncements.[89]

---

[84] See History of Ealing Borough available at https://www.ealing.gov.uk/site/.

[85] See Andrea Pezza and Roberto Mastroianni, 'Striking the Right Balance: Limits on the Right to Bring an Action Under Article 263(4) of the Treaty on the Functioning of the European Union' (2015) 30 *American University International Law Review* 743.

[86] Case C-183/00 *Maria Victoria* Gonzalez Sanchez *v Medicina Asturiana* ECR [2002] 1-3901.

[87] See Joined Cases C-240/98 to C-244/98 *Océano Grupo Editorial SA* [2000] ECR I-4941 [hereinafter *Océano Grupo*].

[88] See Fernanda Nicola and Evelyne Tichadou, 'Océano Grupo: Missed Opportunities and a Second Life for EU Consumer Law' in Davies and Nicola (n 57) 369.

[89] See s V.

C. Pointing at Progress

A third move in our external critique reflects the more utopian side of CLS, which requires pondering what to do post-critique in order to achieve a more equitable and democratic society. Here, scholars may promote ideological progress through legal doctrines, legal education, or judicial and lawyering techniques.[90] A more radical avenue is to show how legal reforms, no matter how well meaning, run out of steam if they are grafted onto larger systemic inequalities,[91] which can only be addressed through a reconceptualisation of basic legal entitlements,[92] transformative institutions,[93] or ideological changes.[94]

This utopian vein characterises Hans-W Mickliz's reflections on the outcome of *Aziz*.[95] This case, decided by a first chamber led by Vice-President Tizzano in the role of reporting judge, is one of the most acclaimed decisions rendered in the aftermath of the financial crisis. The answer of the CJEU amounted to what scholars called an 'earthquake'.[96] The Court held that the Spanish procedural rules impaired the level of protection required by the Unfair Terms Directive[97] and provided, in line with the opinion of AG Kokott, concrete guidance on how to apply the tests of 'significant imbalance' and 'good faith'.[98] The outcome of *Aziz* led to several important reforms of Spanish mortgage enforcement procedures.[99] Most significantly it showed desperate consumers, on the verge of losing their homes and deeply resentful of EU-led austerity policies, that the Court does not ignore humanity.[100]

On the other hand, Micklitz has noted that defining standards of fairness is a much larger issue in an austerity-ridden Europe than the *Aziz* court was willing to concede. It is an issue that encompasses much more than the private law *acquis*, and calls for broader reflections on the meaning of social rights in the

---

[90] See Bill Davies and Fernanda Nicola, 'Introduction to EU Law Stories' in Davies and Nicola (n 57) 1.

[91] Micklitz (n 62).

[92] See Duncan Kennedy and Frank Michelman, 'Are Property and Contract Efficient?' (1980) 8 *Hofstra Law Review* 712.

[93] See Karl Klare, 'Transformative Constitutionalism and the Common and Customary Law' (2010) 26 *South African Journal on Human Rights* 403.

[94] See Gerald Frug, 'The City as a Legal Concept' (1980) 93 *Harvard Law Review* 1062.

[95] See Case C-415/11 *Mohamed Aziz v Caixa d'Estalvis de Catalunya, Tarragona i Manresa* EU:C:2013:164.

[96] Anthi Beka, 'The Ex Officio Doctrine in European Consumer Law: A Procedural Tool Reinvigorating Individual Consumer Litigation' (Doctoral thesis, University of Luxembourg, 2015) 341, 417.

[97] Council Dir 93/13/EEC of 5 April 1993 on unfair terms in consumer contracts; *Aziz* (n 95) paras 57–59.

[98] *Aziz* (n 95) paras 73–75.

[99] The first round of reform was clearly insufficient to meet the standard of protection set by the Dir, as the Court found in Case C-169/14 *Sánchez Morcillo and Abril García* EU:C:2014:2099. More than a dozen references were lodged by Spanish courts in the aftermath of *Aziz*.

[100] Beka (n 96).

EU Charter.[101] It is also problematic to let the Court be the sole social engineer in matters that require a much more robust and open democratic dialogue. While praising the court for 'getting it right' in the particular context of *Aziz*, and for enabling pro-debtor litigation strategies across the EU, Micklitz reminded readers that the problem of mortgage insolvency could be much better handled via a mix of judicial, legislative and administrative solutions.[102] This is the sort of big-picture utopia that the CLS movement recommends, and that we hope to encounter more frequently in the academic commentary of CJEU decisions.

V. Scholarship and the Challenge of Indeterminacy

Foregrounding the distributive stakes of EU law disputes is clearly important when the judgment is cast in formalist terms, with unproblematic reference to the internal logic of the EU legal system. But identifying distributive issues is just as relevant when the court does engage in a balancing of conflicting rights or interests—a seemingly anti-formalist move—and yet portrays the stakes of the case as politically neutral, and eventually frames its result in the language of legal necessity.[103] This was the decision-making move adopted by the CJEU in such cases as *Laval* (C-341/05) and *Viking* (C-438/05), both obviously linked to radical tensions between organised Nordic labour, employers and lower-wage workers coming from newly acceded Member States.[104] In the aftermath of such judgments, a variety of commentators hurried to add texture to the court's analysis and to explain how, following the judgments, a particular vision of societal welfare had been asserted or reinforced.[105]

Competing accounts emerged. Some saw these cases as a regrettable triumph of shallow cosmopolitanism, as an undue challenge to hard-fought labour-capital equilibria, and as a worrisome dismantlement of national inter-class solidarity.[106] Others looked at these disputes from the perspective of Central and Eastern Europe's job seekers and reached very different conclusions. This view

---

[101] Micklitz (n 62).

[102] ibid 12–18.

[103] Lasser (n 41).

[104] ibid. See also Stephen Weatherill, '"Viking" and "Laval": The EU Internal Market Perspective' in Mark Freedland and Jeremias Prassl (eds), *Viking, Laval and Beyond* (Oxford, Hart Publishing, 2014) 36 (decrying the 'ambiguity of the Court'); Alexander Somek, 'Idealization, De-Politicization and Economic Due Process: System Transition in the European Union' in Bogdan Iancu (ed), *The Law/Politics Distinction in Contemporary Public Law Adjudication* (Utrecht and Portland OR, Eleven International Publishing, 2009) 131, 140 ff (criticising in particular AG Maduro's use of the notion of economic due process in his *Viking* opinion).

[105] The literature is too vast to cite here.

[106] See Alexander Somek, 'From Workers to Migrants, from Distributive Justice to Inclusion: Exploring the Changing Social-Democratic Imagination' (2012) 18 *European Law Journal* 711.

emphasised that low-wage migrant workers were seeking not just free movement (an economic right), but also *social* rights (the right to work, the right to decent conditions), which were just as important as the social rights of the allegedly displaced Nordic workers.[107] Still others followed the on-the-ground repercussions of such cases, tracing the ensuing arrangements between social partners in the affected states and economic sectors.[108]

The scholarly debate did not directly steer the court in one direction or another, but it made the crucial point that it was not possible for the Union to move forward without a thorough rethinking of labour-capital relations and without pondering, legally and politically, the distributive consequences of enhanced labour and capital mobility. The debate made clear, in other words, that the terse language of the EC Treaty on matters of free movement would not simply produce market efficiencies (if any), but would more likely trigger competition for finite resources and require a new political and philosophical arrangement. It also made clear that social and economic rights, as spelled out in primary and secondary EU law, would be simply the beginning of politically difficult conversations—not closing lines of cogent legal syllogisms.

Similarly situated at the crossroads of conflicting value choices is a more recent decision, *Alo and Osso*.[109] The case revolved around the possibility for Syrian citizens, found worthy of subsidiary protection in Germany (though not yet eligible for refugee status), to pick and choose where exactly to settle in their host state. Here again, the Court found itself in the midst of conflicting considerations. On the one hand, the fact that both EU citizens and some categories of third-country nationals have the right to elect a place of residence, while subsidiary-protection recipients do not, is a form of discrimination, further complicating an already problematic distinction between 'mobile nationals and immobile aliens' in EU law.[110] A firm judicial stance in favour of equal treatment should have led the court to allow these legal aliens to choose where to live.[111] On the other hand, Germany was seeking a margin of flexibility in designing its immigration policy through a geographic restriction limited in time for those immigrants receiving public benefits. Foremost in the judges' minds were likely the media's images of Molenbeek, the neighbourhood where several of the terrorists behind recent attacks in Paris and Brussels were living, or the deeply disturbing news of riots between xenophobic locals and third-country nationals in many different EU cities. Allowing Member States to direct some of their immigrants to particular

---

[107] Kukovec (n 16) 414–415.

[108] See eg Eva Maria Tscherner, 'Austrian Labour Law after Viking, Laval, and Beyond' in Mark Freedland and Jeremias Prassl (eds), *Viking, Laval and Beyond* (Oxford, Hart Publishing, 2014) 125.

[109] See Case C-443&444/14 *Alo and Osso* EU:C:2016:127.

[110] See Francesca Strumia, *Supranational Citizenship and the Challenge of Diversity: Immigrants, Citizens and Member States in the EU* (Leiden, Brill Academic Publishing, 2013) 105.

[111] See Tamara Perišin, 'Transformation or Reconstitution of National Regulatory Policies at the EU Level: Insiders and Outsiders under Free Movement Rules' (in this volume).

parts of the territory might in some cases foster the goal of cultural, social and economic integration as well as redistribute the fiscal burden evenly among German Länder.[112] In the enormous body of literature comparing the available range of integration tools, Germany could certainly find support for the idea that all urban areas should remain diverse and should host carefully balanced mixtures of people of different backgrounds, especially given the state's allocation of resources for such purposes.[113] The CJEU eventually decided to grant heavier weight to the latter considerations. The holding did narrow down the scope of Germany's policy choices, excluding that a Member State could mandate specific destinations for subsidiary protection beneficiaries on the sole basis of budgetary concerns. At the same time, the Court held that the state should retain the power to choose the migrants' place of residence if this proved necessary to the goals of integration and public safety—a result perhaps perceived as necessary at the time to quell anti-immigrant sentiment at the heart of Europe.

Cases like *Viking*, *Laval*, and *Alo and Osso* prove two points dear to CLS scholars. First, the distributive outcomes of adjudication are sometimes easy to identify as either progressive or regressive, but just as often they are really complicated, and may lead to disagreement even among scholars of equally progressive persuasion. The consequences of a judicial decision might remain under-determined,[114] or even prove wholly ambivalent, due to rapidly changing historical circumstances (and the European Union is certainly experiencing a time of turbulence).[115] Taking a stance may be difficult, and only partly possible. Utopian arguments put forth by legal academia may remain, indeed, utopian, and should be acknowledged as such. In some contexts, uncovering blind spots in the court's reasoning will be all that a scholar can do. As observed above, however, only an honest commentary informed by all relevant distributive possibilities can point in the direction of real progress.

Second, it is often the case that the law upon which judges must base their decision—be it black-letter law, a string of precedents, or relevant *acquis*—often 'runs out', and CLS's insight on the indeterminacy of legal rules should therefore be taken seriously.[116] At the end of the day, many judicial decisions are based on one or another vision of the common good, and involve choices between often

---

[112] See *Alo and Osso* (n 109) para 12 explaining that Germany was attempting: a) to equalise the fiscal burdens of the different Länder receiving the refugees; b) to '[avert the] emergence of points of social tensions'; and c) to '[link] foreign nationals in particular need of integration to a specific place of residence so that they can avail themselves of the integration facilities available there'.

[113] Integration policies in the EU may even draw inspiration from crucial conversations on racial justice in the US. See eg *Fisher v University of Texas at Austin* 133 S Ct 2198 (2016).

[114] See Oliver Wendell Holmes, 'Privilege, Malice and Intent' (1894) 8 *Harvard Law Review* 1.

[115] See Pierre Schlag (n 56) (addressing the plurality of context).

[116] See Mark Kelman, *A Guide to Critical Legal Studies* (Cambridge, Harvard University Press, 1987) (outlining the controversy on law's indeterminacy within the CLS movement). cf Perišin (n 111), suggesting a more univocal account of the effects of decisions like *Alo and Osso*.

irreconcilable world views. Even though judges cast their reasoning in terms of legal necessity,[117] no univocal conclusion can be reached in such disputes simply on the basis of legal rules and principles (free movement, non-discrimination, individual rights, international obligations, etc), which remain ultimately open-ended. This realisation can be painful,[118] not only for judges duly preoccupied with maintaining an aura of sheer objectivity, but also for progressive advocates, who would rather present their own argument as being clearly superior in point of law.[119] The realisation of law's indeterminacy, however, is often a necessary starting point for serious distributive analysis in scholarly circles. Progressive scholars are best positioned to voice the inner limits of legal argumentation, to aid the Court in identifying gaps, conflicts and ambiguities in the law, and hopefully to promote distributive justice and inclusion as paramount goals of the EU legal system. Only by acknowledging 'the inevitability of value-laden choice in adjudication'[120] will legal scholars engage the Court in a continuous dialogue about values and perhaps, by so doing, move forward the ball of substantive justice.

---

[117] Karl Klare, 'Critical Perspectives on Social and Economic Rights: Democracy and Separation of Powers' in Alviar García, Klare and Williams (eds) (n 63) 3 (noting that 'the decision-maker's judgment is a performance enacted to persuade the public that the outcome was required by legal necessity').

[118] ibid. ('Acknowledging that ethical and political choice play a role in adjudication is problematic in legal cultures that socialize participants to believe that such influence is illegitimate.').

[119] ibid.

[120] ibid.

INDEX

Lightning Source UK Ltd.
Milton Keynes UK
UKHW022240240620
365497UK00003B/140